UNFAIR CONTRACT TERMS IN EUROPEAN LAW

The book examines Directive 93/13 on Unfair Terms in Consumer Contracts and its implementation with a twofold aim: first, to understand the extent to which the Directive has influenced and will influence fundamental notions and principles of contract law in the domestic legal systems of the Member States; second, it examines the extent to which the domestic legal traditions of the Member States have influenced the process of drafting of the Directive and, more importantly, will affect the way that the Directive is interpreted and applied in national courts. The focus is mainly on English law (including the 2005 Unfair Terms in Contracts Bill) and on Italian law, but frequent references are made to the French and the German systems.

At the same time, the book has a broader, more 'European' concern, in that it aims to distill from the existing Community *acquis* and from the history and rationale of Directive 93/13 notions and concepts that could guide its interpretation. It is well known that Community law uses terminology which is peculiar to it, and that legal concepts do not necessarily have the same meaning in EC law and in the law of the various Member States: every provision of Community law must be placed in its context and interpreted in the light of its own objectives and rationale, and of the objectives and rationale of Community law as a whole. In this respect, this book aims to identify the contours and features of the emerging European legal tradition, and to assess the impact that this may have on the domestic traditions.

Modern Studies in European Law: Volume 15

Modern Studies in European Law

1 Soft Law in European Community Law
Linda Senden

2 The Impact of European Rights on National Legal Cultures
Miriam Aziz

3 Partnership Rights, Free Movement and EU Law
Helen Toner

4 National Remedies Before the Court of Justice: Issues of Harmonisation and Differentiation
Michael Dougan

5 The National Courts' Mandate in the European Constitution
Monica Claes

6 EU Environmental Law: Challenges, Changes and Decision-Making
Maria Lee

7 European Union Law and Defence Integration
Martin Trybus

8 Principles of European Constitutional Law
Armin von Bogdandy & Jürgen Bast

9 EU International Relations Law
Panos Koutrakos

Unfair Contract Terms in European Law

A Study in Comparative and EC Law

Paolisa Nebbia

•HART•
PUBLISHING
OXFORD AND PORTLAND, OREGON
2007

Published in North America (US and Canada) by
Hart Publishing
c/o International Specialized Book Services
920 NE 58th Avenue, Suite 300
Portland, OR 97213-3786
USA
Tel: +1 503 287 3093 or toll-free: (1) 800 944 6190
Fax: +1 503 280 8832
E-mail: orders@isbs.com
Website: www.isbs.com

Hart Publishing, 16C Worcester Place, OX1 2JW
Telephone: +44 (0)1865 517530 Fax: +44 (0)1865 510710
E-mail: mail@hartpub.co.uk
Website: http://www.hartpub.co.uk

British Library Cataloguing in Publication Data
Data Available
ISBN-13: 978-1-84113-594-6 (hardback)
ISBN-10: 1-84113-594-1 (hardback)

Typeset by Hope Services, Abingdon
Printed and bound in Great Britain by
Biddles Ltd, King's Lynn, Norfolk

A mia Mamma

Acknowledgements

There are a number of people to whom I am indebted.

Many of my colleagues have read, at different stages and in different forms, parts of or all of this work. I would therefore like to thank Hugh Beale, Steve Weatherill and Paula Giliker for their useful suggestions and Takis Tridimas for providing precious guidance when, a few years ago, I first dealt with unfair terms in EC law in my doctoral thesis.

I am grateful to my German colleagues, Peter Rott and Katja Ziegler for answering my questions on German law and to Erika Szyszczak for providing useful feedback on a paper on public services, which constituted the background to chapter 6.

I am very much indebted to Richard Hart, who believed in this project, and to all the staff at Hart Publishing, who have been incredibly helpful.

I also owe a 'thank you' to my own college, St Hilda's, for providing an inspiring and friendly setting for the writing of this book.

Finally, on both a professional and personal level, I wish to thank Professor Marco Ricolfi of the University of Torino who encouraged my first steps in the academic world.

Contents

Table of Cases

ENGLAND

EUROPEAN COURTS AND COMMUNITY DECISIONS

FRANCE

GERMANY

ITALY

1

Introduction

AS THE TITLE suggests, this book aims to be a study in both comparative and EC law. It develops along two intersecting axes, the comparative and the European.

The comparative axis is based on the idea that the fate of any change which is made to the law is that it will be incorporated into the existing tradition and will come to be interpreted in the traditional ways: 'even radical legislation enters a continuing tradition which probably affected the way in which it was drafted and certainly will affect the ways in which it is read and applied.'[1]

The comparative analysis carried out in this book starts from the assumption that law is more than a set of rules, but comprises a set of methods, values, ways of thinking and perceptions of the law's role in the society: it is, in other words, a 'tradition'. The aim of this work is to demonstrate the inescapability of tradition when drafting and, more significantly, interpreting the law. Most studies on the relationship between European and national law are concerned with the impact that the former has on the latter; this book, on other hand, is (also) concerned with the impact that domestic legal systems have on European law, that is, the way that the drafting and the interpretation of Directive 93/13 on Unfair Terms in Consumer Contracts is being affected by national traditions.

The comparative axis also acts as an epistemological tool by which the shortcomings, characteristics, rationales and values of each system reveal themselves with more clarity and vividness by means of comparison: 'Auf Vergleichen lässt sich wohl alles Erkennen, Wissen zurückfüren':[2] accordingly, from a methodological point of view this work aims to demonstrate the essential role played by comparative analysis in the understanding of the effects of European law on national legal systems. Although this work does not directly enter in the debate on harmonisation of private law, it suggests a method to assess the desirability and effect of measures of harmonisation: only comparison can unveil and explain the degree of divergence or convergence of legal systems; broader inferences can then be drawn on the viability and consequences of further measures of harmonisation. In this respect, the choice to concentrate the analysis on the Italian and the English

[1] M Krygier, 'Law as Tradition' (1986) *Law and Philosophy* 237 at 251.

[2] 'All knowledge is based on comparison': Novalis, Works III, ed Minor (Jena, 1907) 45, fragment 229, as quoted in K Zweigert and H Kötz, *An Introduction to Comparative Law*, vol. I (Oxford, Clarendon Press, 1998) v.

legal systems has proved enlightening since the two systems have turned out to be at opposite ends of the spectrum not only in terms of legal techniques and methods, but also in their diverging conceptions of the role of law in society and methods of adjudication. The comparison is completed by frequent references to the French and the German systems, which have been particularly significant in the drafting of the Directive.

The European axis aims to distil from the history and the rationale of the Directive and from the existing European *acquis* notions and concepts that could guide the interpretation of Directive 93/13. It is well known that Community law uses terminology which is peculiar to it, and

> legal concepts do not necessarily have the same meaning in Community law and in the law of the various Member States. . . . Every provision of Community law must be placed in its context and interpreted in the light of the provisions of Community law as a whole, regard being had to the objectives thereof and to its state of evolution at the date on which the provision in question is to be applied.[3]

In this respect, this work aims to identify the contours and features of the emerging European legal tradition and to assess the impact that this has, in turn, on the domestic traditions.

The choice of topics discussed has been made in accordance with the objectives outlined above. This ought to sound a *caveat* for the reader, who should not expect to find in this book a comprehensive study dealing with all issues arising out of the implementation of Directive 93/13: it does not discuss, for example, problems relating to enforcement, sanctions for breach of the fairness test or the exclusion concerning terms that reflect international conventions. The topics that are analysed here have been selected with a view to looking at the dialectical process by which the European and the domestic traditions influence one another: the discussion is therefore limited to those areas which appear to be most significant in this regard.

[3] As first established in 283/81 *CILFIT & Lanificio di Gavardo SpA v Ministry of Health* [1983] ECR 3415.

2

Directive 93/13 and EC Consumer Law and Policy

LIKE MOST COMMUNITY measures in the area of consumer protection, Directive 93/13 (the Directive)[1] has a Janus-faced nature: formally based on article 100a (now article 95) of the Treaty of Rome and therefore aimed at reinforcing the internal market, it also pursues the objective of ensuring protection of consumers against unfair terms throughout Europe.

Compared to national rules on unfair terms, that have the sole purpose of protecting the most vulnerable party to the transaction, Directive 93/13 has therefore one peculiarity: it establishes a link between consumer protection and the internal market. This chapter will investigate this link both in general terms and with specific reference to Directive 93/13. In this latter respect, it must be noted that the pre-existence of different domestic measures controlling unfair terms in most Member States constituted not only a reason that justifies Community intervention to facilitate the establishment of the internal market, but also an important source of inspiration for those who drafted the Directive: the attempt to mirror and combine various domestic solutions in the Directive can often explain its ambiguities and inconsistencies.

Understanding the extent to which the interplay between the internal market and the consumer protection rationale has influenced the drafting of the Directive will provide the necessary background for understanding the Directive's effect on national legal orders discussed in Chapters 5 to 9.

A BRIEF OUTLINE OF DIRECTIVE 93/13

Directive 93/13 applies to all terms contained in contracts with consumers which have not been individually negotiated and introduces a requirement of fairness against which such terms are to be tested. The requirement is based on two main criteria, that the term is not 'contrary to the requirement of good faith' and that it does not cause 'a significant imbalance in the parties' rights and obligations arising under the contract, to the detriment of the consumer' (article 3). Unfairness must be assessed in relation to the time of conclusion of the contract and to all circumstances

[1] Council Directive 83/13 of 5 April 1993 on Unfair Terms In Consumer Contracts OJ L95/29.

surrounding the conclusion, including the nature of the goods or the services provided (article 4(1)). Terms relating to the definition of the main subject matter of the contract or the adequacy of the price or the remuneration are excluded from control as long as they are in plain intelligible language (article 4(2)).

Due to the concern that the notion of unfairness expressed by general clauses would lack sufficient accuracy and precision to be applied in a uniform way throughout the Member States, an annex was attached to the Directive providing an 'indicative and non-exhaustive list' of unfair terms.[2]

The Directive additionally introduces in article 5 a general transparency requirement by imposing that terms offered to consumers are expressed in plain, intelligible language. Where terms are subject to different interpretations, the one which is most favourable to the consumer must prevail.

At the level of enforcement, the Directive provides that terms which do not comply with the requirement of fairness will not be enforceable against the consumer. In combination with this sanction, the Directive requires Member States to introduce 'adequate and effective means' to prevent the use of unfair terms (article 7). For this purpose, Member States must ensure that persons or organisations having a legitimate interest according to national law to protect consumers can take action in national courts or administrative bodies for a decision that contract terms drawn or recommended by sellers, suppliers or their associations are unfair.

THE EC INVOLVEMENT IN CONSUMER POLICY AND THE ROOTS OF DIRECTIVE 93/13

Consumer Policy in the EC

The original EEC Treaty, as signed in Rome in 1957, lacks any explicit reference to the consumer as such. Even though the consumer is mentioned five times,[3] he can-

[2] The Annex contains a list of 17 clauses which may be regarded as unfair. Roughly, those clauses can be classified according to the following four criteria (see R Brownsword, G Howells and T Wilhelmsson, 'The EC Unfair Contract Terms Directive and Welfarism' in Brownsword, Howells, and Wilhelmsson (eds) *Welfarism in Contract Law* (Aldershot, Dartmouth, 1994) 275–84):

1. terms giving a party the control of the terms of the contract or of the performance of the contract (eg point j of the Annex, terms which enable the seller or supplier to alter the terms of the contract unilaterally without a valid reason which is specified in the contract; see also points i, k, l, m, p);
2. terms determining the duration of the contract (eg point g, terms enabling the seller or supplier to terminate a contract of indeterminate duration without reasonable notice; see also point h);
3. terms restraining a party to have the same rights as the other (eg point c, terms making an agreement binding on the consumer whereas provision of services by the seller or supplier is subject to a condition whose realisation depends on his own will alone, see also points d, f, o);
4. exemption and limitations clauses (eg point a, terms excluding or limiting the legal liability of a seller or supplier in the event of the death of a consumer or personal injury to the latter resulting from an act or omission of that seller or supplier, see also points b, e, n, q).

[3] In arts 33 (formerly 39), 34 (formerly 40), 81 (formerly 85), 82 (formerly 86), 87 (formerly 92).

not be considered 'a point of reference or the object of a single policy objective or measure'[4] as the Treaty does not determine his rights and duties, nor impose or allow for active measures to improve his position. The provisions of the Treaty that explicitly refer to the consumer illustrate what could be called a 'productivist'[5] perception of his interests in the common market: the attention to consumption has its 'raison d'être' in the fact that it is directly related to production and distribution. In other words, the Treaty proceeds on the basis that the consumer is the ultimate beneficiary of the economic objectives of the Community: at the European level, consumer law revolves around the application of the substantive provisions of the Treaty which act as an instrument for the achievement of the economically efficient integrated market. For instance, the transformation of relatively small-scale national markets into a large single Community market will stimulate competition and induce producers to achieve maximum efficiency in order to protect and to expand their market share. In this context, competition is regarded as the 'consumer's best friend' and its intensification should serve the consumer by increasing the available choice of goods and services.

The Member States' attitude at the time the Treaty was drafted and their trust in market forces rather than in governmental intervention to correct or replace the functioning of the market may be considered surprising if considered in the light of the general trend towards what is generally called the 'welfare state' (*Etat Providence, Sozialstaat, Stato sociale*), entailing new forms of state control and intervention in the market: the state intervened to devise new principles to govern the operation and the outcomes of the market. Instead of permitting the distribution of wealth to be determined by voluntary choices to enter market transactions, the social security system, funded largely through progressive taxation, reshaped the eventual outcomes of the distribution of wealth,[6] and ideas of social justice justified the channelling and regulation of market transactions. Similarly, employment legislation was passed to confer rights on employees which they could not secure for themselves by contract; landlord and tenant legislation was enacted to give minimum rights to tenants; the increasing awareness of consumers' rights and the development of consumers' representative groups in the late fifties in many European states also involved revising to different extents the classical principles of freedom of contract, *caveat emptor* and fault liability, seen as mechanisms discriminating against consumers and other weaker parties or groups in the society.

In brief, while Member States seemed to assert that the free market mechanisms would benefit consumers at European level, they were at the same time enacting interventionist measures within their territory. This can be explained by the fact that the concern of the European founders at the time was certainly not social policy but the creation of an economically integrated European market; at the same time, nobody was probably aware of the fact that, in the evolution of the

[4] L Krämer, *EEC Consumer Law* (Brussels, Bruylant 1996) 2.

[5] T Bourgoignie and D Trubek, *Consumer Law, Common Market and Federalism* (Berlin/New York, De Gruyter, 1986) 100.

[6] H Collins, *The Law of Contract* (London, Butterworths, 1997) 9.

Community, it would be those interventionist measures themselves which would be considered, at a later stage of the development of European integration, obstacles to market-building.

It did not take too long, however, before the contradiction in Member States' behaviour emerged. In 1961, four years after the signing of the Treaty, the vice-president of the Commission, Sicco Mansholt, acknowledged that 'the general interests of consumers in the Common Market are not represented to the same extent as those of producers'.[7] Therefore, despite the exclusion of consumer protection from the explicit constitutional structure of the Treaty of Rome, the status of the consumer as a partner of the developing structure of Community law and practice started earning recognition, at first largely at an informal level by 'soft law' initiatives. Since the Paris Summit of October 1972 various political declarations insisted on the social dimension of the European Community. The objective of Community policy-making was said not to be confined to the establishment of the internal market, but to promoting an active and comprehensive social policy throughout the Community.

The first Preliminary Programme of the EEC for a Consumer Protection and Information Policy[8] was the Commission's answer to the Paris demand. A second, similar Programme was issued in 1981.[9] Under these programmes, consumers were granted five basic rights (right to protection of health and safety, right to protection of economic interest, right of redress, right to information and education, right of representation).

The roots of Directive 93/13 can be found at those early stages of the development of EC consumer policy. According to the 1975 Programme, the increased abundance and complexity of the goods offered had as a side effect abuses and frustration of the consumer who was no longer able to fulfil the role of balancing factor; as a consequence, producers and distributors had increasing opportunities to determine market conditions. The need had arisen to formulate a specific Community consumer policy aimed at securing, inter alia, effective protection against damage to consumers' economic interests. Within this framework, it would be the Community's task to adopt measures aimed at ensuring that purchasers of goods or services were protected 'against the abuse of power by the seller, in particular against one-sided standard contracts, the unfair exclusion of essential rights in contracts, harsh conditions of credit, demands for payment for unsolicited goods and against high-pressure selling methods'.[10]

The Second Programme for a consumer protection and information policy, referring to the question of unfair contract terms, reported that the Commission had considered that their first step 'should be to draft a discussion paper in which [they] will set out all the problems which this subject involves and the various

[7] Quoted in V Kendall, *EC Consumer Law* (London, Chancery Law Publishing, 1994) 7.

[8] Council Resolution of 14 April 1975 OJ C92, 1.

[9] Council Resolution of 19 May 1981 OJ C133, 1. Both the 1975 and the 1981 Resolutions are expressly referred to in Recital 8 of Dir 93/13.

[10] Council Resolution of 14 April 1975, above n 8, para 19.

options open with a view to harmonising those aspects which may be affected by discrepancies in this area'.[11] The fulfilment of the task of raising the standard of living of European citizens—stated the Programme—requires that disparities between Member States are eliminated so that a high standard of consumer protection against unfair terms can be enjoyed by all consumers throughout the Community. In other words, the existence of a genuine internal market with rules providing the same protection to all consumers appeared to the Council to constitute a considerable direct benefit to the consumer, while, on the other hand, avoiding distortions of competition.[12]

The legislative history of Directive 93/13

Between 1975 and 1977 the Commission prepared a few draft proposals, which were discussed by governments' experts, but in the same years an intense burst of legislative activity on the part of the Member States took place: in 1976 the Federal Republic of Germany adopted a statute on unfair contract terms,[13] in 1977 the UK did so too,[14] and France followed in 1978.[15] The introduction of different regulatory frameworks for unfair terms in several Member States certainly did not facilitate the attainment at Community level of a degree of consensus sufficient to proceed with work in that area; in addition, there were conflicting visions of the appropriate intensity of social regulation on the matter and of the acceptable degree of Community involvement in its realisation. Owing to this, to commitments in other areas and to lack of staff the Commission's work in the field of unfair term halted for almost 10 years.

In 1984 the Commission took the initiative again by publishing a consultation paper entitled 'Unfair Terms in Contracts Concluded with Consumers',[16] which constituted the main background to the Directive; nonetheless, 16 more years had to pass before the Commission put forward its first proposal for a directive on unfair terms.

The first proposal for a Directive on Unfair Terms in Consumer Contracts was submitted by the Commission on 24 July 1990.[17] The Commission's proposal had its first reading in the European Parliament in October 1991, after which the Commission submitted an amended proposal. This was adopted by the

[11] Council Resolution of 19 May 1981 above n 9, para 30.

[12] See the European Parliament's call for the adoption of a Directive on Unfair Terms in its Resolution on the Second Programme (OJ C291, 10 November 1980).

[13] *Gesetz zur Regelung des Rechts der Allgemeiner Geschäftsbedingungen (AGB-Gesetz)* of 19 December 1976.

[14] Unfair Contracts Terms Act (UCTA) 1977.

[15] *Loi sur la protection et l'information des consommateurs des produits et des services (loi Scrivener)*, no 78-23 of 10 January 1978.

[16] Commission Communication presented to the Council on 14 February 1984, *Bulletin of the European Communities*, Supplement 1/84, 5.

[17] Proposal for a Council Directive on Unfair Terms in Consumer Contracts COM (1990) 322 final, [1990] OJ C243.

Commission on 4 March 1992[18] and was a complete reformulation of the original text: discussion in the Council started again on this reformulated text. Four months later, on 29 June 1992, the Council adopted an agreement in principle on a common position: it was during this period that the amended proposal of the Commission was transformed into the text finally approved on 5 April 1993. The final text of the Directive takes up without major modifications the text adopted in June 1992 as the Council did not place heavy emphasis on the opinion of the Parliament on second reading nor on the re-examined proposal of the Commission.[19]

Overall, almost 20 years had to pass before the idea of a directive on unfair terms could be implemented: such a lapse of time, apart from raising obvious criticism on the efficiency of the European law-making process, allowed a radical change in the legal landscape within which the Directive had to be enacted. Year by year, almost all of the Member States enacted their own legislation, which made the adoption of a directive not only partially redundant, but also rather problematic since it had to fit within domestic frameworks which in most cases would not have existed had the Directive been enacted earlier. Accordingly, the innovative force of the Directive turned into a 'disturbing' element for the national legislation that had meanwhile been adopted and the Community legislator ended up following, rather than triggering and leading, law reform in the Member States.

Between 1977 and 1984 and 1984 and 1990, however, relevant changes in the legal framework of the European Community deeply affected the development of the process of market building. Such changes, on the one hand, facilitated the adoption of Directive 93/13, which is based on article 100a (now 95) EC; on the other hand, they lie at the roots of the Directive's tensions and contradictions, which have been highlighted by the more recent developments of the internal market project.

THE RATIONALE OF THE DIRECTIVE: THE INTERNAL MARKET ARGUMENT

Political and legal framework at the time of adoption of Directive 93/13

Qualified majority voting and the minimum harmonisation formula

The introduction by the Single European Act (SEA) of qualified majority voting in the Council via article 95 EC (formerly 100a) allowed an acceleration in the development of indirect consumer protection policy through the possibility that harmonised standards of protection can be put in place at Community level, even without unanimous consensus among the Member States. The introduction of the qualified majority voting must be seen in conjunction with an increasing use of the

[18] Amended Proposal for a Council Directive on Unfair Terms in Consumer Contracts COM (1992) 66 final, [1992] OJ C73.

[19] M Tenreiro, 'The Community Directive on Unfair Terms and National Legal Systems' (1995) *European Review of Private Law* 273–74.

minimum harmonisation formula, which since the SEA has been institutionalised through express incorporation in the Treaty. The replacement of unanimity by majority voting extenuated the ability of individual Member States to resist the will of the Community even when they felt that important questions of social policy were at stake: a state could be obliged by the demand of harmonisation to lower its own existing standards for the sake of complying with the majority's preference for a minimalist Community norm: hence, the minimum harmonisation formula represented a compromise which is to some extent comparable, in its rationale, to the *Cassis de Dijon* mandatory requirements in that market integration should not constitute a threat to certain valuable non-market interests.[20]

From the consumers' point of view, this formula can be considered as the legal response to the concern that positive integration (and therefore common standards) could entail a reduction in the standards which already existed in some states. The traditional idea of pre-emption underpinning the Treaty would in fact entail that national rules should be replaced by Community law and that a field which is occupied by the Community would be barred to national law making. However, it was soon realised that treating national rules of market regulation as mere barriers to trade instead of considering their broader social function would lead to the suppression of long-established and well-developed national initiatives in the field of consumer protection. Accordingly, an attempt had to be made to accommodate those different traditions within a flexible Community framework; to attain this effect, the Community decided that they would establish a minimum standard, but Member States should be entitled to enact or maintain stricter rules if they wanted to.[21]

Accordingly, article 8 of Directive 93/13 entitles Member States to 'adopt or retain the most stringent provisions compatible with the Treaty' in the area covered by the Directive, thus jeopardising the target of achieving similar market conditions throughout Europe. Such a formula would still guarantee that consumers can enjoy the minimum level of protection ensured by the Directive no matter where they chose to buy goods or services; but from the traders' point of view, the fact that disparities can remain to a large extent would entail that they still could not use the same standard form contract throughout the Community. It must be noted, however, that the minimum harmonisation formula was not included in the 1990 and 1992 texts and was slipped in only in the final version, probably under the pressure of some Member States, understandably concerned that the Directive would lower their own standard of protection.

The relationship between internal markets and Directive 93/13

The *Cassis de Dijon*[22] ruling is well known for its dramatic consequences on free movement of goods in terms of securing wider choice for the consumers by

[20] For an overview of this type of legislation, see K Mortelmans, 'Minimum Harmonization and Consumer Law' (1988) *European Consumer Law Journal* 2.

[21] See Council Resolution of 7 May 1985 OJ C136/1.

[22] Case 120/78 *Rewe-Zentral v Bundesmonopolverwaltung für Branntwein* [1979] ECR 649.

allowing recognition of diverse national traditions; of decreasing the Commission's workload in the area of positive harmonisation[23] by reducing the need to adopt common rules; of sweeping away the concerns for the rise of a 'Europroduct'[24] by promoting the circulation of national products.

The *Cassis de Dijon* ruling also had a landmark influence on the understanding of the relationship between national consumer protection measures in Europe and the goal of ensuring the free flow of trade and factors of production. In this respect, various options were available.[25] At one extreme, the Community may have decided that the existence of strong consumer protection at the national level and substantial diversity between national approaches to consumer protection posed no problems for open borders. On the other hand, the European Community may have felt that diverse national consumer laws substantially inhibited intra-European economic activity and that diversity in consumer protection law posed a serious threat to efficient allocation of resources within Europe. In the latter case, implementation of the open borders policy would have required that the Community play an active role in consumer protection.

Cassis de Dijon explicitly states that the diverse national consumer laws can act as a brake on the free flow of goods. However, the absence of Community harmonisation in a specific field would allow Member States to take or maintain reasonable measures to prevent unfair trade practices. The consequence is that

> upholding the national law . . . amounts to a recognition that the State maintains certain powers and responsibilities which are not overridden by the process of market integration. Market fragmentation persists. In such circumstances the limits of negative laws are reached, which implies a need to shift the emphasis towards positive law. Traditionally, this would take the shape of Community legislative action in the field to establish free trade on common rules throughout the Community while ensuring that an appropriate level of protection is also secured.[26]

Accordingly, positive integration in the field of consumer protection remains the only remedy to the diversity of national measures acting as lawful obstacles to trade. This is probably one of the reasons why most consumer measures have been adopted after this seminal judgment was given; the Commission itself has reaffirmed that the development of consumer policy at EU level has been the 'essential corollary of the progressive establishment of the internal market'.[27]

Directive 93/13 must be placed against this background: adopted on the legal basis of article 100a (now 95) EC, it is part of the programme of achievement of

[23] See the positive comment in the Commission Communication concerning *Cassis de Dijon* OJ 1980 C256/2.

[24] See S Weatherill, *EC Consumer Law and Policy* (London, Longman, 1997) 47.

[25] See Bourgoignie and Trubek, above n 5, at 104 ff.

[26] H Micklitz and S Weatherill, 'Consumer Policy in the European Community: Before and After Maastricht' (1993) *Journal of Consumer Policy* 289.

[27] Communication from the Commission to the European Parliament, the Economic and Social Committee and the Committee of the Regions. Consumer Policy Strategy 2002–6 COM (2002) 208 final.

the internal market—while safeguarding consumers' rights, the Directive would help open up the internal market for both consumers and traders by eliminating obstacles and distortions originating from different domestic rules on unfair terms.

More specifically, the contribution of the Directive to 'facilitating the internal market'[28] can be seen under two different perspectives, that of consumers and that of traders. From the consumers' point of view, the Directive would serve to remove obstacles to trade by encouraging them to take advantage of the internal market by cross-border shopping (the concept of the so-called 'confident consumer'):

> it cannot be assumed that consumers who cross frontiers to buy goods or services, or to invest or acquire property in other Member States, have understood and agreed the terms of a contract they have made, if they do not speak the local law, especially if it is complex . . .. Unless there is some assurance that they will not be seriously disadvantaged by unfair contracts, consumers will lack the confidence to use the new possibilities opened up by the completion of the internal market, for example the opportunity to buy goods and services at more favourable prices in other Member States than their country of residence.[29]

This is clear from Recital 5 of the Directive, which states that the lack of knowledge of the rules of the other states may deter consumers from concluding transactions in those states:[30] this reflects the view that the consumer is considered as 'a market player whose action (or inaction) is vital in constructing the single market'.[31] Recital 10 of the Directive adds that 'more effective protection of the consumer can be achieved by adopting uniform rules of law in the matter of unfair terms'. This statement would be true only if the Directive took as its starting point the highest level of consumer protection, which is clearly not the case; it is therefore possible that this paragraph merely seeks to reinforce what is already affirmed in Recital 5.

From the traders' point of view, the Directive would contribute to the removal of obstacles by decreasing the doubts and difficulties involved in cross-border trading (Recital 7), such as, for example, transaction costs and uncertainty as to whether certain contract terms would be valid under another state's law; in addition, the Directive would remove disparities between traders when selling goods or providing services in a State other than their own,[32] thus eliminating distortions of competition

[28] Recital 6 of Dir 93/13.

[29] Explanatory Memorandum to the 1990 Proposal, COM (90) 322 final, 2; see also Recital 6 of Dir 93/13.

[30] The Preamble of Directive 1999/44/EC on Certain Aspects of the Sale of Consumer Goods and Associated Guarantees ([1999] OJ L171/12) also contains a reference to the consumer confidence:

> whereas the creation of a common set of minimum rules of consumer law, valid no matter where goods are purchased within the Community, will strengthen consumer confidence and enable consumers to make the most of the internal market.

[31] D Oughton and C Willett, 'Quality Regulation in European Private Law' (2002) *Journal of Consumer Policy* 303.

[32] See also Recital 7 of Dir 93/13.

(according to Recital 2, 'national markets for the sale of goods and services to consumers differ from each other and . . . distortions of competition may arise amongst the seller and suppliers, notably when they sell and supply in other Member States').

Since the Directive was adopted, however, the constitutional and political landscape of the EC has changed significantly, and such changes have revealed the tenuousness of the link between the internal market and the EC consumer protection policy.

The relationship between article 95 EC and Directive 93/13 in the light of more recent developments

The 'confident consumer' argument

The argument of the confident consumer has been criticised on the mere basis of 'common sense' and 'self-evident knowledge about how consumers act in the marketplace':[33] most consumers are unaware of their rights even under their domestic legal system, and their choices are, in this respect, somehow 'accidental' or merely 'price-driven'.[34] Hence, it is unlikely that lack of knowledge of a foreign legal system would be a significant deterrent from cross-border transactions: linguistic variations and impeded access to justice may be much more serious hindrances in this respect. One could argue, however, that even though consumers do not know their own legal system in detail, they may still believe or suspect (and empirical evidence seems to confirm this) that their own system of protection is better than that of the other Member States, and this belief may prevent them from making full use of the internal market. This may support the argument that a set of minimum rules to be used a 'safety net' would help decrease the number of situations in which consumers feel themselves to be subject to severe injustice when they attempt to use the legal machinery in other Member States.[35]

It is difficult to deny, however, that the argument is a weak one and that the contribution that the Directive brings to market building is, in this respect, pretty insignificant: the lack of knowledge and understanding of the law which is applicable when shopping across the border may appear to be, in truth, a rather negligible obstacle to trade. The weakness of this argument nevertheless depends

[33] T Wilhelmsson, 'The Abuse of the "Confident Consumer" as a Justification for EC Consumer Law' (2004) *Journal of Consumer Policy* 325.

[34] G Astone, 'Commento all'articolo 1469-bis, secondo comma' in G Alpa and S Patti (eds) *Le clausole vessatorie nei contratti con i consumatori* (Milano, Giuffrè, 1997), 102.

[35] Upon these grounds, T Wilhelmsson (above n 33, at 327) argues that only minimum harmonisation can be justified on internal market grounds, while total harmonisation cannot: since consumers are not aware in detail of their legal rights, it would not make a difference to them if these were the same throughout Europe. Although the argument may be a valuable one as far as consumers are concerned, from the traders' point of view total harmonisation is a much more significant contribution to the improvement of the internal market than minimum harmonisation.

on what exactly we perceive as being an 'obstacle to trade': this question is more thoroughly dealt with later in this chapter.

'Obstacles' from the traders' perspective

It has earlier been said that, from the trader's point of view, supplying goods or services in another state creates risks, uncertainties and costs that are mainly due to his lack of knowledge of other states' laws. Cross-border contracts, however, are subject to the Convention on the Law Applicable to Contractual Obligations (Rome Convention)[36] and are accordingly subject to the principle of freedom of choice embedded in article 3. This means that the trader can, by his own choice, select the law applicable to the whole or to a part of the contract. The trader will therefore be able to choose his own law as the law regulating the contract.

The Rome Convention contains in article 5 some special provisions for the protection of consumers aimed at ensuring that a choice of law does not deprive the consumer of the protection afforded to him by the mandatory rules of the law of the country in which he has his habitual residence. These provisions, however, apply only in limited circumstances: they do not apply where the consumer travels to another country to purchase the good or service, unless the journey was arranged by the trader with the purpose of inducing the consumer to buy. In all the other cases, article 5 applies only under the conditions listed at paragraph 2, that is, (a) the conclusion of the contract was preceded by a specific invitation addressed to him or by advertising and he has taken in his country all the steps necessary for the conclusion of the contract; (b) the trader or his agent received the consumer's order in the country of the consumer; (c) if the contract is for the sale of goods, the consumer travelled from his country to another country and there gave his order, provided that the consumer's journey was arranged by the seller for the purpose of inducing the consumer to buy.

If there is no choice of law, the applicable law will be, according to article 4 of the Convention, that of the country where the party who is to effect the performance which is characteristic of the contract has his habitual residence or principal place of business; where under the terms of the contract the performance is to be effected through a place of business other than the principal place of business, the applicable law will be that of the country in which that other place of business is situated. As a result, in most of these cases a trader (as the party who has to effect the characteristic performance) will be acting according to his own law or to a law which he can anyway ascertain in advance (eg the law of the place through which he operates).

The provisions of article 4 do not apply where the contract is made with a consumer, provided that the circumstances listed in paragraph 2 of article 5 apply: in this case, the applicable law will be that of the country in which the consumer has his habitual residence.

[36] [1998] OJ C27/34.

The provisions of the Rome Convention leave little room for cases where the contract would be regulated by a law which is not the one of the trader: in theory, the Directive should be able to remove the obstacles arising in such cases. Nevertheless, as the next section will show, the Directive does even not appear to be able to assist businesses engaged in cross-border trading when the applicable law is not the one of the trader.

The problems created by the minimum harmonisation formula

The minimum harmonisation formula, although coveted at political level, jeopardises the process of market building: market fragmentation targeted by the harmonising measures would still be permitted, as states may make different choices as to what level of protection they want to ensure. The minimum harmonisation formula may certainly be detrimental to, if not in conflict with, market integration to the extent that it does not prevent Member States from adopting or maintaining more restrictive provisions if those are more favourable to the consumers.[37]

The relationship between market integration and consumer protection in the Community framework could therefore be summarised in the following stages:

1. *Partial negative integration*: deregulation does not occur in cases where the European Court of Justice (ECJ) identifies a need to protect consumers. In those instances, domestic regulation stands and market fragmentation persists;
2. *Re-regulation and positive integration*: EC law is adopted in order to achieve harmonisation in the field where market fragmentation persists by setting common rules and standards;
3. *Adoption of the minimum harmonisation formula in re-regulating the market*: because of the minimal character of EC legislation, Member States are allowed to maintain their own regulations. In those cases, market fragmentation would once again persist.

Theoretically, it is possible to imagine cases where the market would not be subject to any variation from stage 1 to stage 3: a domestic measure restrictive of trade would be entitled to stand on the basis of *Cassis*' mandatory requirements first; on

[37] Several examples of this approach to technical harmonisation can be found: Dir 84/450/EEC Relating to the Approximation of the Laws, Regulations and Administrative Provisions of the Member States Concerning Misleading Advertising ([1984] OJ L250/17) allows Member States to maintain or introduce stricter provisions; Dir 85/577/EEC of 20 December 1985 to Protect the Consumer in Respect of Contracts Negotiated Away from Business Premises ([1985] OJ L372/31), Dir 87/102/EEC for the Approximation of the Laws, Regulations and Administrative Provisions of the Member States Concerning Consumer Credit ([1987] OJ L42/48), Dir 90/314/EEC on Package Travel, Package Holidays and Package Tours ([1990] OJ L158/59) adopt similar formulas; Dir 97/7/EC on the Protection of Consumers in Respect of Distance Contracts ([1997] OJ L144/19) allows Member States to adopt more stringent provisions, such as 'a ban, in the general interest, on the marketing of certain goods and services . . . by means of distance contracts' and finally Dir 1999/44/EC on Certain Aspects of the Sale of Consumer Goods and Associated Guarantees ([1999] OJ L171/12) includes the possibility for the Member States to adopt or maintain more stringent provisions to ensure a higher level of consumer protection.

the basis of the minimum harmonisation formula once positive integration has occurred.[38]

The Commission has recently stated that 'the principle of minimum harmonisation in consumer protection legislation was criticised as not achieving the uniformity of solutions for similar situations that the internal market would require'[39] and the latest trend is, in truth, aiming to total harmonisation.[40]

As far as Directive 93/13 is concerned, from the point of view of consumers the 'confidence building' rationale still remains a valid (?) one: the directive ensures a minimum threshold of protection which entails that, although they may not know the law of another state, consumers can expect a minimum level of protection.

As far as traders are concerned, it is difficult to see how a directive containing a minimum harmonisation formula can benefit those who fear that their contract would not be subject to their own law: a trader wishing to offer his goods or services in other Member States would still be obliged to research the legislation in force in each State to ensure he complies with it, doubts and uncertainty would persist, and so would transaction costs. The distortions of competition originated by the fact that traders in one country are subject to more stringent requirements than those in another country would also remain unaffected.

[38] In practice, however, the ECJ attitude to admitting exceptions based on the mandatory requirements has been quite restrictive; justification under the minimum harmonisation formula, on the other hand, would probably enhance remarkably the chances of a domestic measure to be upheld: rather than being simply tolerated, the measure would be fully legitimised under the provisions of a related 'minimal' Directive: see Case 328/87 *Buet v Ministère Public* [1989] ECR 1235. One example of limited harmonisation is operation of the Consumer Credit Directive. Adopted under art 94 (100), it aimed at reducing discrepancies between Member States' laws in consumer credit. Art 15 provided that the Directive should not preclude Member States from retaining or adopting more stringent provisions. Member States took advantage of the provisions to a considerable extent, with the result that the Directive had a modest impact on the original objective of harmonisation (see Commission Report COM (95) 117 final) and the Commission is currently considering reform: see Proposal for a Directive on the Harmonization of the Laws, Regulations and Administrative Provisions of the Member States Concerning Credit for Consumers COM (2002) 443 final. In measures which are only partially or indirectly aimed at consumer protection, more stringent domestic measures to the detriment of harmonisation are allowed less frequently, see, eg, C–386/00 *Axa Royale Belge SA v Ochoa* [2002] ECR I–2209; C–233/94 *Germany v Parliament and Council (Re Deposit Guarantees)* [1997] 3 CMLR 1379.

[39] 'Communication from the Commission to the European Parliament and Council, A More Coherent European Contract Law. An Action Plan' COM (2003) 68 final, 9. See also speech 02/461, available at http://ec.europa.eu/consumers/dyna/speeches/speeches_cons_consint.cfm, of the then Commissioner Byrne, who admitted that

> the history of EU consumer protection measures is largely one of minimum harmonisation. The Member States wanted to retain discretion to add national provisions to those laid down by EU law. However, the downside of this approach has been to dilute the harmonising benefits of EU legislation and also to provide a backdoor means by which internal barriers can be created not only in relation to business, but also to consumers.

[40] See, eg, the more recent directives 2005/29/EC Concerning Unfair Business-to-Consumer Commercial Practices in the Internal Market ([2005] OJ L149/22) and 2002/65/EC Concerning the Distance Marketing of Consumer Financial Services ([2002] OJ L271/16). The Consumer Policy Strategy 2002–6 (Communication from the Commission to the European Parliament, the Council, the Economic and Social Committee and the Committee of the Regions COM (2002) 208 final, 11) envisages moving away from the present situation of different sets of rules in each Member State towards a more consistent environment for consumer protection across the EU.

The ambiguous notion of 'obstacle to trade'

Beyond the problems raised by the minimum harmonisation formula, more radical criticism to the contribution of Directive 93/13 to market building may be made when one looks at the notion of 'obstacle' upon which it is based.

The interpretation of the *Cassis* ruling discussed above is based on the idea that any rule of consumer protection can potentially be an obstacle to trade. On the other hand, this view does not take into account the different kinds of rules which can be grouped under the wide umbrella of 'consumer protection law'. These can be 'technical' rules concerning the product in itself, that is, its composition, packaging, presentation, such as the ones at issue in *Cassis* and in several other *Cassis*-derived cases; but they may also be domestic rules of contract or tort law such as, for example, 'laws of the Member States relating to the terms of contract between the seller of goods or supplier of services, on the one hand, and the consumer of them, on the other hand'.[41]

In *Keck*,[42] the ECJ drew the well-known distinction between rules relating to products themselves and selling arrangements, and established that the latter do not

> hinder directly or indirectly, actually or potentially, trade between Member States within the meaning of the *Dassonville* judgement [. . .] provided that those provisions apply to all affected traders operating within the national territory and provided that they affect in the same manner, in law and in fact, the marketing of domestic products and of those from other Member States.

Under this formal distinction, rules relating to unfair terms are to be considered 'selling arrangements' and would therefore not be deemed to be an obstacle under article 28 EC.[43]

The judgment was accompanied by a widespread critical reaction by academia,[44] advocating a less formalist test rather based on whether

> measures introduced . . . in a Member State . . . apply equally in law and in fact to all goods or services without reference to origin and . . . impose no direct or substantial hindrance to the access of imported goods or services to the market of that Member State.[45]

This has slowly triggered a shift in the court's attitude towards a less formalistic approach which takes into account not only the discriminatory nature of a certain measure, but whether there is a 'substantial hindrance' to market access for for-

[41] Dir 93/13, Recital 2.

[42] C–267 and 268/91 *Criminal Proceedings against Keck and Mithouard* [1993] ECR I–6097.

[43] This does not apply, of course, where the contract is the 'product' itself, such as in the case of banking and insurance contracts.

[44] See, eg, N Nic Shuibhne, 'The Free Movement of Goods and Article 28 EC: An Evolving Framework' (2002) ELR 408; C Barnard, 'Fitting the Remaining Pieces into the Goods and Persons Jjigsaw' (2001) 26 ELR 35; P Oliver 'Some Further Reflections on the Scope of Articles 28–30 (ex 30–36) EC (1999) 36 CML Rev 783; S Weatherill, 'After *Keck:* Some Thoughts on How to Clarify the Clarification' (1996) CML Rev 885.

[45] *Ibid* 896–97.

eign producers,[46] a solution which is partly (but not entirely) in line with the ECJ case-law on the other freedoms.

How would this reasoning apply to the relationship between article 28 EC and domestic contract law rules?

Alsthom Atlantique[47] is a case that involved exemption clauses. Sulzer, involved in a claim for latent defects in two vessel engines provided to Alsthom, was, according to French law, unable to rely on a clause that exempted its liability. This was because a peculiar but consolidated case-law of the Cour de Cassation interpreted the relevant provisions of the French *Code civil* so as to allow clauses limiting liability only where the parties to the contract were engaged in the same specialised field (which was not the case). Sulzer therefore claimed that such case-law distorted competition and hindered, contrary to article 29 (formerly 34) EC, the free movement of goods by putting French undertakings at a disadvantage compared to the foreign competitors who were not subject to such stringent liability. The ECJ held that article 29 EC applied to restrictions on intra-Community trade which placed the export trade at a disadvantage for the benefit of domestic trade. Accordingly, the fact that all traders subject to French law were at a disadvantage, without there being any advantage for domestic production, did not trigger the application of article 29 EC. In addition, parties to an international contract of sale are generally free to determine the law applicable to their contractual relations and can thus avoid being subject to French law.

Leaving aside the issue of choice of law, the case could give rise to further legal issues. One may argue that the French law constitutes a measure having equivalent effect to a quantitative restriction (MEQR) under article 30 (now 28) EC since a foreign trader would feel that his access to the French (consumer) market is restricted by the fear of the French rules of liability (to which, as we have seen, he would be subject only in a very limited number of cases).

In *CMC Motorradcenter v Pevin Baskiciogullari*[48] Motorradcenter, a non-authorised trader in motorcycles that had been the object of parallel import, claimed that an obligation under German law to communicate to the other party to a contract facts which may determine its decision to make the contract was a MEQR within the meaning of article 30 (now 28) EC. The ECJ stated that the possibility that a duty of information in German contract law could deter from business was too remote and too indirect to be an obstacle to trade under article 30 (now 28) EC, but the case was then decided mainly on other grounds.

The issue of the indirectness and remoteness of an obstacle is, however, a very important one. Cases such as *Krantz GmbH v Ontvanger der Directe Belastingen*

[46] See C–405/98 *Konsumentombudsman (KO) v Gourmet International Products AB (GIP)* [2001] ECR I–1795; C–34 to 36/95 *De Agostini* [1997] ECR I–3843.

[47] C–339/89 *Alsthom Atlantique SA v Compagnie de Construction Mécanique Sulzer SA* [1991] ECR I–107.

[48] C–93/92 [1993] ECR I–5009.

and Netherlands,[49] *BASF AG v Präsident des Deutschen Patentamts*[50] and *Graf*[51] provide some enlightenment as to what position the ECJ might take in future cases concerning the relationship between contract law and free movement of goods. In the case of *Krantz*, for example, the issue was whether non-discriminatory domestic tax legislation allowing tax authorities to seize goods in possession of a taxpayer even when they are property of a supplier in another Member State could prevent traders from selling goods to purchasers established in other Member States. Both the Advocate General and the court pointed out that the rules at issue were indistinctly applicable to domestic and imported goods and, in addition,

> the possibility that nationals of other Member States would hesitate to sells goods . . . to purchasers in the Member State concerned because such goods would be liable to seizure by the collector of taxes if the purchaser failed to discharge their Dutch tax debts is too uncertain and indirect to warrant the conclusion that a national provision authorising such seizure is liable to hinder trade between Member States.[52]

The ECJ appears to introduce here a sort of *de minimis* rule[53] according to which a remote possibility that a rule acts as a hindrance to trade is not sufficient to trigger the application of article 28 EC. The concept is comparable to the 'substantial restriction' principle laid down by Jacobs AG in his well-known opinion in *Leclerc Siplec*,[54] particularly where he emphasises the need to consider the direct or indirect, immediate or remote, or purely speculative and uncertain effect of a certain measure.[55] As a result, if the court was to apply a test based on 'substantial restriction' to contract rules on unfair terms (as selling arrangements), the answer would probably be that their divergence does not impede directly and substantially access to the market.

The *Tobacco Advertising* case[56] points in the same direction. In annulling a Directive based on article 95 EC whose purpose was mainly to ban advertising and sponsorship of tobacco products, the ECJ excluded that 'a mere finding of disparities between national laws and of the *abstract* risk of obstacles to the exercise of

[49] C–69/88 [1991] 2 CMLR 677.

[50] C–258/99 [2001] ECR I–3643. See also C–412/97 *Ed Srl v Italo Fenocchio* [1999] ECR I–3845.

[51] C–190/98 *Graf* [2000] ECR I–49.

[52] Above n 49, at para 11.

[53] The application of a *de minimis* criterion to art 28 had in the past been rejected by the ECJ (see Case 177/82 Van de Haar [1984] ECR 1797), while it is a well-accepted rule in competition law. It seems, however, that there is a slight difference between the *de minimis* rule above and the one known in competition law. In competition law, the *de minimis* rule is a quantitative criterion based on the assumption that, because of the size of the parties' market share, an agreement which could potentially restrict trade does not have an appreciable effect on trade; in the area of free movement, on the other hand, *de minimis* appears to rest on a qualitative criterion, ie one where it is the capability itself of a measure to restrict trade which is uncertain.

[54] Opinion delivered in C–412/93 *Societé d'Importation Edouard Leclerc–Siplec v TF1 Publicité SA and M6 Publicité SA* [1995] ECR I–179, see paras 39–42.

[55] For a similar, market-access based approach to the freedom to provide service see *Alpine Investments BV v Minister Van Financiën* [1995] 2 CMLR 209.

[56] C–376/98 *Federal Republic of Germany v European Parliament and Council* [2000] ECR I–8419.

fundamental freedoms or of distortions of competitions' can be sufficient to justify the application of article 95 EC: this would contradict the principle of article 5 EC that the Community has only the powers specifically conferred on it and 'the powers of the Community would be practically unlimited'.

In some ways, the *Tobacco Advertising* case represented an extreme case, since in combination with the fact that the risk of obstacles or distortions was 'abstract', it was clear from the judgment that the measure failed in all respects the proportionality test because of its generality and of the fact it did not ensure the free movement of products in conformity with its provisions.[57] Assuming one could prove that divergence in unfair terms laws restricts trade, the proportionality issue could not be re-proposed in the same terms as in *Tobacco Advertising* because the Directive contributes to market building by promoting consumer confidence.[58]

The fundament question that remains to be determined, therefore, is the extent to which a measure should facilitate trade in order to be legitimised under article 95 EC: in other words, one needs to understand whether building consumer confidence entails eliminating an obstacle to trade which, far from being an 'abstract one', is direct and concrete enough to justify the use of article 95 EC.

Is consumer confidence a sufficient reason to justify the use of article 95 EC?

On the one hand, one could argue that consumer confidence is not a reason to justify the use of article 95 EC, and that

> the shakiness of the factual assumptions and reasoning behind the EC focus on consumer contracts both alerts us to the possibility of an expansion of the province of EC contract law, and leads us to look for more contingent political explanations of the scope of the Directive. Such explanations may take the form that a consumerist movement has percolated into the organs of the EC, particularly the Commission, so that whilst the professed objectives of this regulation are couched in terms of improving the competitiveness of the single market and expanding consumer choice, the real agenda for many participants has been consumer protection as an end in itself.[59]

On the other hand, one can argue that building consumer confidence is still part of the internal market programme. Community action in the last few years[60]

[57] T Tridimas and G Tridimas, 'The European Court of Justice and the Annulment of the Tobacco Advertisement Directive: Friend of National Sovereignty or Foe of Public Health?' (2002) *European Journal of Law and Economics* 174.

[58] Since case C–210/03 *Swedish Match* [2005] 1 CMLR 26 ECJ it appears that, in order to be validly based on art 95, a directive must no longer eliminate both obstacles *and* distortions: the ability to remove either obstacles or distortions is sufficient.

[59] H Collins, 'Good Faith in European Contract Law' (1994) OJLS 237.

[60] See the recent Commission proposals to proceed to a certain degree of harmonisation of contract law: Communication from the Commission to the Council and the European Parliament on European Contract Law COM (2001) 398 final; Communication from the Commission to the European Parliament and the Council, A More Coherent European Contract Law: An Action Plan COM (2003) 68 final; Communication from the Commission to the European Parliament and the Council, European Contract Law and the Revision of the *acquis*: the Way Forward COM (2004) 651 final.

appears to be pervaded by the feeling that a degree of harmonisation of the law of obligations is a necessary and inevitable part of the irreversible process of integration started many decades ago. Uniform conditions as to what contract terms are valid may bring down the psychological, if not practical, barriers that prevent the creation of a truly common market and ultimately of a common feeling of European citizenship.[61]

Against this background, it must be said that the 'appreciability' of an obstacle or distortion is not a predetermined notion: suffice here to recall that from the ECJ's seminal judgments on free movement one gains the impression that even the notion of 'measure equivalent to a quantitative restriction' is, in itself, not a given, but a concept which is somewhat functional to the objective which, within a certain political and economic context, the court seeks to attain.[62]

Cassis de Dijon, for example, represented not only the most robust judicial contribution to the internal market but also the perfect example of purposive interpretation knowingly aimed at promoting market integration and at fending off political stagnation and euro-pessimism, paving the way for the Commission's new regulatory strategy.[63]

The sudden *revirement* in *Keck*, on the other hand, rather than simply representing the ECJ's attempt to 'clarify its case-law' also corresponded to a voluntary self restraint in the free movement of goods. In the first place, the allocation of Community competences following *Cassis* had resulted in a mechanism where 'the broader [is] the catch of article 30 EC [now 28], the broader [are] the legislative competences of the Community'.[64] Any rules which fell under *Cassis* become prey to the Community legislative process under article 95 EC operating by majority voting. *Keck* therefore aimed to make a major contribution to limiting Community governance in a scenario where the growing involvement of the ECJ in regulatory policy and the consequent increase in judicial activism was endangering the court's legitimacy; second, as the harmonisation programme had developed very successfully since *Cassis*, the need for judicial activism as a means of driving the common market agenda had considerably lessened, and the court could shift its focus from 'market building' to 'market maintaining', hence addressing its activism to other, less integrated, areas of the common market.[65]

The post-*Keck* case-law is also significant in this respect, since its confusion as to what constitutes or not an MEQR somehow represents the quest for clarity 'as

[61] See, eg, J Basedow, 'A Common Contract Law for the Common Market' (1996) 33 CML Rev 1182–83.

[62] For an example in the area of freedom of establishment see C Barnard and S Deakin, 'Market Access and Regulatory Competition' in C Barnard and J Scott (eds), *The Law of the Single European Market. Unpacking the Premises* (Oxford, Hart, 2002) 209–12.

[63] See the Commission's White Paper 'Completing the Internal Market' COM (85) 310.

[64] J Weiler, 'The Constitution of the Common Market Place' in P Craig and G De Búrca, *The Evolution of EU Law* (Oxford, OUP, 1999) 372.

[65] M Poiares Maduro, *We, the Court. The European Court of Justice and the European Economic Constitution* (Oxford, Hart, 1998) 99.

to the ultimate constitutional objective of the internal market, in general, and free movement of goods, in particular'.[66]

Accordingly, a decision as to what constitutes an obstacle to trade (or, by reference to *Tobacco Advertising*, as what constitutes a 'direct' and 'concrete' obstacle) is not taken in a *vacuum*, but rather by reference to what should be the objectives and the nature of the internal market.[67] As these are not, in themselves, predetermined, the exact width of Community competence in relation to the internal market is not predetermined either: it largely depends on the interaction between the ECJ and the Community institutions, Treaty articles, secondary Community legislation, at a given historical moment.

We will therefore proceed on the assumption that it cannot be ruled out that consumer confidence is a sufficient reason to use article 95. This assumption, however, will be revisited in the conclusion.

THE CONSUMER PROTECTION ARGUMENT

The much less controversial aim of improving consumer protection is clearly spelled out in Directive 93/13: Recitals 8 and 9 refer to the consumer protection programmes by stating inter alia that 'acquirers of goods and services should be protected against the abuse of power by the seller or supplier, in particular against one-sided standard contracts and the unfair exclusion of essential rights in contracts'.

It could be argued that protection should not be limited to consumers, as it is beyond doubt that businesses, in particular small traders, are in need of protection against one-sided contract as much as consumers; and, as an internal market matter, it is more likely that distortions of competition occur at the level of small traders rather than at consumers' level: a small trader will probably pay more attention than the consumer to the terms of the contract he is about to sign, and accordingly the level and type of protection ensured in a certain country may affect his choice of the contracting party.

Some early proposals envisaged a wider control on unfair terms and the possibility of controlling terms included in all standard form contracts was considered. The difficulties involved in gathering consensus for a set of rules that would be applicable to all standard contracts, the formal inclusion of the Directive in the EC consumer policy programme, the fact that the Directive is a compromise between different schools of thought[68] and, last but not least, a strong lobbying from large enterprises played a remarkable role in bringing the scope of the Directive down to the lowest possible level.

[66] See P Koutrakos, 'On Groceries, Alcohol and Olive Oil: More on Free Movement of Goods after *Keck*' (2001) 26 ELR 401.

[67] P Nebbia, 'Internal Market and the Harmonisation of European Contract Law' in T Tridimas and P Nebbia, *EU Law for the 21st Century: Rethinking the New Legal Order* (Oxford, Hart, 2004) vol II, 96.

[68] See below, pp 89–90.

THE FUTURE OF DIRECTIVE 93/13

The Directive as it is today may be subject to future amendments: article 9 provides that after no more than five years from the deadline for the implementation of the Directive the Commission shall present a report to the Parliament and the Council. Accordingly, in 1999 the Commission invited lawyers, representatives from the Member States, of consumer organisations and of the industry to a conference where the need for changes in the Directive was discussed. From these discussions the Commission drew suggestions and conclusions for its report, which was published on 27 April 2000[69] and not only gives a useful overview on the problems met by the Member States in the implementation of the Directive but also puts forward a few proposals for amendment. In addition, the Commission has created a database accessible via the Internet (CLAB)[70] which collects all the existing case-law in the Member States concerning unfair terms. The database, however, has not been updated since 2001 and the proposals put forward in the 2000 Report have not had any follow-up. Rather than indicating a loss of interest in this matter on the part of the Consumer Protection DG, its most recent initiatives suggests that the problems raised by Directive 93/13 will be now dealt with under the new project for a more coherent contract law, in particular as part of the plan to improve the quality of the EC contract law *acquis.*[71]

[69] Report from the Commission on the Implementation of Council Directive 93/13/EEC of 5 April 1993 on Unfair Terms in Consumer Contracts, COM (2000) 248 final.

[70] CLAB (=European Database on Case Law about Unfair Contractual Terms) can be viewed at: http://europa.eu.int/clab/index.htm

[71] See Communication from the Commission to the European Parliament and the Council. A More Coherent European Contract Law: An Action Plan COM (2003) 68 final para 41 ff.

3

Unfair Terms Regulation: A Comparative Study

SINCE WORLD WAR II, the changing nature of consumption and the emergence of the welfare state has provided the background to dramatic regulatory changes in Europe. Technological developments, changes in the methods of sale and distribution and the increased use of mass methods of manufacture and of standard form contracts have radically changed the economic and social landscape of the last century. Buyers no longer have sufficient knowledge and skill to assess the quality of goods they want to purchase; the retailers' function has been reduced to handling what buyers have already been persuaded to buy by nationally advertised producers; the established balance between buyer and seller (if ever the was any) has been seriously disturbed by the use of standard contracts, necessary to deal with customers on mass scale.

As a consequence, states have taken up control of some aspects of market transactions in an attempt to re-establish bargaining power between the parties by compensatory mechanisms like imposing warranties or prohibiting exemption clauses; they have conferred 'basic rights' to consumers by granting them rights such as health and safety, protection of economic interests, access to justice; they have revised classic principles such as *caveat emptor* and freedom of contract so as to favour the vulnerable or ignorant party to a transaction.[1]

The following pages present an overview of the legislation regulating unfair terms in Germany, France, England and Italy. This is meant to fulfil two purposes: as far as English and Italian law are concerned, the information provided sets out the main features and aims of the two systems of unfair terms control that will be examined in more detail in Chapter 4. As far as German and French law are concerned, the overview provided in this chapter aims to provide a 'platform' of information which will be necessary to understand the comparative references that will be made to these two systems in the course of this book.

[1] N Reich, 'Diverse Approaches to Consumer Protection Philosophy' (1992) *Journal of Consumer Policy* 261.

OVERVIEW

The German AGB-Gesetz and the BGB

In German law, unfair terms were specifically regulated by the 1976 AGB-Gesetz[2] (commonly called AGB-G). This has been repealed by the 2002 reform of the BGB[3] (*Schuldrechtsreform*) and its provisions are now reproduced, with minor variations, in §§ 305 to 310 BGB.

A first set of rules concerns requirements for incorporation. § 305(2) establishes that the person proposing the contract, (the 'user', *Verwender*) must expressly draw attention to any standard terms and conditions applying to the contract. If it is not possible to inform clients expressly, a prominent notice must at least be displayed. Standard terms and conditions do not become part of the contract unless the consumer agrees to them (§ 305(2), BGB). The user must give the other party, in a reasonable manner that also appropriately takes account of any physical handicap of the other party discernible by the user, the possibility of gaining knowledge of their content. There is also the possibility of concluding a framework agreement that will apply to all contracts concluded between the parties (§ 305(3)).

The obligation to draw terms and conditions clearly to the attention of clients really matters only if the terms are physically not part of the contract: no need for such reference arises if the terms are included in the contract form. The same applies to the obligation under paragraph 3: the provision only refers to cases where terms and conditions are not physically incorporated in the main contract.

The above provisions do not apply in contracts with a business party (*unternehmer*): in these cases, the pre-AGB-G case-law on the general principles of contract law still applies. In practice, this entails that there is a duty to refer to the general terms, but no duty to communicate them to the other party,[4] who has anyway the right to gain knowledge of them upon reasonable conditions.[5] There is no need for any express reference to terms and conditions if the parties are under a long-standing commercial relationship (*ständige Geschäftsbeziehungen*) whereby they had in the past adopted such terms; or when terms are common usage in a certain trade. Special incorporation rules exist for terms concerning the provision of certain public services.[6]

'Unexpected' terms are not part of the contract. Terms are considered 'unexpected' if they contain obligations which are so unusual that consumers would not normally expect to encounter them in a contract (§ 305c BGB). This reflects pre-existing case-law.[7] Paragraph 2 of the same article contains the familiar principle

[2] Gesetz zur Regelung des Rechts der Allgemeinen Geschäftsbedingungen of 9 December 1976.

[3] Bürgerliches Gesetzbuch.

[4] See, eg, BGH (Bundesgerichtshof) 11 May 1989, WM (Wertpapier Mitteilungen) 1989, 1227, 1228.

[5] BGH 3 December 1987, BGHZ (Bundesgerichtshof in Zivilsachen) 102, 293.

[6] See § 305a BGB.

[7] BGH 11 November 1968 NJW 1969, 230.

(added only by the 2002 amendment)[8] that where the general terms and conditions are obscurely worded, the interpretation which is less favourable to the person proposing them, normally the seller, applies (§ 305c(2) BGB).

The BGB then contains a 'grey' and a 'black' list of unfair terms. The grey list under § 308 contains terms which present a substantial risk that the client will be disadvantaged. However, whether an unfair disadvantage exists depends on the specific circumstances and accordingly the validity of such terms is subject to judicial appraisal (these terms are called *Klauselverbote ohne Wertungsmöglichkeit*): for this purpose, the German legislator uses terms such as 'reasonable',[9] 'particular importance',[10] 'unreasonably high',[11] 'inadequately specified',[12] which are explicitly meant to provide judges with sufficient flexibility for a case-by-case analysis.

§ 309 lists terms whose invalidity is not subject to any appraisal (*Klauselverbote mit Wertungsmöglichkeit*). These include, for example, terms in which the seller excludes all liability for defective goods, restricts his liability to repairing the defective good, or refers the client exclusively to third parties (eg the manufacturer).

The two lists are completed by a closing provision, § 307, laying down a general test (*Inhaltskontrolle*) for terms that do not fall within §§ 308–9: standard business terms are invalid if, contrary to the requirement of good faith (*Treu und Glauben*), they place the contractual partner of the user at an unreasonable disadvantage (*unangemessene Benachteiligung*). The latter is the key requirement to the fairness test. In determining whether there is a significant disadvantage the judge shall identify and weight the interests of the two parties under the type of contract under discussion as a whole and the aims of the contract.[13]

This provision is particularly important for fairness control in business-to-business contracts, since the lists under §§ 308–9 are only applicable to contracts which are not made with an *unternehmer* (as clarified by § 310). This does not mean, of course, that a term which falls within one of the two lists but which is

[8] The use of contract terms which are incorrect or obscure was anyway considered in breach of § 9 AGB-G (now § 307 BGB), and the principle of transparency was considered to be 'inbuilt' in the system of the AGB-G.

[9] See, eg, § 308 no 4:

> the stipulation of the user's right to alter or depart from the promised performance, unless, taking into account the user's interests, the stipulation to alter or depart from performance is reasonable for the other party.

[10] See, eg, § 308 no 6:

> a provision which provides that a declaration by the user of particular importance is deemed to have been received by the other party.

[11] See, eg, § 308 no 7(a):

> a provision by which, in the event that one of the parties to the contract terminates the contract or gives notice to terminate it, the user can demand (a) unreasonably high remuneration for the utilisation or use of a thing or a right or for performance made.

[12] See, eg, § 308(1):

> a provision by which the user, in derogation from legislative provisions, reserves the right to an unreasonably long or inadequately specified additional period within which to perform.

[13] C Witz, *Droit privé allemand. Droits subjectifs* (Paris, Litec, 1992) 353.

contained in a business-to-business contract may not be declared unfair under § 307.

The second paragraph of § 307 specifies that in case of doubt an unreasonable disadvantage is assumed if a provision cannot be reconciled with essential basic principles of the statutory rule from which it deviates. This reflects previous case-law on § 242 BGB holding that a term that modifies the 'directing image' (*Leitbild*) of the contract given by default rules is contrary to good faith; but academics and courts tend to distinguish between default rules based on consideration of equity (*Bestimmungen mit Gerechtigsgehalt*), that is, those that reflect the need to protect the weak party, from those that simply have a practical use (*Bestimmungen mit Zweckmässigkeitfunktion*),[14] and only non-compliance with the former may be considered as giving rise to unfairness.

Terms are also presumed to be unfair where they restrict essential rights or duties resulting from the nature of the contract in such a manner that there is a risk that the purpose of the contract will not be achieved (§ 307(2)2). So, for example, an exemption clause may be considered to be unfair when it touches upon the cardinal obligations (*Kardinalpflichten*) of the contract, that is, those that are of fundamental importance for the achievement of the aims of the contract. Naturally, these provisions only introduce a presumption that can be rebutted, for example by proving that the disadvantage is compensated by another advantage granted to the customer.[15] Where an individual term or condition is ineffective, the rest of the contract nevertheless remains in force (§ 306(1) BGB), and legal provisions, where applicable, replace the ineffective terms and conditions (§ 306(2) BGB).

Implementation of Directive 93/13 (the Directive) took place in 1996 by the simple insertion of two new paragraphs, § 12 on international applicability and § 24a on consumer contracts. The effect of the latter provision is to ensure that, with specific regard to consumer contracts, some minor discrepancies between the AGB-G and Directive 93/13 are ironed out so that the former can guarantee at least the same level of protection as the latter. Accordingly, § 24a introduced a presumption that standard terms are proffered by the business party; stated that terms which are pre-established fall within the scope of control even if they are intended for use only once; required that in determining unreasonable detriment under § 9 the circumstances at the time of the conclusion of the contract are taken into account. The transparency principle was not mentioned until the 2002 reform, but this has now been remedied, as earlier mentioned, by § 307(1).

[14] Such as, eg, terms on prescriptions, compensation or choice of forum.

[15] It must be noted, in this respect, that the Bundesgerichtshof tends to reject the argument that an unfair term can be compensated by a lower price on grounds that risks should be allocated rather to customers in general (maybe by imposing a higher price) than to the specific customers who happen to be the victims of the unfair term (BHG 12 May 1980 BGHZ 77, 126, 131).

The French *loi Scrivener*

The French law against unfair terms dates back to 1978 when the so-called *loi Scrivener*[16] was enacted. This contained, in chapter 4, the rules on unfair terms and was consolidated, together with other provisions, in the *Code de la consommation* in 1993. Provisions on unfair terms now constitute articles L 132.1 to L 132.5 of that *Code.*

The provisions only apply to contracts concluded between professionals and consumers or non-professionals. According to the pre-Directive test of fairness, a term was unfair 'if it seems to be imposed on the non-professional by an abuse of the economic power (*abus de la puissance économique*) of the other party, to which it confers an excessive advantage (*avantage excessif*)'. Hence, various requirements had to be fulfilled: the term had to be imposed, it had to confer an excessive advantage, and there had to be an abuse of economic power (although this requirement was usually considered to be automatically fulfilled by the existence of an excessive advantage); moreover, control was only limited to certain types of clauses, such as terms concerning certain aspects of the price and its actual payment, the determination of subject matter, the delivery of the goods bought, the allocation of risks, responsibilities and warranties, conditions of performance, termination. All of these criteria have been removed by a 1995 amendment (adopted to transpose Directive 93/13),[17] except that of 'excessive advantage' that has now become the cornerstone of the fairness test. In order to implement the Directive correctly, the 1995 law also required that the unfair nature of a term must be appreciated taking into account the circumstances surrounding the conclusion of the contract, as well as the other terms of the contract; it introduced the 'core terms' exclusion; it transposed the indicative and non-exhaustive list of unfair terms of Directive 93/13.

The original formulation of the *loi* did not envisage any forms of judicial control. The Conseil d'Etat was in charge, upon consultation with a 'Commission for Unfair Terms' of issuing secondary legislation (*décrets*) containing lists of terms that were prohibited. This turned out to be a failure: only one list containing three terms (one of which was then struck down by the Conseil d'Etat itself) was issued. The Commission for Unfair Terms also issued (and still does so) recommendations containing lists of potentially unfair terms but these are not binding: however, judges often refer to such recommendations in order to decide whether a term is fair or not. Concerned by the risk of excessive judicial interference with contractual freedom, the *loi* established that judges were only allowed to apply the *décrets* but had no freedom to carry out a fairness test. However, given the idleness of the legislator, the Cour de Cassation decided in 1991[18] that a term could be declared unfair on the sole basis of the *loi Scrivener*, even if a *décret* prohibiting that term had not been adopted. This solution is now reflected in a more recent

[16] *Loi Scrivener* no 78-23 of 10 January 1978.
[17] *Loi* no 95-96 of 1 February 1995.
[18] Cour de Cassation Civile 1ère 14 May 1991 D 1991 J 449 (with a comment by J Ghestin).

version of the *Code de consommation* which, in accordance with Directive 93/13, envisages both the ex ante and the ex post forms of control.

The common law remedies and the Unfair Contract Terms Act 1977 (UCTA)

Generally speaking, even a superficial analysis of doctrines such as consideration, incorporation of terms, undue influence, interpretation, implied terms and mistake shows that, behind the facade of the 'hands off' approach to contracts, there exists a clear reluctance of courts to allow exploitation of the others by means of a contract.[19] Elements of fairness permeate the law, even though one may wonder whether these elements are sensibly put together to form a coherent general requirement of fairness as a prerequisite to contracting. The determination of whether a contract has been formed, on what terms and whether it is vitiated often allows references to notions adjacent to fairness.[20]

It is evident, however, that the doctrines deployed in order to avoid enforcement of unfair transactions rarely refer to fairness as a relevant consideration but rather are 'used instrumentally to achieve the outcome of invalidating the contract or a noxious term'.[21] In other words, a court will stress any elements of procedural impropriety that it can discover rather than address directly the unfairness of the bargain. Substantive unfairness may provide the motive for intervention, but the formal legal reason given for upsetting the contract will be formulated in terms of a procedural defect, such as deception, manipulation or unfair surprise. The result is that although it may seem plausible that courts are concerned with substantive unfairness in a particular case, since their formal reasons for the decision inevitably latch on to a procedural impropriety, the case for believing that substantive unfairness is crucial to the decision may be regarded as unproven.

Accordingly, for the purposes of our analysis it is important to bear in mind that, if any reason of substantive fairness underlies a decision, it is unlikely that it would be clearly stated: this applies especially to the remedies elaborated by the common law, since the Unfair Contract Terms Act 1977 (UCTA) opened the route to more open judicial reasoning.

Remedies against unfair terms in England are stratified at different levels of legal sources, having been partially elaborated by courts (common law remedies), and partially introduced by means of the Unfair Contract Terms Act 1977. The common law rules developed by courts consist in (or, more correctly, consist in a particular use of) rules on incorporation of terms and interpretation. Rules concerning the so-called fundamental breach and breach of a fundamental term are also a part, even though slightly outdated, of this framework. Rules on incorporation of terms into the contract are based on the principle that a certain term will

[19] P Atiyah, *An Introduction to the Law of Contract* (Oxford, Clarendon Press, 1995) 282–96.

[20] G Howells and S Weatherhill, *Consumer Protection Law* (Aldershot, Ashgate, 2005) 263.

[21] H Collins, *The Law of Contract* (London, Butterworths, 1997) 254.

only operate if it has been incorporated into the contract upon which it purports to have effect. In cases where a contract is partly oral and partly written, the party seeking to rely on the clause may have to show that he has incorporated it into the bargain: in cases of this type, the question of what should constitute sufficient notice of a written term for it to be regarded as part of the agreement has given judges rather wide room for action in excluding the enforceability of burdensome terms.

Once an exclusion clause has, by whatever means, been incorporated into a particular contract, the next tier of judicial control consists in checking whether that clause is apt, as a matter of interpretation, to cover the particular event which has arisen. Two main sets of rules have been created in this respect: the rule of construction *contra proferentem* and of negligence liability.[22] Both rules aim to exclude that a certain exemption clause applies to a certain event on grounds that such an event is not covered by the clause when correctly interpreted.

Finally, fundamental breach and breach of a fundamental term are also part of this framework, but lost their importance since they started being considered as rules of construction rather than substantive rules. According to such rules, the possibility of relying on an exemption clause can be barred on grounds that it is the content of the clause itself that renders it unenforceable.

Judicial motivation to use indirect routes such as the ones described above to attack clauses perceived to be unfair was dramatically reduced by the adoption of the Unfair Contract Terms Act 1977. In spite of its name, the Act does not deal with all types of unfair terms, but only with exemption clauses;[23] nevertheless, it is the most important legislative limitation on the effectiveness of unfair terms.

First, it renders totally ineffective certain types of restrictions or exclusions of liability: according to section 2(1), a person who acts in the course of business cannot by any contract term or notice exclude or restrict his liability for death or

[22] Some texts also mention the rule of 'strict construction' of exclusion clauses: its content and rationale, however, are comparable to the *contra proferentem* rules, with the only practical difference that a term may be subject to 'strict interpretation' in favour as well as against the *proferens.*

[23] The notion of 'exclusion clause' under the Act is wide enough to cover clauses which seek to achieve this effect indirectly. According to s 13 the notion of 'exclusion or restriction' includes:

—clauses making the liability or its enforcement subject to restrictive or onerous conditions;
—clauses excluding or restricting any right or remedy in respect of the liability;
—clauses excluding or restricting rules of evidence or procedure.

The intention is clearly to embrace terms which, although they do not specifically exclude or restrict liability, have a similar effect, and thus to prevent the evasion of the Act. In practice, then, one party will be prevented from doing things such as imposing a short time limit within which claims must be brought (see eg *Thomas Witther Ltd v TBP Industries Ltd* unreported, 15 July 1994 in R Lawson, *Exclusion Clauses and Unfair Contract Terms* (London, Sweet & Maxwell, 2000) 106), or excluding a particular remedy (such as rejection or set-off) without affecting another (see *Stewart Gill Ltd v Horatio Myer & Co Ltd* [1992] 2 All ER 530 and the comment by E Peel, 'Making More Use of the Unfair Contract Terms Act 1977: *Stewart Gill v Horatio Myer*' (1993) MLR 98–103; see also *Esso Petroleum v Milton* unreported, 5 February 1997 in Lawson, *Exclusion Clauses,* 106 fn 5), reversing the burden of proof and so on. Valid agreed damages clauses and agreements to submit present or future differences to arbitration, on the other hand, are commonly considered not to be subject to the Act, see G Treitel, *The Law of Contract* (London, Sweet & Maxwell, 1999) 228.

personal injury resulting from negligence. Negligence is defined by section 1(1) to include 'breach . . . of any obligation arising from the . . . terms . . . of a contract, to take reasonable care'. On the other hand, it is clear that section 2(1) does not apply if the breach of contract or duty is committed without negligence: clauses purporting to exclude liability for such breaches, however, may be ineffective under other provisions of the Act.

Second, the Act continues the effect of previous legislation concerning defective or dangerous goods. Section 6 restricts the ability of sellers of goods to exempt themselves from liability for breach of the stipulations implied in contracts of sale or hire-purchase under the Sale of Goods Act 1979: in particular, it prohibits exclusions or restrictions of liability for breach of stipulations as to title[24] (s 6.1)[25] and it prohibits exclusions or restrictions of liability in relation to statutorily implied terms as to correspondence of goods with the description or sample, and as to their quality or fitness for a particular purpose[26] (s 6.2). It must be noted that this latter provision applies only to cases where the buyer is dealing 'as a consumer'.[27]

Finally, section 5 of the Act prohibits the exclusion or restriction of negligence liability of a manufacturer or distributor of goods by means of a written guarantee, subject to the requirement that the goods are of a type supplied for private use or consumption and the loss or damage has arisen from the goods proving defective while in consumer use.

Save for the instances examined above, where the 1977 Act prohibits absolutely the exclusion or restriction of liability, the contract terms controlled by the Act are subject to a test of reasonableness. Thus, under section 2(2) a contract term or notice by which a party acting in the course of business seeks to exclude his liability for negligence giving rise to loss or damage other than death or personal injury must comply with such a requirement.

A large number of contractual terms are subject to the reasonableness test under section 3, entirely dedicated to liability arising in contract. According to this provision, the following terms in a contract with a consumer or on standard terms are valid only if they satisfy a judicially administered test of reasonableness: (1) terms that exclude or restrict the other party's liability when in breach of contract. This refers to 'any liability' and not only to negligence liability; (2) terms that entitle the other party to be able to render a contractual performance substantially different from that which was reasonably expected of him or to render no performance at all. According to section 6(3), the reasonableness requirement must be fulfilled by

[24] Implied by s 12 of the Sale of Goods Act 1979.

[25] It must be noted that s 6.1 applies not only to business liabilities but also to those arising under any contract of sale of goods or hire-purchase agreement: accordingly, even a private seller is subject to this provision.

[26] Ss 13–15 of the Sale of Goods Act 1979.

[27] As far as other contracts for the supply of goods are concerned (eg, exchange, pledge or hire) when by statute those contracts contain implied terms as to title, correspondence with the description, quality or fitness for a particular purpose, a person acting in the course of business cannot in a contract with a consumer exclude or restrict liability in this respect (s 7 UCTA).

a term in a contract for the sale or hire-purchase of goods purporting to exclude or restrict liability for breach of statutorily implied terms where the buyer or hire-purchaser deals otherwise than as a consumer.[28] UCTA also amends section 3 of the Misrepresentation Act 1967 so as to subject terms excluding or restricting liability for misrepresentation to the requirement of reasonableness.

It must be also noted that UCTA only applies at the level of individual contract. There is no provision for collective or public enforcement action against unfair terms since English law is not familiar with the concept of representative action.

Finally, a few prohibitions are scattered in sectoral legislation such as, for example, the one on consumer credit, fair trading, transport, employment and social security.[29] Because of their specificity, those provisions are outside the scope of the present work.

The Italian civil code

The Italian civil code (hereinafter 'cc'), which dates back to 1942 but is still deeply rooted in the ideology of the Enlightenment, does not envisage any form of direct and substantive control on fairness of contract bargains: private law, as *jus privatorum*, is the law of private individuals and as such shall encourage them to pursue their interests by allowing them a high degree of autonomy and self-determination and by ensuring in the first place formal equality before the law: in the name of 'laissez-faire' parties are free to pursue their own interests and neither the legislator nor the judge has the power to interfere and modify rights and duties freely undertaken by the parties.

Accordingly, control on the content of the contract takes place only in few exceptional cases listed in the Italian civil code.[30]

Outside those exceptions, it is not possible to interfere with the contractual arrangement of the parties and distribute the risk according to a model which is different from the one envisaged by the parties: the contract is a private matter between parties to which the judge has no access, save of course cases where the

[28] A similar rule applies to other contracts for the supply of goods under s 7(3); additionally, in those contract terms excluding or restricting liability for breach of implied terms as to title to, or quiet possession of the goods, are also subject to the test of reasonableness. Furthermore, s 4 of the Act introduces the requirement of reasonableness for contract terms where a consumer undertakes to indemnify another person in respect of a business liability incurred by the other for negligence or breach of contract.

[29] See, eg, s 173(1) and (2) of the Consumer Credit Act 1974; s 151 of the Road Traffic Act 1960; s 1(3) of the Law Reform (Personal Injuries) Act 1948.

[30] Those are cases where performance becomes impossible (*impossibilità sopravvenuta della prestazione*, arts 1218, 1256 cc) or too burdensome (*eccessiva onerosità*, art 1467 cc); cases where one party agrees to an extremely disadvantageous contract for the reason that he finds himself in a situation of danger or need and the other party takes the opportunity to derive an unfair profit for himself (*rescissione di contratto concluso in stato di pericolo*, art 1447 cc, and *per lesione*, art 1448 cc); cases where a term imposes too burdensome duties on the party at fault in case of trivial breach or delay in performance (*clausola penale*, arts 1382, 1384 cc).

lawfulness (*liceità*) of the transaction is at stake (arts 1325, 1349(2), 1343, 1345, 1346, 1354, 1895, 1904, 1963, 2035, 2103(2), 2265, 2744 cc).

That the modern age had brought relevant changes to the process of contract formation and to its content, however, was a well-known and much discussed issue at the time when the 1942 civil code was adopted. The attention of the legislator was particularly attracted by the emergence of standard terms contracts (the closest translation to '*condizioni generali di contratto*'). Those are contracts the terms of which do not represent the result of a process of negotiation and the final convergence of the parties' will; rather, terms are imposed by one party (usually the one with the stronger bargaining position) on the other by using a standard form adopted for a number of similar transactions.

The use of such tools was considered entirely positive, in that it laid down uniform conditions of contract for everybody and saved the costs and time of negotiation by allowing an immediate and fast conclusion of the contract: one only had to adhere to the contract.[31] However, since the beginning of the twentieth century the need to regulate this type of contract had been felt for the reason that it left no room for individual choice, and no possibility of discussing or modifying the content of the contract. The Italian civil code boasts the peculiarity of being the first in Europe to address specific norms to this phenomenon and to face the conflict between the need to protect the party who cannot choose the content of the contract and the wish to encourage business activity, clearly facilitated by the use of standard terms contracts.

For this purpose, articles 1341 and 1342 cc were introduced. They apply to *condizioni generali di contratto* (standard terms of contract) that is, to those terms which are contained in the so-called *contratti d'adesione*[32]. Those are contracts where one party adheres to a contractual text which is pre-formulated by the other party in order to regulate in a uniform way certain contractual relationships.

Article 1341(1) cc provides that standard terms of contract prepared by one of the parties are effective as to the other, only if at the time of formation of the contract the latter knew of them, or should have known of them by using ordinary diligence (*onere di conoscenza o di conoscibilità*). Article 1341(2) cc adds that in any case some specific types of clauses (commonly known as *clausole vessatorie*) are not effective unless specifically approved in writing. Such clauses are those which establish, in favour of him who has prepared them in advance, limitations on liability, the power of withdrawing from the contract or suspending its performance, or which impose time limits involving forfeitures on the other party, limitations on the power to raise defences, restrictions on contractual freedom in relations with third parties, tacit extension or renewal of the contract, arbitration clauses, or derogations from the competence of courts

[31] For this reason they were also called 'automatic' contracts 'as they conclusion is very fast, almost mechanic' see M Galizia, *Industrialismo e nuove forme contrattuali* quoted in G Alpa, *Il diritto dei consumatori* (Bari, Laterza, 1999) 157.

[32] The words *contratti d'adesione* and *condizioni generali di contratto* are used interchangeably in the Italian legislation and case-law.

Article 1342 adds that in contracts made by subscribing to forms or formularies prepared for the purpose of regulating certain contractual relationships in a uniform manner, terms added to such forms or formularies prevail over the original terms of said forms or formularies when they are incompatible with them, even though the latter have not been struck out. This does not affect the application of article 1341(2).

The essence of those two provisions can be summed up in the following rules: according to article 1341(1) the simple fact that the adherent had the possibility of becoming aware of a certain term is sufficient to make such a term binding; to compensate for failure to respect the principle that the contract results from parties' freedom, article 1341(2) imposes the formal requirement that the adherent's attention must be drawn on the most burdensome terms; according to article 1342, in standard terms contracts, forms and formularies, added terms prevail over the pre-determined ones, on the assumption that the former are the result of a bargaining process.[33]

Those rules are to be read in conjunction with the relevant rules of interpretation laid down in article 1370 cc and codifying the ancient principle of *interpretatio contra proferentem:* terms contained in standard terms contracts or in forms or formularies which have been prepared by one of the contracting parties must be interpreted, in case of doubt, in favour of the other party.

Finally, article 1229 cc imposes a blanket prohibition on terms that exempt or limit one party's liability for cases of fraud (*dolo*) or gross negligence (*colpa grave*) by making them void (*nulli*); nor can a party exempt or limit liability in cases where the act of the debtor or his auxiliaries constitutes a violation of duties arising from rules of public order. It must be noted that this article applies not only to contractual relationships, but to any type of obligation (*obbligazione*).

For many years the Italian system has not provided for any sort of administrative control on unfair terms.[34] Recent regulation for specific sectors has introduced some general and indirect forms of administrative control on contract terms promoted by bodies outside the public administration, the purpose of which is not to protect the consumers' interests but to assure compliance with the 'general public interest'.[35]

[33] F Lapertosa, 'La giurisprudenza tra passato e futuro dopo l'avvento della nuova disciplina sulle clausole vessatorie' Foro Italiano 1997 V 357.

[34] R De Negri, 'Report on the Practical Implementation of Directive 93/13/EEC in Italy' in *The Unfair Terms Directive: Five Years On* Acts of the Brussels Conference 1–3 July 1999 (Luxembourg, Office for Official Publications of the European Communities, 2000) 304.

[35] Among the most important bodies of administrative control, CONSOB (Commissione Nazionale per le Società e la Borsa; for the control of companies listed in the stock exchange) and the Autorità Garante della Concorrenza e del Mercato (the antitrust national authority) must be mentioned. Moreover, it is necessary to mention the supervision of the Bank of Italy on the activities of banks and financial intermediaries and of ISVAP (Istituto per la Vigilanza sulle Assicurazioni Private e di Interesse Collettivo) on the activities of insurance companies. The administrative control of contractual frameworks carried out in such fields, however, aims mainly at preserving competition and ensuring clarity of information for the market and not at balancing the substance of the contract. Maintenance of competitive markets is not, however, a sufficient means to ensure the fairness of

In addition, if the review of unfair terms has been within the exclusive power of the judicial system, it must be said that the scantiness of the means of protection is increased by the absence of any form of class action that could extend the effect of the final decision *ultra partes;* the possibility for consumers' associations to activate controls was heavily penalised by the lack of legislative tools, as well as by the lack of economic resources. In fact, the Italian consumers' associations, unlike those of other countries, were not admitted until recently to any official financial support and existed merely on a voluntary basis.

THE RATIONALE OF UNFAIR TERMS CONTROL IN ITALY AND ENGLAND

Standard form contracts versus inequality of bargaining power

The French and the German systems of control provide the perfect example of two types of approach, reflecting two different schools of thought, that can be taken towards unfair terms control.

According to one school of thought, the reason for intervention against unfair terms lies in the use of standardised contract terms in market transactions. Although this facilitates market transactions by saving time and money, it presents the inherent danger of depriving one party of the possibility of revising the terms of the contract in detail, and thus requires some external control on the fairness of the transaction. This approach is well represented by the German BGB (and the previous AGB-G), whose provisions apply to contracts on standard terms and conditions of business where there had been no individual negotiation (*Individualvereinbarungen*), including business-to-business contracts, and only in a few cases subjects contracts with non-professionals to a stricter control.

The other school of thought is biased in favour of the consumer as the potentially weaker side of the transaction, exploited by the superior economic power of the 'professional' side. The stronger market power in the form of superior negotiation and information power leads to one-sided abuse of both freedom of contract and freedom of choice. Contract terms that are so determined can be disadvantageous to one party to a contract and question the equilibrium paradigm of liberal market theory. From this perspective, the need for market control arises from the notion of abuse of economic power.[36] This view is well evident in the French *loi Scrivener*, where the motive for intervention lies mainly in the need to prevent the abuse of power to the detriment of the more vulnerable party, the consumer.

The following section will seek to identify which of these views prevails in English and Italian law. It must be noted that one approach does not necessarily exclude the other, and it is possible (as with English law) to find traces of both approaches in one single domestic system.

contractual transactions, see P Nebbia, 'Standard Form Contracts between Competition Law and Unfair Terms Control' (2006) ELR 102.

[36] L. Krämer, *La CEE et la protection du consommateur* (Bruxelles, Bruylant, 1988) 168.

Standard form contracts

In England, academic writings and policy documents emphasised since the 1940's how the ever-increasing use of standard contracts began to reflect a structure of the market where well-organised business imposes take-it or leave-it terms upon consumers who are unable to protect themselves against this power.[37]

The inadequacy of the common law to deal with standard term contracts first emerged in the infamous case of *L'Estrange v Graucob*[38] where, in holding the plaintiff bound by his signature on a standard form contract, Maugham LJ lamented:

> I regret the decision to which I have come, but I am bound by legal rules and cannot decide the case on other considerations . . . I could wish that the contract was in a simpler and more usual form. It is unfortunate that the important clause excluding conditions and warranties is in such a small print.[39]

Less than fifty years later, the problem of standard contract terms had found a vivid description in Lord Reid's well-known analysis of the two problems generated by standard form contracts:[40] first, a problem of information, in that a customer would often not read contract terms or would not understand their impact on his situation; he would therefore be later taken 'by unfair surprise'; second, a problem of lack of any room for bargaining, in that the customer may find that the business is unwilling to remove or alter any unwanted terms. Most of the common law cases on unfair terms actually concern cases where standard form contracts were at issue.

The problem of standard contract terms is also addressed by UCTA: section 3 provides that judicial control can be triggered not only in consumer contracts but also in cases where both parties are acting 'in the course of a business' but one deals 'on the other's written standard terms of business'. The need to extend section 3 to standard form contract was explained by the Law Commission in the following terms:

> The case for controlling clauses is evident in a situation where one party acts in the course of a business and the other does not. Injustice may arise because the consumer will frequently not understand the implication of the terms of the contract and, even if he does, he may not have sufficient bargaining strength to prevent their inclusion in the contract. But these factors are not limited to consumer contracts. In many cases a person acting in the course of a business is in a very similar position to the consumer . . . We believe that the situations where control is necessary (even though both parties to the contract are acting in the course of a business) arise where one party requires the other to accept terms which the former has decided upon in advance as being generally

[37] An influential source for those considerations was Kessler's discussion of contracts of adhesion in the US, see F Kessler, 'Contracts of Adhesion: Some Thoughts about Freedom of Contract' (1943) *Columbia Law Review* 629.

[38] [1934] 2 KB 394.

[39] *Ibid* 405.

[40] *Suisse Atlantique SA v Rotterdamsche Kolen Centrale* [1967] 1 AC 361, 406.

> advantageous to him, and the customer must either accept those terms or not enter into the contract: that is, where there is a standard form contract.[41]

The above extract illustrates clearly the close link between arguments concerning standard form contracts and arguments concerning inequality of bargaining power. It should be noted, in this respect, that although inequality of bargaining power has never achieved the status of a doctrine in itself, it has been the object of judicial concern, often expressed by Lord Denning in terms that still have wide echoes in the English legal environment.

In Italy, the 1942 legislator was also very much concerned with the use of standard contract terms as a threat to contractual freedom as well as a means of concluding contracts that would encourage rapidity of exchanges. For the Italian legislator the widespread use of contract forms, rather than underlining a situation of disparity between the proponent and the adherent, marks the end of the classical concept of contract, where the two parties gradually come to an agreement that strikes a balance between the interests of both.[42]

This emerges from some unambiguous passages contained in the *Report to the King on the Civil Code*:

> the need to ensure the uniformity of the content of all the relationships of identical nature, for a more precise determination of the risk involved, the trouble of negotiating with customers . . . the need to simplify the organisation and the management of the enterprise induce the enterprise to draft forms, the text of which cannot be discussed by the customer if he does not want to withdraw from the bargain. Such a way of making a contract cannot be considered illegal just because it is not based on negotiation and discussion of the terms but one is forced to comply with the pre-arranged terms. The modern economic reality is based on a quick conclusion of transactions due to the acceleration of the phenomenon of production: the need to have free bargaining must surrender to this reality as it would bring disadvantages that cannot be overcome. On the other hand, the use of contracts of adhesion has given rise to abuses in those cases where the predetermined forms contain terms that put the customer entirely in the hands of the enterprise . . . Artt.170 and 171 [ie 1341–42] attempt at remedying this abuse by making enforceable only those terms that the customer knew or should have known when making the contract; and, in addition, terms which bind in a burdensome way the adherent are not enforceable, unless attention is specifically drawn to them.[43]

It is therefore clear that the policy choice expressed by the legislator does not aim to protect the weak party to the transaction, but rather to serve business activity. This is even more evident if one considers that:

[41] Law Commission, *The Law Commissions' 1975 Report: Exemption Clauses: Second Report* Law Com no 69, para 147.

[42] G Chinè, *La contrattazione standardizzata* in M Bessone, *Trattato di diritto privato* vol III *Il contratto in generale* (Torino, Giappichelli, 2000) pt II, 494.

[43] *Relazione al Re*, 78, quoted in G Alpa and G Rapisarda, 'Il controllo giudiziale nella prassi' in G Alpa and M Bessone (eds) *I contratti standard nel diritto interno e comunitario* (Torino, Giappichelli, 1991) 79.

1. Article 1341(1) cc in practice puts the customer in a rather difficult position. Usually, the customer has no time to read long terms: the customer is, by definition, a 'person in a hurry'.[44] If the rationale of the article is to facilitate commercial transactions in cases where there is no time for negotiation, how can the legislator then expect that the customer has the time to read and think over the terms of the contract offered to him? Paradoxically, this may favour those who insert in the contract unintelligible clauses, written in small print or hardly visible.
2. Article 1341(2) cc does not really offer any substantive protection but only excludes validity of standard terms in cases where they are not specifically signed. The signing of the contract may make the customer aware of the content of the contract (provided that he has read and understood every single term, which is actually rather unlikely) but guarantees to the enterprise the possibility of inserting clauses of any type and effect, which can be neither negotiated nor modified by the other party. In other words, nothing prevents the enterprise from using the harshest terms as long as the requirement of specific written approval is fulfilled.
3. Article 1342 cc has in practice negligible importance as terms subsequently added to the standard form are an extremely rare occurrence; and, in any event, it does not provide any substantive protection but rather consolidates the principle that a negotiated term cannot be unfair.

The rule of interpretation of standard form contracts, article 1370cc, is of little assistance: as later[45] discussed, it has had such poor judicial use, that its role in the defence of the weak party is almost non-existent.

In other words, one can say that the rules contained in articles 1341–42 cc are laid down to preserve the principle that contracts are made by agreement, rather than to address inequality of bargaining power. It comes as no surprise that, as the use of standard form contracts affects the traditional process of formation of the contract, the relevant rules are located in the section of the civil code concerning the agreement (*accordo*) of the parties:

> the location of such rules within the structure of the Code shows that the aim pursued by them is to regulate a peculiar way of concluding contracts in order to guarantee as much as possible the existence of the usual assumptions (*presupposti*) for the conclusion of contracts; certainly the aim was not that of limiting the autonomy of the parties by envisaging a control that goes beyond compliance with formal requirements.[46]

[44] G Alpa, *Il diritto dei consumatori*, above n 31, at 161.

[45] See ch4, p 55.

[46] S Patti 'Introduzione' in G Alpa and S Patti (eds) *Le clausole vessatorie nei contratti con i consumatori* Milano, Giuffrè, 1997) xlvii.

Inequality of bargaining power

Inequality of bargaining power is expressly acknowledged as being relevant to the reasonableness of a term by two provisions of UCTA: first, the strength of parties' bargaining position is one of the guidelines for the application of the reasonableness test under Schedule 2; second, some UCTA provisions, such as section 3, apply only when one of the parties acts 'as a consumer'.

In practice, when dealing with parties of comparable bargaining power, judges have been reluctant to upset contractual terms:

> It is always relevant to have in mind when construing a contract between commercial parties that the primary purpose of the relevant provision may simply be one of division of risk, often insurable risk . . . A court, particularly a court accustomed to deal with commercial contracts, should show no reluctance to give full effect to the provisions of the contract. It also has to be borne in mind that commercial contracts are drafted by parties with access to legal advice and in the context of established legal principles as reflected in the decisions of the courts. Principles of certainty, and indeed justice, require that contracts be construed in accordance with the established principles. The parties are always able by the choice of appropriate language to draft their contract so as to produce a different legal effect.[47]

The judgment seems to suggest that in a commercial context, where parties have full understanding of the meaning and effect of contract terms, none of those can turn out to be a 'bad surprise' for any of the parties: as long as they can be 'reasonably expected', they are fair. On the other hand, if one party cannot read, understand or change the terms of the contract, at least he should not to be caught by 'unfair surprise': he must be able to find in the contract what he—or a reasonable person in his shoes—expects, or what is more likely to correspond to his intention. In other words, the judicial test on unfair terms is based on whether an ordinary person would reasonably expect to find a certain term; or whether an ordinary person would reasonably interpret the intention of the parties so as to cover a certain event.

For this reason, for example, judges seem to be less prepared to accept incorporation by course of dealing in a consumer context. In *Hollier v Rambler Motors Ltd.*[48] the Court of Appeal held, inter alia, that three or four transactions made by a consumer with a business in the course of five years were not sufficient to establish the 'course of dealing' needed to incorporate certain terms, included in forms only occasionally signed by the plaintiff. Commenting on that decision in *British Crane* Lord Denning observed 'that was a case of a private individual who . . . had signed forms on three or four occasions. The plaintiff there was not of equal bargaining power with the garage company . . . The conditions were not

[47] Hobhouse J. in *EE Caledonia Ltd v Orbit Valve Co Europe* [1993] All ER 165 at 173. On the fracture between consumer and commercial law in general, see R Brownsword, 'The Two Laws of Contract' (1981) SJ 279–81.

[48] [1972] 2 QB 71.

incorporated'.[49] Had the parties both been business men, contracting on equal terms, the result might well have been different.

In Italy, as already mentioned, formulation in advance and general use are the reasons justifying legislative intervention, and the causal link with inequality of bargaining power does not appear to be particularly relevant in the eyes of the Italian legislator:[50] the requirement that the contract must be drawn for general use seems to exclude that one party is able to rely on articles 1341–42 cc in cases where he has been unable to negotiate its content but the contract in itself is drawn for individual use.[51]

That the rationale is not to protect the weak party to the transaction is also confirmed by the fact that the aforementioned articles contain no reference to the *status* of the parties: they therefore apply to contracts concluded not only between consumers and enterprises but also between enterprises themselves, no matter what their position and their bargaining strength are.

Most of the time, the fact that the term must be unilaterally drafted[52] and that the economic position of the parties is irrelevant has gone to the disadvantage of the parties who attempted to claim that they were not bound to comply with the requirements in article 1341 as they were not in a position of economic superiority. On the other hand, the fact that the adherent was in a particularly weak position has been held irrelevant in those cases where unilateral pre-drafting was absent.[53] The irrelevance of parties' position is judicially confirmed by the case-law on the so-called *clausole bilaterali.*

Clausole bilaterali are terms which give a specific right or deprive of a specific right both parties to the contract, that is, which apply in favour of or to the detriment of any of the parties so as to maintain formal equality between them. The characteristic of *bilateralità* is attached mainly to terms which allow parties to terminate or to suspend the performance of the contract *ad nutum* (without

[49] *British Crane Hire Corp Ltd v Ipswich Plant Hire Ltd* [1975] QB 303 at 310.

[50] P Nebbia, 'The Implementation of Directive 93/13 in Italy and in the United Kingdom: a Comparison' in H Schulte-Nölke and R. Schulze (eds) *Europaïsche Rechtsangleichung und nationale Privatrechte* (Baden-Baden, Nomos, 1999) 312.

[51] See A Tullio, *Il contratto per adesione—tra diritto comune dei contratti e la novella nei contratti dei consumatori* (Milano, Giuffrè, 1997), 11–17; S Troiano 'L'ambito oggettivo di applicazione della Direttiva CEE del 5 Aprile 1993: la nozione di clausola "non oggetto di negoziato individuale"' in M Bianca and G Alpa (eds) *Le clausole abusive nei contratti stipulati con i consumatori* (Padova, Cedam, 1996) 599.

[52] In this respect, it is irrelevant whether the proponent himself drafted the contract or not: contracts drafted by professional associations or third parties with particular technical-legal knowledge are also covered as long as they are then imposed by one party on the other. This is the case, for example, of *norme bancarie uniformi,* draft terms agreed by the *Associazione Bancaria Italiana* (ABI) and widely used by banks in the contractual relationships with customers.

[53] In Corte di Cassazione (Cass) 27 April 1991 no 4638 in Giurisprudenza Italiana Massimario 1991, for example, the plaintiff had bought a pre-made wooden house. The contract contained a choice of forum clause, which the plaintiff claimed to be invalid on grounds that it had not been specifically approved pursuant to art 1341(2) cc. The court considered that there was no doubt that the plaintiff was the 'weak' party and the seller/defendant was the 'strong' one; however, the contract had been drafted and typed at a notary's office and this excluded unilateral determination of the contract: the rationale of the rule, ie to make the party aware of the content of the contract, did not apply in this case and there was therefore no need for specific approval.

notice); or to terms that allow tacit extension or renewal of the contract. Such terms may be considered as *vessatori* under article 1341(2) on grounds that, as a matter of fact, the same clause can have remarkably different effects depending on the party which relies on it. The issue has been the object of an oscillating attitude of the Corte di Cassazione which, without any apparent logic, has held from time to time that such terms are *vessatori*, other times that they are not. However, a systematic analysis of the case-law reveals that terms which refer to the possibility of suspending or withdrawing from the contract are usually held non *vessatori*, while terms concerning renewal and extension have been the subject of a gradually more evolutionary approach.

As to the first type of terms, the common reasoning one can find behind the decisions on their validity and enforceability is that, since the same right is guaranteed to both parties (it is interesting to note that in two of the 'leading' cases one party is FIAT, in another AGIP, both against small enterprises),[54] there seems to be no reason why the term should be more burdensome for one party than for the other; on the other hand, the situation covered by article 1341 is one where the term is in favour of one party only, thus making the position of the weak party particularly burdensome.

A recent approach of the Corte di Cassazione to tacit renewal or extension of the contract seems to consider that such terms, even though bilateral, may have a particularly burdensome effect on the weak party: the reasoning of the court refers to the different position of the parties, and considers that the proponent has a better chance to assess in advance the advantages flowing from the insertion of a term of that type in the contract.[55] This seems to be one of the very few cases where the Corte di Cassazione shows willingness to go beyond the sterile wording of article 1341(2) in order to ascertain in practice, on grounds of the advantages and disadvantages actually conferred on the parties by the contract, whether its terms are fair or not, and accordingly whether or not they meet judicial support. The different treatment of the first and the second type of terms examined remains, however, an unexplained mystery.

IMPLEMENTATION OF DIRECTIVE 93/13 IN ENGLAND AND IN ITALY

While Germany and France were able to implement Directive 93/13 with relatively few amendments to the existing law, both England[56] and Italy chose to enact new legislation. Doubtlessly, since the philosophy underlying the Directive seems to be

[54] Cass 4 July 1986 no 4540 in Giurisprudenza Italiana Massimario 1986 and Cass 27 February 1990 no 1513 in Giurisprudenza Italiana Massimario 1990; see also Cass 22 January 1991 no 544 in Giustizia Civile 1991, I, 853.

[55] See Cass 27 February 1998 no 2152 in Foro Italiano 1998 I 1051, but also Cass 8 October 1968 no 3161 in Foro Italiano 1969 I 383.

[56] It must be noted that, although UCTA contained separate provisions for England (together with Wales and Northern Ireland) and Scotland, the Government has decided that the new Regulations apply to the UK as a whole. In the course of this work, however, reference will continue to be to 'England'.

a combination of the French and the German approaches to unfair terms control,[57] it was an easier task for the latter two countries to transpose it. In Italy, no proper system of unfair terms control was in place, so there was nothing to amend: legislation had to be adopted *ex novo*. In England (from whose system the Directive has also partly borrowed), on the other hand, control was inspired by reasons concerning both inequality of bargaining power and use of standard form contracts: accordingly, since both the Directive and UCTA reflect, in different ways, a combination of two different philosophies, it would have technically been quite complex to make the necessary amendments to UCTA.

As a result, the UK Government chose to implement the Directive by making separate regulations, the Unfair Contract Terms Regulation 1994,[58] later replaced by the Unfair Contract Terms Regulations 1999[59] (UTCCR), and by leaving in place all of the pre-existing controls on contract terms.

The decision to create two separate statutory regimes for unfair terms, rather than to amend the 1977 Act, was justified by the Government on grounds that

> the test of fairness in the Directive has similarities to the test of reasonableness to which a majority of the terms within the scope of the Act are subject. The existence of this similarity should reduce any problems arising from the overlap between the two measures.[60]

Similarity between the two tests would sound like a good reason to merge them into one, rather than to keep them separate. The words of the Department of Trade and Industry (DTI), in charge of drafting the implementing measure, actually reveal different reasons for a cautious approach to implementation:

> Community legislation derives from a number of jurisdictions which have very different legal systems, and embodies linguistic and legal concepts which are not always easy to translate into UK law. The Department considered implementing Regulations which would clarify the Directive or align certain concepts more closely with those familiar to UK lawyers. However, having regard to the case-law of the European Court, the Department has concluded that to attempt this would be unlikely to be helpful.[61]

These words reflect the Government's anxiety that any attempt to implement differently the Directive and to co-ordinate it with the previous law would open the UK to an action for infringement, especially having considered the lack of time and the complex issues that surrounded the process of implementation.[62]

Nevertheless, some provisions of the first implementing measure, the 1994 Regulations, appeared not to be in perfect conformity with the Directive. In response to legal proceedings brought by the Consumers' Association for judicial review of the

[57] See Ch 5, pp 89–90; ch 8, p 143.

[58] SI 1994, No 3159.

[59] SI 1999, No 2083.

[60] DTI, *Implementation of the EC Directive on Unfair Terms in Consumer Contracts (93/13/EEC). A Consultation Document* (London, DTI, 1993) 1.

[61] DTI, *The Unfair Terms in Consumer Contracts Regulation 1994. Guidance Notes* (London, DTI, 1995) para 2.3.

[62] H Collins, 'Le clausole vessatorie nel Regno Unito' (1997) *Rivista Trimestrale di Diritto Procedura Civiile* 455.

Regulations,[63] and in order to ensure faithful transposition of the Directive, the Government adopted the Unfair Terms in Consumer Contracts Regulations 1999, which repealed the 1994 Regulations. The main innovation of the 1999 Regulations is to include consumers associations among the entities which, with the Director General of Fair Trading (now the Office of Fair Trading (OFT))[64], are entitled to bring preventive actions against traders who use or recommend unfair terms. Other changes include: (1) amending the definition of 'seller' and 'supplier' so as to extend the scope of the Regulations to contracts which are not sale or supply of goods;[65] (2) eliminating Schedules 1 and 2[66] to the 1994 Regulations which 'embody material coming from the recitals to the Directive, not its main text'[67] (the practical impact of the amendment, however, is minimal since, as OFT acknowledged, 'regard must still be made to the Recitals in interpreting the 1999 Regulations');[68] (3) make the *contra proferentem* rule inapplicable to proceedings brought for an injunction.

The Office of Fair Trading has so far played a key role in the enforcement of the Regulations: having set up a special unit to deal with the complaints and to disseminate information about the Regulations, it usually approaches traders using unfair terms by negotiation, persuasion and consensus, first issuing warnings and advice and seeking informal undertakings and uses the threat of litigation as a last resort to obtain from business undertakings to alter terms and cease the use of those considered unfair.[69]

The Government has recently admitted that the dual regime of the 1977 Act and the 1999 Regulations has become most intricate and incomprehensible and is therefore considering 'the feasibility of a single, unified regime to replace UCTA and UTCCR',[70] which should not involve any significant increase in the extent of controls over terms in consumer contracts nor any significant reduction in consumer protection.

In Italy, the measure implementing Directive 93/13 in Italy, Legge 6 February 1996 no 52, inserted at the end of Title II (Book IV) of the civil code five articles—articles 1469-bis to 1469-sexies.

[63] Case C–82/96 Reference for a preliminary ruling by the High Court of Justice, Queen's Bench Division, by order of that court of 28 February 1996, in the case of T*he Queen against Secretary of State for Trade and Industry, ex p Consumers' Association and Which (?) Ltd* OJ C145 18 May 1996, 3. Following the enactment of the new Regulations the action was abandoned.

[64] See s 2 Enterprise Act 2002.

[65] DTI had understood that the Directive 'can apply only to contracts for sale of goods or services' and had therefore drafted the 1994 Regulations accordingly: above n 60, at 4.

[66] Sch 1 contained a list of contracts and particular terms excluded from the scope of the Regulations; Sch 2 a list of factors to be taken into account in making the assessment of good faith.

[67] (1999) 8 *Unfair Contract Terms Bulletin* (OFT), 3. Interestingly, the DTI previously emphasised that 'recent case-law of the ECJ has confirmed the importance of the recitals or "whereas" clauses of a Directive in interpreting the articles of the text'; see above n 61, at 1.

[68] *Unfair Contract Terms Bulletin*, previous n, at 3.

[69] R Bradgate, 'Experience in the United Kingdom' in *The Unfair Terms Directive: Five Years On* above n 34, at 47.

[70] Law Commission and Scottish Law Commission, *Unfair Terms in Contracts A Joint Consultation Paper* Law Commission Consultation Paper no 166/Scottish Law Commission Discussion Paper no 119 (2002) 2.

Implementation of Community law into the Italian legal system is usually made through delegated legislation, the so-called *decreti legge*, which are free standing in the sense that they are independent and separate from the legislation contained in the codes.[71] In the case of Directive 93/13, however, the implementation was made through an amendment to the civil code and therefore required the adoption of a *legge*, a hierarchically higher form of legislation than a *decreto legge*.

The choice of inserting the new provisions in the civil code rather than adopting a *decreto legge* can be explained by the wish to maintain the primacy of the code as focal point and primary instrument of the contract law system over the increasing amount of free-standing legislation, and, at the same time, by the desire to highlight the innovative importance of the Directive within the Italian law of contract; at the same time, the choice of Title II (contracts in general) for the insertion of the new law emphasises its nature as a law of general application in contract law: 'the Directive introduces *general principles* which are applicable to an indefinite number of adhesion contracts for the simple fact that those are made between the consumer and the professional'.[72] Nevertheless, the text finally adopted does not appear to make any attempts to adapt the new law to the framework of the code, but merely reproduces the text of the Directive, thus appearing very much as a free-standing piece of legislation 'inside the tortured body of our old civil code'.[73]

The Italian implementation was subject to an infringement procedure, at the end of which Italy was condemned for not having included, among those against whom action can be taken, sellers, suppliers or their associations which *recommend* the use of (as opposed to use) unfair terms. This has now been remedied by article 37 of the consumer code.[74]

[71] This type of legislation is adopted through a faster procedure than the one required for *Leggi* (acts of the Parliament) and is expressly recognised as a tool of implementation by the so-called *legge La Pergola* (L 9 March 1989, no 86), which lays down general provisions for the fulfilment of Community obligations. For a survey on the implementation of consumer directives in Italy see S Cotterli and P Martinello, 'Implementation of EEC Consumer Protection Directives in Italy' (1994) *Journal of Consumer Policy* 63–82.

[72] Presentation to the *Camera dei Deputati* of the 1994 Bill, *Camera* internal paper no 1882 of 16 January 1995 in E Cesaro, 'La Direttiva CEE n. 93/13 del 5/4/1993 in materia di clausole abusive. Raccolta di documenti' (1995) II *Rivista di Diritto dell'Impresa* 323 ff.

[73] L Bigliazzi Geri 'Commento subarticle 1469-bis comma I' in M Bianca and F Busnelli (eds) *Capo XIV bis cc:dei contratti del consumatore* (Padova, Cedam, 1999) 793.

[74] C–372/99 *Commission v Italy* [2002] ECR I–819. The other grounds of infringement were: (1) The Italian legislator had limited the scope of application of art 1469-bis ff. to 'contracts for the supply of goods or services', while the Directive targets all types of consumer contracts; (2) art 6.2 of the Directive (which prevents parties from opting for a less favourable *régime* than that of the Directive) was implemented by art 1469-quinquies so as to mean that parties cannot choose a law that deprives the consumer of the protection granted by that 'article'—instead of that 'chapter'; (3) art 1469-quater did not reproduce the co-ordination between art 5 and art 7.2 of the Directive, with the result that the principle of interpretation in favour of the consumer would also apply to preventive actions. Following the opening of the infringement procedure, the Italian Government agreed to amend the articles related to the above three infringements by Legge No 526 of 21 December 1999, but refused to remedy to the fourth infringement until the consumer code was adopted.

More recently, the Italian Government has adopted a consumer code (*Codice del consumo*)[75] with the primary purpose of collecting together and systematising the cluster of *decreti* used to implement Community consumer law. Articles 1469-bis to 1469-sexies have been repealed upon adoption of the consumer code, and the provisions on unfair terms are now contained, almost unaltered,[76] in Part III, Title 1 of the consumer code (arts 33–8). The adoption of the consumer code marks a seminal change in the approach of the Italian legislator to the 'consumer', whose existence had not found any space in the Italian legal system until it was introduced by the Community legislator: and, even then, its existence was merely tolerated and the relevant provisions were slipped into the Italian legal system through the backdoor of the *decreti*.

Thirty years after the birth of the Community consumer policy, the consumer code is now meant to become the 'general law of the consumer'[77] laying down the general principles, the definitions and the detailed rules that regulate the most important aspects of the economic life of citizens. The code entitles organisations representing consumers and professionals and the Chambers of Commerce, industry, craftsmanship and agriculture to apply to ordinary civil courts to obtain an injunction against the use of unfair terms by traders or by their organisations Preventive actions represent, as yet, the greatest majority of cases decided by Italian courts and in this respect the work carried out by Italian courts of first instance is comparable to that of the OFT. It must be noted, however, that although courts may order that a measure is published in one or more newspapers (of which at least one must have national circulation) the quantity of information available on Italian cases is not comparable to that available on the OFT's work. There is, as yet, no official instrument for the dissemination of information concerning cases on unfair terms: this is left to normal case-reporting which does not occur on a regular basis and hence does not guarantee that information on the practical application of the Directive is easily available.

[75] D Lgs 6 September 2005.

[76] One main change is in the legal consequences of a finding of unfairness. Under the old law, an unfair term was to be declared by the judge *inefficace*; under the new law, it is *nullo*. The main consequence is that the unfairness of a term can now be declared by a judge by his own motion. Also, 'unfair' terms gain back their original name of *vessatorie* instead of *abusive*, which was the term adopted by the clumsy formulation of articles 1469-bis ff.

[77] A Gentili, 'Codice del consumo ed esprit de géométrie' (2006) 2 *I contratti* 159, at 165.

4

Unfair Terms Control in England and Italy

THIS CHAPTER FOCUSES on the different types of unfair terms control in place in England and Italy before the implementation of Directive 93/13 (the Directive). Those can be broadly divided into two categories, formal and substantive controls.

The term 'formal controls' is meant to include all rules which do not involve a direct assessment of the substance of contractual terms, but rather compliance with certain general, formal, requirements for their validity and enforceability. So, for example, giving appropriate notice to a term or complying with certain formalities required for its acceptance does not entail an assessment of its fairness but rather concerns the question whether the term is to be considered or not as part of the contract. Formal controls, however, may often provide the indirect means for more substantive control of fairness on particularly burdensome terms.

'Substantive controls', on the other hand, aim to address directly the content of contractual terms, which accordingly may be totally forbidden (blanket prohibitions, 'black lists') or subject to judicially administered tests.

The analysis of the scope and rationale of unfair term control in Chapter 3 and of the content and practical application of such control in this chapter will reveal that decisions on whether a term is unfair or not may vary depending not only on the legal tools that are available to the judiciary, but also on the different methods that judges may adopt in the process of decision making. This point will then gain particular importance in the context of the definition of the exact role that the fairness test contained in Directive 93/13 needs to play within national legal systems, which is discussed in Chapter 8.

FORMAL CONTROLS

As previously mentioned, the application in England of formal controls based on rules of incorporation and interpretation hides a more penetrating and substantive investigation on fairness: however, the legal reason given for upsetting the contract would still be disguised under formal argumentation based on whether and on what terms a contract has been formed. On the other hand, formal procedural requirements imposed by Italian law for the approval of certain terms, originally justified by their burdensome nature, do not appear to have been developed so as to offer a more substantive protection in favour of the most vulnerable parties.

A comparison of the different development followed by formal controls in the two legal systems can therefore offer useful insights of the different legal techniques for regulating contract formation and interpretation; but, above all, it allows a better understanding of the relationship between the law and the context where it is applied.

Rules on incorporation

As already briefly discussed, rules on incorporation focus on the question of whether a certain term is part of the contract.

In England, the harsh rule laid down in *l'Estrange v Graucob*[1] excludes that a term which is part of a signed contract is not incorporated.[2] Besides the few cases of fraud, misrepresentation[3] and *non est factum*[4] in signed contracts, attention has therefore concentrated on other issues, such as incorporation of notices, incorporation of terms in unsigned documents, incorporation by course of dealing. In Italy, on the other hand, the case-law has concentrated on the interpretation of articles 1341–42 cc in respect of signed contracts.

The first rule concerning incorporation in England is that no exclusion clause is effective unless adequately brought to the other party's attention before or at the time the contract is made.[5] Cases of this type are quite straightforward and leave some room for interpretation only on the question of who makes the offer and who makes the acceptance and at what point the contract is concluded.

In Italy, absence of case-law on the time of incorporation is actually rather surprising. In at least one case decided at last instance it is made clear that reference to the moment where the party concluded the contract excludes the enforceability of clauses where the adherent has the opportunity to know them after the conclusion of the contract: so, the *clausole generali di contratto* inserted in a receipt sent after the conclusion of the contract are not enforceable as the requirement of *conoscenza* or *conoscibilità* applies at the moment when the contract is made, unless it is otherwise clear that the party knew them or should have known them.[6]

More radical divergence between the two systems emerges when tackling the issue of the steps that have to be taken to bring a clause to the attention of the other

[1] [1934] 2 KB 394.

[2] But note the *dictum* of Evans LJ, in *Ocean Chemical Transport Ltd* [2000] 1 Lloyd's Rep 446 at 48.

[3] See, eg, *Esso Petroleum v Mardon* [1976] 2 All ER 5.

[4] See, eg, *Gallie v Lee* [1970] 3 All ER 961.

[5] See the leading case *Olley v Marlborough Court Ltd* [1949] 1 KB 532.

[6] Corte di Cassazione (Cass) 9 October 1962 no 2890 Giurisprudenza Italiana Massimario 1962. See also Cass 7 June 1988 no 3846 Giurisprudenza Italiana Massimario 1988.

party. In England, it was established in *Parker v South Eastern Railway*[7] that a term will only become incorporated in the contract if notice of it has been given and that notice is reasonably sufficient in all the circumstances of the case. This is a question of fact, 'in answering which the tribunal must look at all the circumstances and the situation of the parties'.[8]

Although the question of the reasonableness of the steps taken is one of fact, the test is an objective one so that the personal circumstances of the plaintiff are irrelevant provided that the notice is reasonably sufficient for a person normally entering into such a transaction. So, for example, in *Thompson v L.M. & S Ry*,[9] the plaintiff was unable to read the terms and conditions contained in the company's timetable (to which the ticket she bought referred), which was available for customer purchase. Although she was illiterate, the Court of Appeal held that the notice in the ticket was clear and the terms in the timetable were incorporated in the contract. The case was an extreme one, since the likelihood of the timetable being bought (let alone read) by a passenger was, to say the least, remote. The same result, however, would not be achieved where the person seeking to rely on the clause knows of the particular disability of the other party: in an earlier case,[10] some reliance was placed on the fact that the other party was a steerage passenger and so belonged to a class of persons who could not be expected to read clauses in small print and therefore much more strenuous efforts to bring the conditions to the attention of the passengers were required. The two cases are not easy to reconcile since, in practice, the probability that a passenger in the first case buys and reads the timetable is no higher that the probability that a steerage passenger in the second case reads the small print.

Rather, the rule that a clear reference to the standard terms may be enough to incorporate them in the contract can be explained in practical terms by the impossibility of including sometimes lengthy lists of terms in a ticket; and the real issue lies in whether the customer could expect or not that a certain term would be introduced.

On the basis of the principle of parties' reasonable expectation, courts created what may be called a 'special notice' test which requires that a party who seeks to rely on a particularly onerous or unusual term may have to take special steps to

[7] (1877) 2 CPD 416.

[8] *Hood v Anchor Line* [1918] AC 837 at 844. Later cases refined more precisely the rules by stating, for example, that a clause will not be incorporated if there are no words on the face of the document drawing attention to it or if the words are made illegible by a date stamp or if the exemption clause is buried in a mass of advertisements. One other factor that will affect the reasonableness of the notice is the kind of document in which the exclusion clause is contained:

> there may be cases in which a paper containing writing is delivered by one party to another in the course of a business transaction, where it would be quite reasonable that the party receiving it should assume that the writing contained in it no condition, and should put it in his pocket unread. (Mellish LJ in *Parker v South Eastern Railway Co Ltd* previous n, at 422)

See an application of the principle in *Chapelton v Barry Urban District Council* [1940] KB 532.

[9] [1930] 1 KB 41.

[10] *Richardson, Spence & Co Ltd v Rowntree* [1894] AC 217.

bring that term 'fairly and reasonably' to the attention of the other party.[11] The rationale of the rule seems to be that only if a clause is of a type commonly found in a particular class of contract can a party reasonably be expected to be aware that such term is incorporated in the contract.

In a later case, *Interfoto v Stiletto*, the test was slightly reformulated so as to shift focus from the 'type' of clause to its per se harshness. The plaintiffs sought to rely on a term in a contract for the hire of photographic material which imposed a heavy charge for its late return. The court had evidence that the terms used by other suppliers were comparable, even though the amounts charged were much lower. The shift in approach is clear in Dillon LJ's judgment, stating that 'if one condition in a set of printed conditions is particularly onerous or unusual, the party seeking to enforce it must show that that particular condition was fairly brought to the attention of the other party';[12] Bingham LJ, on the other hand, first highlighted that the type of conditions applied by the plaintiffs were regularly encountered in this business, and accordingly they were incorporated into the contract; however, the customers had to be relieved from responsibility since 'the plaintiffs did not do what was necessary to draw this unreasonable and extortionate clause fairly to their attention'.[13]

This approach was taken further in *AEG Ltd v Logic Resources Ltd*.[14] The plaintiff, a multi-national company, had supplied to the defendant equipment of a certain specification. On the reverse were printed extracts from the conditions of sale and a notice that a full set of terms would be available upon request. The defendant did not request it. The case concerned the issue whether a certain burdensome clause could be thereby held incorporated or not. In holding that the term was 'particularly onerous' and accordingly not incorporated the court had no evidence that this was not the practice of other similar business: on the contrary, it appeared that in commercial practice the term at issue was not an unusual one. The majority of the Court of Appeal however held that, in applying the test of incorporation, it was appropriate to consider the construction and effect of the particular clause in the specific case, which made it 'unacceptably onerous'. This would explain the decision of the majority in *AEG* where the real objection of the court appears to have been that the clause was, in effect, unreasonable. On this approach, the test of incorporation becomes a (hidden) test of reasonableness, the criteria of which are not spelled out. Since this type of test would involve a direct attack on freedom of contract which many judges would feel uncomfortable with, courts usually prefer the 'particularly onerous or unusual' formulation above described.[15]

As a result, the relationship between the doctrine of informed notice and the principle of contractual freedom seems to assume, on the one hand, that in the

[11] *Thornton v Shoe Lane Parking* [1971] 2 QB 163.

[12] [1989] QB 433, 439.

[13] *Ibid* 445.

[14] [1996] CLR 265; see also *Circle Freight International Ltd v Mideast Gulf Exports Ltd* [1988] 2 Lloyd's Rep 427 and *Keeton Sons & Co v Carl Prior Ltd* [1986] Butterworths Trading Law Cases 30.

[15] See R Bradgate, 'Unreasonable Standard Terms' (1997) MLR 586–89.

modern standard form contracts it is unusual that the offeree reads and consents to the terms of the contract; on the other hand, it prescribes that if the general expectations of the offeree are not met, owing to the existence of an unusual or unexpected clause, of which he had no notice, then the clause is an unfair one. There is no need that every term of the contract is an exact reflection of the agreement of the parties: it is sufficient that the terms are usual and within the general expectations of the offeree. Actual knowledge and assent to the terms are only required for onerous or unexpected clauses.[16]

The 'reasonable expectation' criterion also features in cases where one party attempts to incorporate terms in a contract on ground of previous oral or written dealings between the parties containing such terms (the so-called incorporation by course of dealing): there, the simple fact that one party knows that the other is contracting on certain terms, previously communicated, is enough to incorporate those terms in the contract (although, as mentioned above,[17] this is less likely to happen in the context of consumer contracts).[18]

A requirement that standard terms and conditions are drawn to the customers' attention also exists under German law (§ 305(2) BGB) but it appears to have been slightly under-used. This is probably for two reasons: first, because the substantive requirement of § 307 and the lists of §§ 310–11 can already provide sufficient grounds for challenging unfair terms; second, because the incorporation rule applies only if the standard terms are not part of the contract but are physically separate from it. In addition, one needs to recall that such rules do not apply to business-to-business contracts. § 305c on 'unexpected terms' comes closer to English law: a term is considered as 'unexpected' if, for example, 'it contains terms that are alien to the type of contract at issue',[19] or modify abnormally the subject matter of the contract;[20] if it is too far from the directing image (*Leitbild*) of the contract;[21] if it betrays the legitimate expectation of the customer.[22] A term is not 'unexpected', however, if the customer has become aware of it before or during the conclusion of the contract.

In Italy, the requirement of *conoscenza* or *conoscibilità* in article 1341(1) cc has not contributed much to unfair terms control. There has been widespread agreement at academic level that *conoscenza* or *conoscibilità* must concern not only the existence but the actual content of the terms,[23] even though, according to the parameter of

16 G Gluck, 'Standard Form Contracts: the Contract Theory Reconsidered' (1979) ICLQ 90.

17 See Ch 3, p 38.

18 See *British Crane Hire Corporation Ltd v Ipswich Plant Hire Ltd* [1975] QB 303 and *Laceys'Footwear Ltd v Bower* unreported, 18 April 1997 in R Lawson, *Exclusion Clauses and Unfair Contract Terms* (London, Sweet & Maxwell, 2000) 24.

19 C Witz, *Droit Privé Allemand. Droits Subjectifs* (Paris, Litec, 1992) 173.

20 Eg a term requiring the tenant to later acquire the property, BGH (Bundesgerichtshof) 8 June 1979, NJW 1979, 2388, 2388.

21 Eg a renewal clause of 10 years for the installation of an automatic distributor machine, BGH 29 February 1984, NJW 1985, 53, 55.

22 Eg a term that clarifies that the party is only an intermediary, while he gave the impression that he was going to be the party obliged to perform, BGH 18 October 1973 BGHZ 61.

23 See, eg, G De Nova,'Le condizioni generali di contratto' in P Rescigno (ed) *Trattato di diritto privato* (Torino, Giappichelli, 1995) 123; G Chinè 'La contrattazione standardizzata' in M Bessone (ed) *Trattato di Diritto Privato* vol.III *Il Contratto in generale* pt II, (Torino, Giappichelli, 2000), 503.

ordinary diligence, such a knowledge must only be superficial and not full and detailed. In the case-law, however, only a few judgments hint at translating *conoscibilità* into a duty to draft terms in clear, intelligible language.[24] At the last instance, the Corte di Cassazione has simply affirmed that terms must be known by using 'ordinary diligence', that is, by what we should reasonably expect from the mass of customers in relation to certain types of transaction, without further specifying what this in practice entails. In this perspective, the actual content and the potential harshness of a contract term bear no relation with its 'physical availability': the question is not whether a certain term could 'reasonably be expected' in a contract, but whether a 'reasonable person' should be expected to read the contract terms. This is sufficient to legitimise all forms and types of unfair terms while preserving the principle that a contract requires the parties' agreement in order to be valid.

Yet, the requirement of *conoscenza* or *conoscibilità* could have acted as the cornerstone for a new, groundbreaking type of control, where courts could take on an active role in imposing on the proponent a duty to ensure full knowledge and understanding of the content of the contract; such a duty may vary, according to the court's view of the particular case, from an obligation to emphasise terms in proportion to their harshness, to a more substantive requirement to make sure that the other party actually understands what he is agreeing to.[25]

Analysis of the case-law flourished around article 1341(2) cc is not more comforting.

The rationale of the rule is to draw the customer's attention to the consequences and importance of certain particularly harsh terms. This is, and has been interpreted as, a merely formal requirement which is independent of whether the adherent was actually aware of such terms. In the same way as effective knowledge of terms is irrelevant in the application of article 1341(1), so is effective knowledge or understanding of the *clausole vessatorie* irrelevant to the application of article 1341(2).

Litigation has mainly revolved around the modalities required to specifically approve a *clausola vessatoria.* Even though the literal text of article 1341 seems to require that each *clausola vessatoria* is specifically approved in writing, it is a consolidated trend just to require that all the *clausole vessatorie* are approved as a single block. In practice, the system is based on a double signature: the first is a simple acceptance of the contract; the second is aimed at approving as a block all the *clausole vessatorie.* This is the necessary and sufficient condition of enforceability of those clauses.[26]

[24] See, eg, Corte d'Appello di Napoli, 3 April 1970 Dir Giur 1970, 548.

[25] G Alpa, *Il diritto dei consumatori* (Bari, Laterza, 1999) 164.

[26] A number of judgments also specify how in practice reference to *clausole vessatorie* should be made: eg, reference to their number (such as 'I specifically approve the terms listed under nos 1, 2, 3, etc. of the contract') is now safely considered as sufficient to fulfil the requirement. According to a widespread view, this would be suitable to exclude the danger of reckless acceptance since this type of reference enables the customer to identify, in the contractual document, terms which are particularly burdensome and accordingly understand their specific content. See, eg, Cass 9 February 1998 no 1317 Giurisprudenza Italiana Massimario 1998; Cass 20 June 1997 no 5533 Giurisprudenza Italiana Massimario 1997.

More interesting litigation has arisen in relation to the question whether the list in article 1341(2) is exhaustive, that is, whether terms not contained in the list in that article need specific written approval or not. The majority of academics and of the case-law consider the list contained in article 1341(2) as exhaustive, with the exception of few isolated commentators and few decisions of lower courts.[27] This conclusion is achieved by means of a strict legal reasoning based on the exceptional character of article 1341 with regard to the general principle of liberty of the forms;[28] a different but comparable reasoning is based on the argument that, by imposing the extra requirement of written approval in a set of special cases, [29] article 1341(2) creates an exception to the rule laid down in article 1341(1) that a term shall be deemed effective if known or knowable to the other party; in both views, however, article 1341(2) is considered as an exception, and must therefore be given a narrow interpretation. This is directly confirmed by the Report to the civil code which describes the list as 'subject to extensive interpretation (*interpretazione estensiva*) but not to analogy (*interpretazione analogica*)'.[30] According to the Corte di Cassazione,[31] analogy is used when

> the need arises to regulate one case not provided for by the law; one would then refer to the rules applicable to a similar case, that is, a case which is based on the same assumptions. Accordingly, interpretation by analogy is a process that aims to determine the rationale, the underlying principle from which rules derive in order to establish if, within those rules, one can also include the case which has not been provided for. Extensive interpretation, on the other hand, occurs only when the case apparently not provided for is the same as the one provided for, and therefore it must be considered as being implicitly within the rule.

According to this formalistic reasoning, courts have held that penalty clauses, forfeitures, terms that allow the seller to increase the price of the goods after the contract is made do not fall under article 1341(2); terms which reverse the burden of proof or terms which prevent one party from requesting the other party's performance before carrying out their own performance, since they limit one party's defences, do fall within the list.

In practice, it is difficult to see how terms such as forfeitures differ from terms having the effect of limiting one party's defence.

The formalism of courts' reasoning and the general scenario as presented here is disappointing if compared with the potential of article 1341(2), which could have been fruitfully combined with article 1341(1) to achieve a more penetrating control of contract terms: while it is widely assumed that written specific approval

[27] See, eg, Tribunale di Milano 21 June 1984 Banca, borsa, tIt cred. 1986, II, 503.

[28] M Bianca 'Condizioni generali di contratto. Diritto Civile'in *Enciclopedia Giuridica* VII (Roma, Treccani, 1988) 5.

[29] G Sicchiero, 'Condizioni generali di contratto'in (1992) II *Rivista di Diritto Civile* 472.

[30] Relazione no 1046 del Ministro Guardasigilli al libro IV del CC, Delle Obbligazioni para 612 (quoted in G Alpa and G Rapisarda, 'Il controllo giudiziale nella prassi' in G Alpa and M Bessone (eds) *I contratti standard nel diritto interno e comunitario* (Torino, Giappichelli, 1991) 79.

[31] Cass Sezioni Unite 14 July 1990 no 5777 in Giustizia Civile 1991, I, 79.

of a term pursuant to article 1341(2) entails automatic satisfaction of the requirement of *conoscenza* and *conoscibilità* under article 1341(1), this is not in fact self-evident. Accordingly, written specific approval could be considered not sufficient to satisfy article 1341(1), with the result that the two paragraphs could act as a two-tier control instead of being mutually exclusive: however, as such a solution must necessarily be attached to a different understanding of the duty of *conoscenza* and *conoscibilità*, it comes as no surprise that it has not raised any interest in courts.

Rules on interpretation

The second set of rules that can be used to indirectly control unfair terms are rules of incorporation, such as the English rule of construction *contra proferentem* and of negligence liability.

The *contra proferentem* rule simply requires that a person who seeks to exclude liability by reference to an exemption clause must do so by using words which clearly and unequivocally apply to the case in hand. Thus, a provision that a seller gives 'no warranty, express or implied' does not protect him from liability for breach of a condition;[32] nor does a clause protecting him for 'breach of implied conditions and warranties' cover breach of an express term of the contract;[33] the list of examples could be long as the case-law is rich in applications of this device.[34]

The rule on negligence entails that in order to exclude liability for negligence (to the extent that UCTA today permits), clear words must be used since courts regard it as 'inherently improbable that one party to a contract should intend to absolve the other party from the consequences of his own negligence'.[35]

The precise rules were laid down by Lord Morton of Henryton in *Canada Steamship Lines Ltd v The King*:[36]

[32] *Wallis, Sons & Wells v Pratt & Haynes* [1911] AC 394.

[33] *Webster v Higgins* [1948] 2 All ER 127.

[34] On the other hand, a clause which places an upper limit on the damages recoverable, while still to be construed *contra proferentem*, will not be construed quite as strictly as an exclusion clause. This was made clear in *Ailsa Craig Fishing Ltd v Malvern Fishing Co and Securicor* [1983] 1 WLR 964 where Lord Fraser explained that strict construction is not applicable when considering the effect of clauses merely limiting liability:

> Such clauses will of course be read *contra proferentem* and must be clearly expressed, but there is no reason why they should be judged by the specially exacting standards which are applied to exclusion and indemnity classes. The reason for imposing such standards on these clauses is the inherent improbability that the other party to a contract including such a clause intended to release the *proferens* from a liability that would otherwise fall upon him.

[35] The principle is neatly illustrated by the example of *White v Warwick* [1953] 2 All ER 102: the plaintiff hired a bike from the defendants. A term of the agreement stated that 'nothing . . . shall render the owners liable for any personal injuries to the riders of the machine hired'. The saddle tipped over while the plaintiff was riding it and he suffered several injuries. He brought an action, suing alternatively for breach of contract and in tort for negligence. Since liability could be grounded in either negligence or strict liability for breach of contract, the Court of Appeal felt able to hold that the exclusion clause extended only to a claim concerning the latter. Accordingly, the defendants remained liable in negligence.

[36] [1952] AC 192, 208.

> (1) If the clause contains language which *expressly* exempts the person in whose favour it is made . . . from the consequences of the negligence of his own servants, effect must be given to that provision . . . (2) If there is no express reference to negligence, the court must consider whether the word used are *wide enough*, in their ordinary meaning, to cover negligence on the part of the servant of the *proferens*. If a doubt arises on this point, it must be resolved against the proferens . . . (3) If the words used are wide enough for the above purpose, the court must then consider whether the 'head of damage may be based on some ground other than that of negligence . . . The 'other ground' must not be so fanciful or remote that the *proferens cannot be supposed to have desired protection* against it.[37] (emphasis added)

More recently, the House of Lords has expressed doubt as to whether this should be understood as a mechanistic rule:

> The question . . . is whether the language used by the parties, construed in the context of the whole instrument and against the admissible background, leads to the conclusion that they [the parties] must have thought it went without saying that the words, although literally wide enough to cover negligence, did not do so. This in turn depends upon the precise language they have used and how inherently improbable it is in all the circumstances that they would have intended to exclude such liability. In applying the *Canada Steamship* guidelines, it must also be borne in mind that . . . they date from a time before the Unfair Contract Terms Act 1977, when the courts had no remedy but construction to relieve consumers from the burden of unreasonable exclusion clauses.[38]

It is, at any rate, reasonably clear that if negligence is the only possible ground for liability, more general words can be used in exemption clauses since those clauses will 'more readily operate to exempt liability':[39] however, cases involving consumers' claims do not always follow this route. In *Hollier v Rambler Motors*,[40] for example, the court rejected the argument that, because liability only appeared to lie in negligence, 'no sufficiently clear words are required': when this is the only source of liability, the law may more readily operate to give sanction to the exclusion clause, but 'the law goes no further than that'. The decisive test was stated to be what an ordinary person in the position of the plaintiff would have thought the effect of the clause was. Only if he thought that negligence was the most likely cause of loss and that therefore the clause covered liability for such negligence would the clause protect the defendant. In that case the ordinary person would not have contemplated that the clause covered negligence, but would have thought it was only a warning that the defendants were not liable for damage done by fire in the absence of fault.

[37] See also: *Monarch Airlines Ltd v London Luton Airport Ltd* [1997] CLC 698; *Lamport & Holt Lines Ltd v Coubro & Scrutton* 1982 Lloyd's Rep 42; *Industrie Chimiche Italia v Nea Ninemia Shipping Co* [1983] 1 All ER 686.

[38] *HIH Casualty and General Insurance Limited and Others v Chase Manhattan Bank and Others* [2003] UKHL 6 at para 63. Words of caution against a mechanistic application of the *Canada Steamship* guidelines can also be found in *Hollier v Rambler Motors (AMC) Ltd* [1972] 2 QB 71, 80 and in *Gillespie Brothers & Co Ltd v Roy Bowles Transport Ltd* [1973] QB 400, 419.

[39] *Rutter v Palmer* [1922] 2 KB 87.

[40] Above n 38.

This approach pushes the law to its limits: as noted,[41] it seems improbable that the defendants intended such a clause to be a warning that they were not liable in the absence of fault. In addition, it is difficult to find a reason to decide this case in a way different to the one in *Alderslade v Hendon Laundry Ltd*,[42] where, on a similar set of facts (concerning the delivery of handkerchiefs to a laundry for washing) it was decided that construing a certain exemption clause so as to exclude negligence would be to leave it 'without any content at all'.

Rules on fundamental breach and breach of fundamental term, now seldom used, also deserve to be mentioned. The words 'fundamental breach' and 'breach of a fundamental term' retain different meanings but in practice have been used interchangeably in cases where a breach of a contract is so totally destructive of the obligations of the innocent party that liability for such a breach cannot be excluded or restricted by means of an exemption clause.[43] Those doctrines first arose in shipping cases about deviation and were then developed by courts to protect consumers as rules of substantive law.[44] Having enjoyed some popularity for a couple of decades, these doctrines underwent a gradual decline as it appeared that, when applied to commercial transactions negotiated at arm's length, they were liable to upset perfectly fair bargains for the reasonable allocation of contractual risk: they were an indiscriminate tool for the control of exemption clauses Accordingly, in *Suisse Atlantique*[45] and later in *Photo Production Ltd v Securicor Transport Ltd*[46] the House of Lords put forward the view that although there was recent authority in favour of the substantive doctrine of fundamental breach, it preferred the view that the doctrine was one of construction only. As Lord Reid noted, exemption clauses

> differ greatly in many respects . . . but this rule appears to treat all cases alike. There is no indication in the recent cases that the courts are to consider whether the exemption is fair in all the circumstances or is harsh and unconscionable, or whether it was freely agreed by the customer.[47]

If special rules are needed to protect consumers, they should, Lord Reid continued, be provided by the Parliament.

The House of Lords, however, did not overrule any of the previous cases on fundamental breach but rather explained them as applications of a rule of con-

[41] E Barendt, 'Exemption Clauses: Incorporation and Interpretation' (1972) 35 MLR 644, 646–47.

[42] [1945] 1 KB 189.

[43] This is actually the definition of 'fundamental breach'. 'Breach of a fundamental term', on the other hand, describes a category of terms, express but more often implied, which is narrower than a condition of the contract. A fundamental term 'underlies the whole contract so that, if it is not complied with, the performance becomes totally different from that which the contract contemplates' (*Smeaton Hanscomb & Co Ltd v Sassoon I Setty, Son & Co* [1953] 1 WLR 1468, 1470). A detailed and complete account of such doctrines and of their development is given by D Yates, *Exclusion Clauses in Contracts* (London, Sweet & Maxwell, 1982).

[44] See, eg, *Karsales v Wallis* [1956] 1 WLR 936.

[45] *Suisse Atlantique Société d'Armement Maritime SA v Rotterdamsche Kolen* [1967] 1 AC 361.

[46] [1980] AC 827.

[47] *Suisse Atlantique Société d'Armement Maritime SA v Rotterdamsche Kolen*, above n 45, at 404.

struction.[48] In *George Mitchell v Finney Lock Seeds Ltd*,[49] however, it was finally clearly stated that 'the passing of the Supply of Goods (Implied Terms) Act 1973 and its successor, the Unfair Contract Terms Act 1977, had removed from judges the temptation to resort to the device of ascribing to words appearing in exemption clauses a tortured meaning so as to avoid giving effect to an exclusion or limitation of liability when the judge thought that in the circumstances to do so would be unfair'.[50] The doctrine of fundamental breach remains, as a rule of interpretation, only to the limited extent that it does not entail the adoption of a strained construction of the exemption clause.

Of all the interpretation rules which flourished in the UK in support of weak parties, Italy recognises only the *contra proferentem* rule embedded in article 1370 cc. This article unfortunately lacks almost any practical applications due to the position assigned by the Italian civil code to objective, as compared to subjective, rules of interpretation. The code provides for two types of rule of interpretation, subjective (articles 1362–66 cc) and objective (articles 1366–71 cc):[51] subjective norms prevail over objective norms, which only supplement the former. The reason for this is that the objective meaning of a certain term is irrelevant when the subjective research of the meaning brings to a useful result.[52] In the first place, one should apply the rules that are aimed at researching the real intention of the parties, such as article 1362cc ('in interpreting a contract one must find what the common intention of the parties was, and not limit oneself self to the literal meaning of the words; in order to find out the common intention of the parties one must take into account their behaviour as a whole, even after the conclusion of the contract'): only if any interpretative doubt remains, can one resort to the rules of objective interpretation.[53] The residual role played by objective rules of interpretation explains why, in practice, article 1370 has received no application.[54]

[48] See the comments made by G Treitel in his case note (1966) MLR 552.

[49] [1983] 2 AC 803.

[50] *Ibid*, 810.

[51] Art 1366 (interpretation of the contract according to good faith) involves both subjective and objective interpretation.

[52] See, as one of the many examples, Cass 10 January 1981 no 228 Giurisprudenza Italiana Massimario 1981; see also F Carresi, *Dell'interpretazione del contratto. Commentario Scialoja-Branca* (Bologna, Zanichelli 1992); G Criscuoli, *Il Contratto* (Padova, Cedam, 1996) 335–47.

[53] See Cass 20 January 1989 no 345 Giurisprudenza Italiana Massimario 1989

> Resorting to the so called rules of objective interpretation laid down in arts 1366–1370 or to the subsidiary criteria in article 1371 of the Code is allowed only in cases where the so-called subjective interpretation of arts 1362–1365 is not sufficient.

[54] See a recent example in Cass 27 May 2005 n 11278 I Contratti 3/2006. See also Cass 19 July 1991 no 8038 Giurisprudenza Italiana Massimario 1991. An insurance company brought an action against the insured for the recovery of money paid to an injured party to an accident which was due to the fault of the insured. The action was based on the fact that the insurance cover did not apply in the cases where the insured 'is not enabled to drive in pursuance of the law in force'. The insured had passed the tests for obtaining his driving licence, but the licence had not yet been issued. The insurers claimed that the term meant that the insured who does not hold a proper driving licence would not be covered. The insured claimed inter alia that the contract, if interpreted according to the parties' intention as

Formal controls: a few comments

The difference in treatment of unfair terms (and the notion of 'unfair term' itself) in Italy and in England is remarkable.

Until UCTA, incorporation and interpretation were the only ways of attacking unfair terms in England and were, as a consequence, widely used. The panorama which emerges from the English case-law is that of a rather confused set of remedies open to over-use and abuse if not carefully weighted, as noted in *Suisse Atlantique*, but at the same time regrettably incapable of providing satisfactory solutions to 'deserving' case. The insufficiency of the indirect controls of unfair terms is thus evident and it is no surprise that judges such as Lord Reid called for parliamentary intervention:

> There is no indication in the recent cases that the courts are to consider whether the exemption is fair in all the circumstances or is harsh and unconscionable or whether it was freely agreed by the parties And it does not seem to me to be satisfactory that the decision must always go one way . . . This is a complex problem which intimately affects millions of people and it appears to me that its solution should be left to the Parliament. . . . there will certainly be a need for urgent legislative action but that is not beyond reasonable expectation.[55]

On the other hand, such doctrines were not in themselves meant to provide a direct form of control of contract fairness and it is therefore understandable that they were unable to offer adequate protection. However, the fact that fundamental breach and breach of a fundamental term declined relatively fast as an explicitly recognised consequence of the creation of more convenient statutory remedies nevertheless proves judges' willingness to adapt the available legal techniques and concepts to socio-economical needs and to avoid results that would be unacceptable from a moral point of view.

A recurrent argument in English courts' reasoning is based on parties' reasonable expectation: this usually involves an abstract assessment, based on the idea that a term is unexpected when an ordinary customer would not expect the term to be included in the contract or that it has a certain meaning. In some cases, however, the 'reasonable expectation' is used by courts as a tool to discard a particularly onerous term, with little regard to the fact that the term at issue may actually be in common use (hence expected) and a shift can be noticed towards an

prescribed by art 1362, would extend to cover this case; that an interpretation according to good faith would bring to the same conclusion; and anyway, art 1370 suggests the adoption of the most favourable interpretation for the customer. The court disagreed and claimed that reference to art 1362 and to the 'common intention of the parties' brought to a different conclusion: the wording of the clause meant that completion of the whole procedure to obtain the driving licence was necessary: it was well understood by the parties that the requirement of being 'enabled to drive in pursuance of the law in force' was not fulfilled until the actual document was issued. The court also added that, once ascertained the common intention of the parties, there was no need to resort to the other criteria as art 1362 prevails over all other criteria of interpretation.

[55] *Suisse Atlantique Société d'Armement Maritime SA v Rotterdamsche Kolen* above n 45, at 406.

approach where 'the effect of a particular clause in a particular case is relevant'.[56] Similarly, cases such as *Hollier v Rambler Motors* can be explained by the desire to protect the particularly vulnerable party to the transaction, rather than in terms of the expectations that a disclaimer may generate.

As to Italy, the overview of the above case-law shows a stubborn and formalistic respect for the words and the intention of the 1942 legislator: with few exceptions, there seems to have been little or no attempt at turning into a more penetrating and substantive control the poor tools provided by the civil code;[57] in addition, the narrow interpretation given to the list in article 1341(2) has left with no remedy parties to contracts that contain terms certainly not less burdensome than the ones included in the list.

SUBSTANTIVE CONTROLS

Controls that tackle the substance of a term itself are rare in Italian law, while pretty familiar to English lawyers. It must be noted, however, that some provisions of the *codice civile* expressly prohibit certain burdensome terms in specific types of contracts: for example, the combined operation of articles 1784 and article 1785-quater cc has the effect of prohibiting all terms which exclude or limit the landlord's liability for things kept in a hotel, for the loss or damages to which he is responsible.

This reflects the Italian legislator's concern for the existence of unbalanced terms in certain contracts, but also reflects its reluctance to impose a more general tool of control which would work as a powerful and possibly unpredictable means to upset any type of contractual arrangement.

Blanket prohibitions

The hierarchy of values underlying UCTA is clearly identifiable when looking at what type of blanket prohibitions the Act imposes. It ensures, for example, a minimum standard of protection when human life and integrity are at stake: nobody can escape liability for undermining such supreme values, and the quality of the other party, the legal framework within which liability arises and any other surrounding circumstances are irrelevant.[58] The rationale for such a strict prohibition can easily be found in the idea that 'a civilised society should attach greater importance to the human person than to property' . . . and accordingly there was

[56] Evans LJ in *Ocean Chemical Transport* [2001] 1 All ER (Comm) 519.

[57] See, eg, M Bessone, 'Contratti di adesione, "potere normativo d'impresa" e problemi di "democratic control" in (1973) *Rivista Trimestrale di Diritto Pubblico* 2028; S Patti, 'Responsabilità precontrattuale e contratti standard' in P Schlesinger (ed) *Il codice civile: Commentario* (Milano, Giuffrè, 1999) 329 ff.; V Roppo, *Contratti standard* (Milano, Giuffrè, 1975) 38 ff.

[58] The only limitation to this provision is the requirement of negligence: UCTA would otherwise introduce a regime of strict liability for death and personal injuries, however caused.

'. . . a *prima facie* case for an outright ban on clauses totally excluding [but UCTA also applies to clauses limiting] liability for death or personal injury due to negligence'.[59]

At the same level of protection UCTA places the economic interest of those, whose position is presumed to be one of inferiority (consumers): accordingly, certain basic rights, such as the ones relating to sections 13–15 of the Sale of Goods Act, cannot be taken away by terms what would 'deny [the consumer] what the law means him to have'.[60]

The equivalent Italian provision is, to some extent, the prohibition of article 1229 cc. The rationale of the provision is to ensure a minimum level of diligent performance under any contractual or tortious relationship and to ensure respect of the fundamental principle of *ordine pubblico* contained in article 31 *preleggi*, according to which any act or law of the Italian state, of a foreign state, of any other body or institution, or any agreement between private parties have no effect in the Italian territory if they are contrary to public order or public morals (*ordine pubblico* or *buon costume*). Most cases arising from article 1229 concern the actual meaning of *ordine pubblico*, understood by courts as 'a set of duties aimed at satisfying interests, the safeguard of which responds to fundamental needs of the society, that is, duties concerning the safeguard of a party to an obligation in his physical/moral integrity.[61] In practice, this has been understood as forbidding terms which exempt liability for death and personal injuries or for breach of rules of criminal law.

Judicially administered tests

The limits of Italian law in the area of unfair terms become more evident when dealing with judicially administered fairness tests. While English law leaves plenty of room for judicial discretion in the assessment of unfair terms, Italian law creates no judicially administered test of fairness; nor have courts attempted in any way to give any significant contribution to the protection of vulnerable parties. Comparison with English law is therefore impossible, and the few comments one can make on Italian law refer to academic comments rather than to the actual law.

Reasonableness under UCTA

The cornerstone of the control under UCTA is the requirement of 'reasonableness'. The reasons for its adoption lie in its flexibility and the opportunity it leaves open to give special treatment to special cases, without interfering unduly with contractual arrangements:

[59] Law Commission, *The Law Commissions' 1975 Report: Exemption Clauses: Second Report*, Law Com Report no 69, para 68.

[60] *Ibid* para 68.

[61] M Bianca, *Diritto Civile* (Milano, Giuffrè, 1994) 67.

> The objection that the introduction of a general reasonableness test would involve unjustifiable interference with freedom of contract is essentially an objection to any general control over exemption clauses . . . It is valid only to the extent that there is true freedom of contract to interfere with, and the objection has no validity where there is no real possibility of negotiating contract terms, or where a party is not expected to read a contract carefully or to understand its implications without legal advice. In our view no legislative formula can distinguish between situations where there is genuine freedom of contract and those where there is not. Only individual scrutiny of all the circumstances to take into account, the strength of the bargaining position of the parties, the knowledge and understanding of the term in question, the extent to which one party relied on the advice or skill of the other, and every other relevant fact, can lead to a valid distinction. This is why a reasonableness test is needed.[62]

The guidelines to the reasonableness test are contained in three different places in the Act: the general test is set out in section 11(1); for cases concerning sections 6 and 7 UCTA, the guidelines are specified in Schedule 2; and, where there is a restriction of liability to a specified sum of money, section 11(4) applies. The reasonableness test, however, is one and the same and the criteria provided by UCTA are considered to be non-exhaustive: courts therefore look at a number of factors other than the ones listed there.[63] In truth, judges have leeway at a number of points: for example, firstly, they can select the relevant reasonableness factors (and there the choice is practically unlimited, eg consent, insurance, fault, bargaining position, etc.); secondly, they can specify the requirements for any particular reasonableness factor (eg, what is precisely required for there to be consent? Is simple non-objection sufficient or are there more stringent requirements?); thirdly, the directional pull of any particular reasonableness factor must be identified, that is, judges can determine in whose favour a certain factor lies; finally, the reasonableness factors are weighted, individually and in aggregate. Taking into account infinitely various factual situations makes it difficult to derive authoritative guidance from the particular rulings: in other words, the leeway in identifying, specifying, applying and weighting the reasonableness factors gives little value to decisions as precedents: accordingly,

> there will sometimes be room for a legitimate difference of judicial opinion as to what the answers should be, where it will be impossible to say that one view is demonstrably wrong and the other demonstrably right. It must follow, in my view, that, when asked to review such a decision on appeal, the appellate court should treat the original decision with the utmost respect and refrain from interference with it unless satisfied that it proceeded on some erroneous principle or was plainly and obviously wrong.[64]

[62] *The Law Commission's 1975 Report: Exemption Clauses* above n 59, paras 65–67.

[63] That the list is not exhaustive is confirmed by the Law Commission itself, when stating that

> no such list can ever be complete. The omission of a matter which may well be relevant in a particular case may carry the implication that it should be disregarded, and the inclusion of particular matters may mean that they receive more importance than they merit. If however, the matters listed are introduced by words indicating that regard should be had to all the circumstances of the case the Law Commission think that the risk that other relevant matters will be disregarded is slight. (*The Law Commission's 1975 Report: Exemption Clauses*, above n 59, para 185)

[64] Lord Bridge in *George Mitchell v Finney Lock Seeds* [1983] 2 AC 803. 815–16.

In such a panorama, where the role of appellate courts is restricted to a 'Wednesbury' sort of jurisdiction,[65] trial judges are free to decide UCTA cases on their own particular facts and with 'minimal citation of authority'.[66]

Nevertheless, from the analysis of the wide range of circumstances that judges take into account it is possible to divide the reasonableness guidelines into two main categories.

At one end, there are circumstances that are taken into account at a more abstract level, that is, outside the specific context where the contract is signed: such are, for example, the nature and the location of terms and whether their size and prolixity or clarity make them easily understandable or not;[67] the position of the party who intends to use the contract in terms, for example, of its importance in the market (eg monopoly) or availability of insurance;[68] as well as availability of alternative, less burdensome, terms, for example possibility to introduce less burdensome terms upon payment of a higher sum;[69] the content and capriciousness of the term at issue and similarity with other contracts in use[70] (in cases of limitation clauses, the size of the limit compared with other limits in widely used standard terms may also relevant);[71] whether compliance with a certain term (eg a time limit for notification of a loss in an insurance contract) is practicable.

On the other hand, certain aspects of the reasonableness test can be assessed only in relation to a specific contract when signed by a specific customer: this includes in the first place the strength of the bargaining position of the parties,[72] also taking into account the question of how far it would have been practicable and convenient to go elsewhere[73] (courts are usually unenthusiastic about intruding 'into contracts between commercial parties of equal bargaining strength, who should generally be considered capable of being able to make contracts of their

[65] J Adams and R Brownsword, 'The Unfair Contract Terms Act: A Decade of Discretion' (1988) LQR 99.

[66] Lord Wilberforce in *Photo Production v Securicor Transport* [1980] AC 827, 843.

[67] *Wight v British Railway Board* [1983] CL 424; *Stag Line v Tyne Shiprepair Group Ltd* [1984] 2 Lloyd's Rep 210.

[68] *Photo Production Ltd v Securicor Transport* [1980] above n 56, at 827; *Singer Co (UK) Ltd v Tees and Hartlepool Port Authority* [1988] 2 Lloyd's Rep 164; *Flamar Interocean Ltd v Denmac Ltd* [1990] 1Lloyd's Rep 434; *Frank Maas v Sansung* [2004] EWHC 1502 (Comm) QBD.

[69] *Woodman v Photo Trade Processing Ltd* unreported, 3 April 1981, Exeter CC in R Lawson, *Exclusion Clauses and Unfair Contract Terms* (London, Sweet & Maxwell, 2000) 163.

[70] *Rasbora Ltd v JCL Marine Ltd* [1977] 1 Lloyd's Rep 645; see also *Stag Line v Tyne Shiprepair Group Ltd* [1984] 2 Lloyd's Rep 210, where the operation of a term depended on where a ship happened to be when a casualty occurred and whether it was convenient and economic to return it to the repairer. Similarly, a term may be unfair if it limits liability where the seller provides, under the same contract, two or more activities or functions in respect of which the nature of the work undertaken, the incidence of risk as between the parties, and the effect of a breach of duty by the defendants are all of different character, yet these are treated without distinction by the limitation of liability, see *Overseas Medical Supplies Ltd v Orient Transport Services Ltd* [1999] 1 All ER (Comm) 981.

[71] *Sonicare International Ltd v East Anglia Freight Terminal Ltd* [1997] 2 Lloyd's Rep 48, 55.

[72] UCTA Sch 2 (a).

[73] *Singer Co (UK) Ltd v Tees and Hartlepool Port Authority* [1988] 2 Lloyd's Rep 164, 169 and *St Albans City and District Council v International Computers Ltd* [1996] 4 All ER 481.

choosing and expect to be bound by their terms');[74] but this may also comprise the difficulty of the task and the practical consequences of the reasonableness decision (ie sums of money involved and capability of each party to bear the loss),[75] the party's knowledge of the existence and the content of the term and his appreciation of its significance,[76] availability of legal or specialised advice;[77] whether the customer contemplated the risk that the good supplied may not satisfy its special needs and whether the parties negotiated who should carry the risk.[78] Such guidelines can be considered to be of 'contextual' nature, in that they are attached to the events and circumstance concerning the contract subject matter of the dispute.

Drawing a clear-cut distinction between those two categories may be misleading, since most of the reasonableness criteria can be applied in both an abstract and a contextual fashion: capacity to bear the loss, for example, may vary from customer to customer, but one may guess that, in the context of consumers contracts, some losses will be very burdensome for all of them; likeliness to insure may be considered as an abstract factor if taking up insurance is a common custom in a certain type of trade; knowledge of the existence or extent of a term can entail an assessment of whether any ordinary customer, rather than the specific plaintiff, would have known and understood the meaning and implications of the term.[79]

The 'chameleonic' nature of the reasonableness criteria can be seen by comparing the following two cases.

In the well known case of *Smith v Eric Bush*,[80] the decision that the exclusion of liability of the negligent surveyors was unreasonable was also determined by the fact that the purchaser belonged to group of people 'buying at the bottom end of the market, many of whom will be young first-time buyers . . . likely to be under considerable financial pressure' and by the fact that the loss resulting from the surveyors' negligence was 'unlikely to cause significant hardship if it has to be borne by the surveyor but it is, on the other hand, quite possible that it will be a financial catastrophe for the purchaser who may be left with a valueless house and no money to buy another'. The reasoning seems to suggest that, had the customers been a wealthy family buying a manor house, the exemption may have been held valid.

In *Heathmill Multimedia v BT* the issue was whether a limitation to a certain sum of BT's liability for defaults in the telephone lines was valid. In holding that it was, the High Court emphasised

> the fact that the small business customer with four lines and the larger customer with 500 or 1,700 lines is subject to the same maximum figure . . . A business with many lines may suffer no actual loss when the service fails because it is able to make alternative arrangements but it is still entitled a maximum compensation of £20,000. On the

[74] Compare, eg, *Granville Oil & Chemicals Ltd v Davies Turner & Co Ltd* [2003] EWCA Civ 570 [2003] and *Overseas Medical Supplies*, above n 70.

[75] *Smith v Eric S Bush* [1989] 2 All ER 691.

[76] *MacRae and Dick Ltd v Philip* [1982] SLT 5.

[77] *Walker v Boyle* [1982] 1 All ER 634.

[78] *Watford Electronics Ltd v Sanderson Ltd* [2001] EWCA Civ 317.

[79] See *Overseas Medical Supplies* above n 70.

[80] Above n 75.

other hand, in some cases, . . . the limit of £20,000 may result in a customer receiving inadequate compensation': and 'the effect of the limits . . . are sufficient to adequately compensate customers in the vast majority of cases where the service fails.'[81]

Nevertheless, as BT offers its service to millions of customers in a world of standard form contracts, the Court held that it could not be exposed to different risks depending on the customer they deal with.

The first case provides an interesting contrast to German law: in applying § 307 BGB (previously § 9 AGB-G) German judges have explicitly refused to assess the 'unreasonable disadvantage' in relation to the specific situation of the consumer: the analysis is carried out at a more general level, according to the interests which are typical of those to whom such term is presented: the individual circumstances of the specific case are not take into any account and the approach is a 'general' one (*generalisierende Betrachtungsweise*).[82] The reason for this is to encourage the elaboration of a set of rules that can then be used to assess the fairness of a certain term in all contracts that are within the same category.

Italian law and unfair terms: unused tools

As already mentioned, there are basically no provisions in the Italian civil code which entrust judges with the task of assessing the fairness of a term. Accordingly, the scope of this section is necessarily limited to a brief analysis of how other existing provisions of the civil code could have been used as possible devices to monitor the fairness of contract terms.

A general principle underlying the whole Book II (obligations)[83] is good faith, which is also specifically mentioned in articles 1175 (fair behaviour), 1337 (good faith in negotiation and pre-contractual liability), 1358 (behaviour of parties while condition is pending), 1366 (interpretation according to good faith) and 1375 (performance according to good faith) cc; in addition, a duty of good faith is specifically mentioned by the *Relazione al Codice Civile* with regard to *contratti d'adesione.* There seems, however, to be no judicially elaborated definition of its content and its exact meaning: courts have never attempted to clearly express and rationally systematise the criteria and guidelines that from time to time brought them to decide that a certain behaviour was or was not 'in good faith'.[84] Decisions concerning good faith are traditionally justified by simply declaring that a certain

[81] [2003] EWHC 690 para 65.

[82] BGH 8 January 1986 NJW 1986, 2102, 2103; BGH 1 July 1987, NWJ 1987, 2575, 2576

[83] There are two different notions of good faith, an objective and a subjective one (*buona fede oggettiva e soggettiva*). Subjective good faith refers to the subjective state of mind of a person: in this sense, a person who (wrongfully) believes himself to be acting in accordance with the law is 'in good faith'; a person who is ignorant of the fact that, by doing something, he will damage someone else's rights is 'in good faith'; and so is the person who, without fault, acts in reliance on a certain situation which is later discovered not to be true. For the purposes of this work, only objective good faith will be discussed.

[84] This has been done in an admirable way by German courts, which have elaborated a consolidated set of cases where good faith could be used with predictable results, see eg D Medicus, *Allegemeiner Teil des BGB* (Heidelberg, Müller, 1997) 56–60.

behaviour complies or does not comply with 'correctness and loyalty';[85] 'respect of the word given and protection of the expectations raised';[86] 'solidarity':[87] the exact parameters that make good faith a (decisive) argument in favour of one party are not expressed, and it is therefore difficult to identify the causal relationship between the final decision and good faith as a criterion for such a decision. Additionally, courts have sometimes been reluctant to use good faith as a *ratio decidendi* for fear of undermining legal certainty and predictability of decisions. A rather well known example of such a reluctance is a judgment delivered by the Corte di Cassazione in 1966 stating that 'a behaviour which is contrary to loyalty, correctness and social solidarity cannot be unlawful and cannot be a source of liability for damages as long as it does not entail at the same time a violation of someone else's rights embedded in other rules'.[88] In other words, simple violation of good faith may be deprived of legal consequences unless there is a concurrent violation of other legally protected rights.

The analysis of some decisions can nevertheless reveal the existence of model situations and recurrent types of conflict where good faith has been successfully applied.[89] In principle, good faith seems to come into play when assessment of conflicting interests is required, and no contractual or legal provision provides a solution for such conflict; good faith, as a 'closing' rule, plays an integrative role in respect of the contract or the law.

So, for example, in cases concerning conflicts on the modalities of exercise of a certain right given to a party by the contract or by the law, good faith prevents the exercise of that right in a certain way when there is another way of exercising the same right which is less burdensome to the other party: good faith thus guarantees a satisfactory achievement of both parties' interest (ie a better fulfilment of the purpose of the contract) by avoiding an improper use of rights and duties granted or imposed on them by the contract or by the law. Thus, for example, the behaviour of a creditor who takes legal action against a debtor who pays a debt by means of an unsigned (hence not payable) cheque was considered as contrary to good faith:[90] respect of the interest of the debtor and compliance with good faith would require that, before taking legal action, the creditor informs the debtor of the mistake and gives him the opportunity to make a proper payment. In other cases, good faith serves to impose on the parties duties which are not imposed by the contract or by the law: accordingly, one party to a contract must give to the other party all the information which is necessary to that party in order to perform the contract; a creditor must inform the person who guarantees repayment of

[85] F Galgano, *Diritto Privato*, 1981 (Padova, Cedam, 1981) 321; Cass 16 February 1963 no 357 in Foro Padano 1964, 1284.

[86] P Rescigno, *Manuale di diritto privato italiano* (Napoli, Jovene, 1977) 647.

[87] S Rodotà, *Le fonti di integrazione del contratto*, Milano, Giuffrè,1969; Cass 5 January 1966 no 89 in Foro Padano 1966, I, 524.

[88] Cass 16 February 1963 no 375, Foro Padano 1964 1284.

[89] In this respect, excellent work has been done by A D'Angelo, 'La tipizzazione giurisprudenziale della buona fede contrattuale' (1990) *Contratto e Impresa* 702–55.

[90] Tribunale di Bologna 21 July 1970 Giurisprudenza Italiana 1971, I, 2, 211.

someone else's debt that the debtor, to whom he keeps on lending money, is in financial difficulties; a landlord who receives from the tenant notice to quit must inform the tenant that the notice was not signed (hence ineffective) so as to give him the possibility to remedy the mistake and avoid tacit renewal of the contract. The duties imposed by good faith range from simple information, as in the cases above, to the obligation to take a certain action or to refrain from taking a certain action (eg failure of an employee, absent from work for health reasons, to stay home to facilitate a speedy recovery may be contrary to good faith); finally, good faith has been used to solve conflict of interests where circumstances unforeseen by the parties at the moment of conclusion of a contract, without rendering performance impossible, affect the balance of interests envisaged in the contract. In those instances, judges have referred to good faith as a means to fairly allocate risks between the parties, to preserve the economical balance of the agreement initially envisaged by the parties and to avoid unfair enrichment.

In practice, good faith is a tool to integrate the contract or the law, and to impose duties and obligations which are ideally instrumental to the achievement of the purpose of the contract; in other words, good faith is understood as a means to guarantee that the economic and legal balance established by the parties is achieved in accordance with, and beyond, the provisions of the contract or of the law. The purpose of good faith is ultimately to ensure that parties' actions are always directed towards the achievement of the purpose for which they originally made the contract.

In relation to unfair terms, the good faith clause could have been usefully applied so as to increase the duties imposed on the proponent in relation to *conoscenza* and *conoscibilità* of the terms; and to make sure that, in making the contract, parties take into account each others' interests so as to realise a fair balance. In practice, good faith has not found any application of this type.

Another criterion which may have usefully been applied to unfair terms is that of *meritevolezza*: according to article 1322, the interest pursued by the parties in the contract must be one that deserves protection (*meritevole di tutela*). The control of *meritevolezza* is carried out on the aim of the contract, but could also be carried out on the single terms: on those grounds, it would be possible to declare terms not enforceable when they impose a heavy burden on the customer without a corresponding advantage: the interest of the enterprise to harm the consumer through a certain term cannot be considered as *meritevole di tutela*.

Public order and public moral are also general clauses of the *Code civil* which could have been applied to unfair terms: in France, for example, courts have elaborated the concept of 'ordre public technologique' by considering the highly specialised technical knowledge enjoyed by the enterprise as opposed to the naïve reliance of the consumer: in this context, the use of technological information cannot be made against the consumer and in this sense an unfair term, if not counterbalanced by some other advantage, can be unenforceable.[91]

[91] M Bessone, 'Controllo sociale dell'impresa e ordine pubblico tecnologico' in (1973) *Politica e Diritto*, 777 ff.

Finally, all the techniques of interpretation of the contract could have allowed some form of manipulation of the contract in order to balance the content of the obligations of the parties, to interfere with the economic arrangements made by them, and to improve the position of the weak party.

DIFFERENT METHODS OF ADJUDICATION

Theories and models of contract (ie principles and concepts relating to contract law, such as the principle of freedom of contract) have a fundamental importance in that they constitute the primary instrument of legal discourse: the actual legal material (ie legislation and case-law) is meaningless and fragmented unless it is shaped, arranged and systematised by the legal doctrine along the lines of certain principles, concepts and models relating to a certain area or sub-area. On the other hand, the choice of the principles, concepts and models which are deemed to become the guidelines for systematisation has its roots outside the law, in the field of the moral and social values of a given society. Accordingly, a contract theory, with its models, concepts and principles, plays a key role in a legal system since it can be considered as the door through which the legal material and the society are connected; in other words, the legal material relating to the area 'contract law' is systematised by the legal doctrine in accordance with certain principles and concepts, that is, to a certain type of contract model which is in itself related to wider social and moral principles and ideologies.

In both Italy and England the prevailing contract model according to which legal doctrine shaped and arranged the legal material was for a long time based on the ideology and values of the past century (ie laissez-faire and freedom of contract).

In England, the awareness of new needs and realities, however, triggered the judicial development of remedies and rules which, while still being based on the traditional models and principles (eg freedom of contract), aimed to give an adequate response to the new social and economic framework: in other words, if on the one hand the available remedies based on the traditional model of contract were pushed to their limits, on the other hand fairness, social equality and re-balancing of the bargain did not become the dominant paradigms and underlying principles of contract law: the legal principles and models of the past century remained unchanged, acting as brakes on legal change. In other words, England did not adopt a more general doctrine of 'contract fairness' or 'contractual balance', or 'good faith'; rather, it preferred to give individual solutions to deserving cases through the formal rules of incorporation and interpretation, applied with reference to the criterion of 'reasonable expectation', trimmed in accordance with parties' bargaining position. The adoption of Unfair Contract Terms Act 1977 marked a real change against the 'hands-off' approach of courts to contracts, providing them with a new contract theory and, as a consequence, with open tools for re-arranging the contractual agreement, in some cases opening the way to a 'bifurcation' of contract law, 'one for the consumer and the other one for the commercial sector'.[92]

In the pre-UCTA and UCTA case-law one can identify two methods of adjudication. One method is based on the 'reasonable expectations' of the customer as a yardstick to determine the reasonableness of a term, or whether it is incorporated into a contract, or how it has to be interpreted: as earlier discussed, if terms are usual and within the 'general expectations' of the offeree they will be deemed to have been incorporated in the contract; the decisive test for interpretation is often based on what an ordinary person in the position of the customer would have thought the effect of a clause to be; most of the 'abstract criteria' earlier identified in the context of UCTA are also based on the concept of 'reasonable expectations' as they often entail taking into account whether a certain term is in common use in a certain trade, whether insurance is usually taken up in business sector at issue, whether a term operates capriciously (hence unexpectedly), whether compliance with a certain requirement is generally practicable for the customer.

The other method entails an assessment of the fairness of contract terms that depends on the specific circumstances surrounding the conclusion of the contract. These are the criteria which have earlier been identified with reference to UCTA as 'contextual guidelines', that is, those that involve the analysis of the specific contract signed by the specific parties to the contract subject to judicial dispute; this method of adjudication also explains the existence, in the pre-UCTA case-law, of cases such as *AEG Ltd v Logic Resources Ltd* where, although the term at issue was not unusual and could therefore be 'reasonably expected', it was still considered as unfair; or *Hollier v Rambler Motors*, where one would find it difficult to believe that the ordinary customer would not have expected that the exemption clause covers negligence.

That existence of a contextual method of adjudication is confirmed (and, in this specific case, criticised) by Beale[93] in a comment to *Phillips Products Ltd v Hyland*:[94] while the Court of Appeal stressed that the question in the case was not whether the clause at issue was fair in other similar contracts, but in relation to the particular contract at issue, Beale suggested that such an approach was mistaken: while individual circumstances could be taken into account in rendering negative any unreasonableness,[95] the normal question should be 'whether the clause is a fair one for the normal run of contracts rather than for the individual customer'.

A contextual method of adjudication may occasionally entail shifting the focus of the reasonableness test under UCTA from the moment of incorporation of a clause (ie whether the clause is a reasonable one to incorporate) to the moment of

[92] R Brownsword, 'The Two Laws of Contract' (1981) SJ 279. In favour of a special *lex mercatoria* for the business-to-business contracts see, recently, A Schwartz and R Scott, 'Contract Theory and the Limits of Contract' (2003) 113 *Yale Law Journal* 2.

[93] H Beale, *Unfair Contract in Britain and Europe* (1989) Current Legal Problems 208.

[94] [1987] 2 All ER 620.

[95] Eg, the absence of bargaining power or choice would not necessarily count against a clause, if the customer was important enough to have choice but did not exercise it: this would actually be an argument in favour of the clause.

reliance (ie whether the clause is a reasonable one to rely upon). In *Rees-Hough Ltd v Redland Reinforced Plastics Ltd*,[96] for example, the decision against the reasonableness of certain terms was also dictated by the fact that the defendants had never sought to rely upon them in his past dealing with the plaintiff: this estopped them from relying on such terms in the case at issue. The essence of the estoppel argument is that the *proferens* has not previously relied on the protective term, which sends out the signal that the term will not be relied upon: accordingly, it would not be fair to rely on the clause. The relevant question to be asked under UCTA, however, is whether the term at issue is a fair and reasonable one to be included in the contract, not to be relied upon. The point had been discussed during the drafting of UCTA between the English Law Commission (supporting a reliance-based test) and the Scottish Law Commission (supporting an inclusion-based test). The view of the latter prevailed since it appeared to make it easier for the parties to ascertain in advance the range of the obligations they undertook: a contracting party must be in a position to assess its risks before he enters into the contract. The test of reasonableness, referred to the moment of incorporation, had the advantage of placing judges behind a veil of ignorance concerning post-formation circumstances, with the result of increasing commercial calculability and security:[97] however, judicial response appears not to have always respected the choice of the legislator.

'Contextual justice' is, to some extent, a natural result of the inductive nature of the common law legal reasoning: as opposed to the civil law reasoning, which is based on abstract normative propositions, the common lawyer 'commence à partir du particulier, d'où l'obsession anglaise des faits':[98] accordingly, the circumstances surrounding the conclusion of a certain contract act as structuring elements of legal reasoning more than they do in civil law thinking. Second, familiarity with 'personalised' justice is certainly stronger in England than in any civil law system, given that England has for centuries accepted equity as a source of law: accordingly, tailor-made, rather than 'standard' solutions are more easily accepted in English courts.

Compared to the English system, Italian law on unfair terms presents different—almost opposite—features. First, 'the existence of specific rules about general conditions of contract has brokered the constructive contribution of Italian courts, which limited themselves to the pure application of the articles specifically dedicated to the point'.[99] Wherever the poor cover provided by articles 1341–42cc applies, judges (and practitioners alike) refrain from resorting to more general principles like that of good faith, thus showing a sort of unspoken mistrust for

[96] (1985) 1 Cons LJ 67.

[97] Adams and Brownsword, 'The Unfair Contract Terms Act' above n 65, at 118–19.

[98] G Samuel, 'Entre les mots et les choses: les raisonnements et les méthodes en tant que sources du droit' (1995) *Revue Internationale de Droit Comparé*, 512.

[99] R De Negri 'Report on the practical implementation of Directive 93/13/EEC in Italy' in *The Unfair Terms Directive, Five YearsOn* (Luxembourg, Office for Official Publications of the European Communities, 2000) 304.

such ambiguous clauses, and in the strictest respect of the principle *lex specialis derogat legis generalis.* In addition, in examining the relevant case-law one cannot avoid noticing that most of the actions involving articles 1341–42cc are also based on other grounds: matters concerning those provisions seem to be considered as 'ancillary' and never dealt with great attention, as if they could support only marginally the plaintiff's (or defendant's) claim.

Second—and more importantly—the legal material developed by courts has always adhered rather faithfully to the classical principles and to the 'neutral' model of contract, the only attempts at change being embedded in a few obscure decisions of first instance courts. This may probably be explained by the wish to preserve the coherence of the private law system but above all by the habit of considering law, especially private law, as a closed system, relegated outside the political, social and economical realities. The problem of unfair terms is a social problem, and the Italian private lawyer has traditionally considered social problems as outside his competence, thus restraining his field of action strictly to the data provided by positive law, and avoiding, in accordance with the kelsenian approach, any contamination of his judgments by 'metalegal' considerations:[100]

> the attitude is that the law is a self-contained discipline or phenomenon that can be understood and perfected by systematic study. It is summed up in the phrase *legal science*, which carries with it the assumption that the study of law is a science, in the same way as the study of other natural phenomena—say those of biology of physics—is a science . . . The theoretical structure of legal science consists of general concepts and institutions of a high order of abstraction, arranged and interrelated in a systematic way. The components . . . of the structure are strictly legal, and indeed it is believed that their purity, and hence their validity, would be destroyed by the introduction of non-legal elements.[101]

Another reason for the mistrust of lawyers in any form of substantive control of *condizioni generali di contratto* can be found in the concern not to threaten any further the principle of contract freedom. This principle already appeared to be reduced by the prohibitions contained in the Italian civil code and by the automatic insertion of *clausole imperative* (art 1339 cc). While it would be possible, however, to admit that the legislator can bring limitations to private autonomy, the idea that such an autonomy may be subject to a judicial or administrative power entitled to assess parties' choices is unacceptable to many; for those who see in freedom of contract a constitutional value, the idea of such a control may even raise a suspicion of unconstitutionality.

[100] M Bianca 'Le tecniche di controllo delle clausole vessatorie'in M Bianca and G Alpa (eds) *Le clausole abusive nei contratti stipulati con i consumatori* (Padova, Cedam, 1996) 357.

[101] M Cappelletti, *The Italian Legal System. An Introduction* (Stanford, Stanford University Press, 1967), 1970–71.

5

Subjective Scope of Application

ACCORDING TO ARTICLE 1, Directive 93/13 (the Directive) applies to contracts concluded between a seller or supplier and a 'consumer', defined by article 2 as 'any natural person who . . . is acting for purposes which are outside his trade, business and profession'.

The notion of 'purpose' in the Directive must in principle be understood as referring to the objective destination of the good or service acquired;[1] the scope of such notion is therefore clear in several cases, where the nature of the goods or services purchased (eg a kitchen or a health insurance policy) or the status of the customer (eg a student, a retired person or a housewife) may leave small room to doubt that a transaction has destinations other than 'consumption', that is, satisfaction of personal (or family) needs.[2] The formula used by the Directive, however, leaves several 'grey areas': those are, for example, cases where the type of the goods or services purchased (eg cars, computers) or the status of the customer (eg a lawyer, a doctor) is not a definitive indicator of the nature of the transaction, or cases where goods or services are purchased by traders or professionals who intend to use them for both personal and business purposes.

This chapter first explores the 'grey areas' left by the definition in the Directive; it then moves on to considering the extent to which Member States remain free to determine the scope of application *ratione personae* of the protection.

THE CONSUMER IN EC LAW

The notion of consumer that one can find in EC law is not a uniform one, but varies in accordance with the different focuses and objectives of EC policies and legislation.

Under article 81(3) EC, for example, anti-competitive agreements may be granted an exemption if they contribute 'to improving the production or distribution of goods or to promoting technical or economic progress, while allowing consumers a fair share of the resulting benefit'. It is clear that, for the purposes of

[1] G Cian, 'Il nuovo capo XIV-bis del codice civile, sulla disciplina dei contratti dei consumatori' Studium Juris 1996, 414; U Ruffolo, 'Le clausole "vessatorie", "abusive", "inique" e la ricodificazione negli artt.1469-bis–1469sexies cc' in U Ruffolo (ed) *Clausole vessatorie e abusive Gli artt.1469-bis e seguenti del codice civile e i contratti del consumatore* (Milano, Giuffrè, 1997) 29.

[2] F Astone, 'Commento all'article 1469-bis 2° comma' in G Alpa and S Patti (eds) *Le clausole vessatorie nei contratti con i consumatori* (Milano, Giuffrè, 1997) vol I, 108.

this article, a 'consumer' is not necessarily a member of the public who purchases goods or services for personal use: undertakings which acquire products in the course of their trade also qualify as consumers[3] since the objective of this provision is to ensure, by means of competition law, the enhancement of the general welfare.[4]

'Consumer law' is, on the other hand, commonly considered as a set of rules and principles specifically designed to protect the consumer in his relationship with the enterprise; this includes a range of measures which cover different aspects of market transactions, from advertising, labelling and negotiation to health and safety of products and contract terms. Intervention is from time to time justified by the subject matter of the contract (eg consumer credit), by the use of a particular selling technique (eg doorstep or distance sale) or by the wish to impose specific duties in relation to the sale of a certain product (eg product safety or sale guarantees): the presence of more of one of these variables seems to create the need to protect the weaker party. The target of achieving protection of a specific category of customers or buyers distinguishes directives related to consumer protection from other directives such as banking and insurance where consumer protection is only an indirect aim.

Even within the limited area of 'consumer law', however, the need to give account of a pluralistic reality entails that one may identify different approaches to the question of who the 'consumer' is: 'the definition of consumer depends on the object and extent of the protection that one wants to ensure'.[5]

Most of the directives which are commonly considered as the 'consumer directives', as well as the Brussels Regulation,[6] rely on a 'transaction' definition, according to which the consumer is a natural person who, in transactions covered by the measure concerned, is acting for purposes which are not within his trade or profession.[7] All the contract directives use this (or a similar) definition, with the exception of the Package Travel Directive.[8]

The directives on product liability[9] and product safety[10] contain a definition of producer, but not of the other party, which is referred to as 'the injured person' or

[3] See, eg, *Kabel-und Metallwerke Neumeyer AG and Etablissements Luchaire SA Agreement* [1975] OJ L222/34.

[4] Even in competition law, however, the notion of consumer may be narrower than the one above presented: in *Pavlov*, for example, the ECJ decided that, for the purposes of the application of art 82 EC, self employed medical specialists were acting as undertakings rather than consumers when setting up a professional pension scheme (C–180/98 *Pavlov and Others v Stichting Pensioenfonds Medische Specialisten* [2000] ECR I–6451). The aim pursued by this interpretation is primarily to ensure the broadest application of EC competition law.

[5] F Picod and V Christianos, 'Consommateurs' Répertoire Communautaire Dalloz, April 1996.

[6] Council Regulation 44/2001 on Jurisdiction and the recognition and enforcements of judgments in civil and commercial matters [1972] OJ L12/1.

[7] The formula was actually first used in the Brussels Convention (see also case 150/77 *Bertrand v Paul Ott* [1978] ECR 1431) and later adopted in Community secondary legislation.

[8] Council Dir 90/314/EC on Package Travel, Package Holidays and Package Tours (Package Holidays Directive) [1990] OJ L158/59.

[9] Dir 85/374/EEC on the Approximation of the Laws, Regulations and Administrative Provisions of the Member States Concerning Liability for Defective Products [1985] OJ L210/29.

[10] Dir 2001/95/EC on General Product Safety [2002] OJ L11/4.

'the consumer' (with no further definition). This approach can be explained by the awareness that some measures need to cover wide economic categories so as to include those who act in a professional capacity: the primary focus of those directives is the general responsibility of producers for the product so that there is no need to restrict the obligations of the producer to any particular category of consumers:[11] it would be both impractical and morally unacceptable to prescribe different degrees of product safety or liability according to the use the purchaser makes of the product. Similarly, the misleading advertising directive extends its protection to all persons carrying out a trade or business or a profession as well as consumers (understood in a broad sense): again, this is because the directive itself is justified by the need to ensure a fair market for all economic agents.

As a result, when further investigating the notion of consumer elaborated at EC level, one needs to be mindful of the fact that each piece of EC consumer legislation must be read in the light of the context and the specific policy reasons that led to its adoption.

The notion of consumer in the ECJ case-law and in Directive 93/13

There are two possible approaches to the interpreting the definition of consumer contained in Directive 93/13.

One approach is to restrict the scope of protection to purchases which are exclusively aimed at satisfying personal needs: a consumer is a person who actually consumes the good or service bought, that is, he does not use any further the goods or services for the purpose of producing or distributing other goods or services.[12] Under this perspective, which may be called 'function-based approach', the purpose of the law is not necessarily to protect the weak party as such, but to protect the party who satisfies family and personal needs.

A different solution, which may be called 'competence-based', suggests that a consumer is anyone who is in a position of technical inferiority compared to the counterpart, who, because of his business, is an expert in that field. On these grounds, one acts for purposes which are within his trade or profession only when making a contract which is an immediate and direct expression of his trade, where he has technical knowledge and competence; the fact that goods may be instrumental to the profession does not exclude that the status of consumer and protection should be extended to businesses whenever they are acting outside their field of competence.[13]

[11] It must be noted, however, that damage caused by death or personal injury is always compensated, while damage to property will be compensated only if the product is of the type ordinarily intended for private use or consumption (art 9(b) Dir 85/374).

[12] G Stella Richter, 'Il tramonto di un mito: la legge uguale per tutti (dal diritto comune dei contratti al contratto dei consumatori)' (1997) II *Giustizia Civile*, 202.

[13] See, eg, V Roppo, 'La nuova disciplina delle clausole abusive nei contratti tra imprese e consumatori' (1993) I *Rivista di Diritto Civile* 283; L Gatt, 'Ambito soggettivo di applicazione della disciplina. Il consumatore ed il professionista' in Bianca-Busnelli (ed) *Commentario al capo XIV bis del*

In the seminal decision in *Di Pinto*,[14] the ECJ had to adjudicate, for the purposes of the Doorstep Sales Directive, upon the status of traders in respect of contracts where they agreed to advertise the sale of their business in a periodical published by Di Pinto. The court rejected the argument that such traders could be considered as consumers. It established a close connection between the act performed and the subjective state of the person involved: acts which are preparatory to the sale of a business are managerial acts performed for the purpose of satisfying needs other than the family or personal ones; in relation to such acts, a normal well-informed trader cannot claim to be surprised as he would be would aware of the value of his business.

A comparable, function-based solution was adopted by the court in cases involving other EC measures containing a similar definition, *Benincasa*[15] and *Dietzinger*[16]. In the latter case focus on the objective element of the transaction is particularly evident since a guarantee given by Dietzinger for the repayment of his father's business debt was considered as made 'in the course of his business'. Dietzinger, nevertheless, had provided the guarantee outside his business or profession: he did not run a financing company, nor did the guarantee fall in any other way within his trade or profession: the guarantee was provided on a one-off basis in order to support his father. The court emphasised the objective elements related to the contract itself and concluded that a contract of guarantee made by a natural person who is not acting in the course of his trade or profession does not come within the scope of the Directive where it guarantees repayment of a debt contracted by another who, for his part, is acting within the course of his trade or profession.

This approach leaves some doubts as to the status of those who purchase a good or a service that should serve both professional and personal needs.[17] The problem is that when a contract simultaneously serves both private and trade or professional needs, it may be possible to determine the proportion of the contract within each category; but it is not possible to deem the customer to be, in that proportion or indeed in any other proportion, a consumer and a non-consumer in relation to one and the same contract.

Codice Civile: dei contratti del consumatore (Padova, Cedam, 1999) 150–51 and L Gatt, 'L'ambito soggettivo di applicazione della normativa sulle clausole vessatorie (nota all'ordinanza di rimessione)' (1998) *Giustizia Civile* 2341–58. This view is also inspired by the case-law developed in other countries, like France and England.

[14] C–361/89 *Criminal Proceedings against Di Pinto* [1991] ECR I–1189.

[15] C–269/95 *Francesco Benincasa v Dentalkit Srl* [1997] ECR I–3767, concerning the definition of consumer in what was at the time the Brussels Convention on Jurisdiction and the Enforcement of Judgments in Civil and Commercial Matters [1972] OJ L299/32.

[16] C–45/96 *Bayerische Hypotheken und Wechselbank AG v Edgar Dietzinger* [1998] ECR I–1199 concerning the definition of consumer in the Doorstep Sales Directive.

[17] P Rossi, 'Il concetto di consumatore e l' ambito di tutela della disciplina dei contratti del consumatore' (1998) *Rassegna Giuridirica dell' Energia Elettrica* 459–60. In favour of the criterion of prevalence to be assessed on a case-by-case analysis is the Law Commission, see Law Commission and Scottish Law Commission, *Unfair Terms in Contracts. A Joint Consultation Paper* Law Commission Consultation Paper no 166/Scottish Law Commission Discussion Paper no 119 (2002) (hereinafter Law Commission Consultation Paper no 166) para 4.155.

The question has recently been brought to the attention of the ECJ the case of *Gruber v Bay Wa*,[18] where the court was asked whether a farmer who bought tiles for the roofing of his farm, which was also his private dwelling, was or not a consumer for the purposes of the special rules of jurisdiction for consumer contracts under article 13 of the Brussels Convention (now Regulation 44/2001). The court ruled that this depended on which purpose, the private or the professional one, was predominant, and established that the status of consumer can only be granted where the link between the purpose for which the goods or services are used and the trade or profession of the person concerned is negligible and 'so slight as to be marginal'.[19]

In coming to this conclusion, the ECJ considered that the rules of jurisdiction for consumer contracts represent a derogation from the general principles established by the Convention and must therefore be narrowly interpreted: the Convention itself does not appear to favour the attribution of jurisdiction to the courts of the claimant's domicile. In addition, the special protection under article 13 is justified only for contracts concluded outside and independently of any trade or professional activity or purpose, solely for the purpose of satisfying an individual's own needs in terms of private consumption. Such protection is unwarranted in the case of contracts made for the purpose of a trade or professional activity.

The decision may be subject to three main criticisms. First, the reason why the professional purpose of the contract (even when it is not prevailing, but simply not 'marginal') must necessarily attract the application of the ordinary rules of jurisdiction is not explained. Jacobs AG suggests that 'inasmuch as a contract is entered into for the customer's trade or professional purposes, he must be deemed to be on an equal footing with the supplier. And that position of equality—his deemed business and legal experience, and resources, vis-à-vis those of the supplier—cannot be undermined by the fact that the contract also serves private purposes': this argument, however, seems to rely on criteria drawn from the competence-based approach, previously rejected by the court.

Second, it is not clear what a 'negligible' or 'marginal' link in practice means: would the purchase of car to be used 70 per cent for personal use and 30 per cent for professional use be considered or not as a 'consumer contract'?

Third, the ruling assumes that it is possible to distinguish between the professional and the commercial use of a good or a service. While this can be done in the case of a car or a computer, it is impossible to draw such a distinction in the case, for example, of a doctor having his medical practice in his own house: would the contract for the supply of electricity or water be considered a consumer contract? To what extent is it possible to argue that the link with the profession is 'negligible'?[20]

[18] C–464/01 [2005] ECR I–439.

[19] *Ibid* para 39.

[20] The issue is addressed by the Law Commission's Consultation Paper no 166, above n 17, at paras 3.36–3.38. The Law Commission states that a definition of consumer as 'an individual who makes the contract for purposes which are not related to any business of his' would totally exclude that a mixed contract could be considered as a consumer contract in the case where the buyer buys primarily for

It is submitted that there are other indicators that, in a case of this type, should be used to decide whether there is or not a consumer contract. Dealing as a business often entails several advantages: one usually has a stronger bargaining power, can gain access to stores that sell to traders/retailers only and, above all, is able to recover value added tax on the purchases made. In those cases, it is submitted that the one who chooses to enjoy such benefits (by, for example, using stationery with his business letterhead or asking for a VAT receipt) should not be able to enjoy, at the same time, the benefits connected with the status of a consumer; in deciding whether to apply or not the consumer rules a court should therefore investigate such matters.

Bearing in mind that, as earlier discussed, each piece of EC consumer legislation must be read in the light of the context and the specific policy reasons that led to its adoption, one may wonder whether judgments rendered by the ECJ in contexts other than that of Directive 93/13 can be relevant for the interpretation of the latter.

While the value of the rulings in *Di Pinto* and *Dietzinger* in this respect is beyond doubt,[21] the issue is less clear with regard to the decision in *Bay Wa*.

The ECJ makes it clear that the provisions of the Convention must be interpreted by reference principally to the scheme and purpose of the Convention, and that article 13, being a derogation from a rule of jurisdiction laid down in the Convention itself, must be narrowly construed. The same reasoning would not apply in the context of Directive 93/13 (although one could argue that since its provisions are an exception to the principle of contractual freedom, their scope of application should be construed narrowly).

There is no reason, however, why the remaining part of the reasoning in *Bay Wa* could not be 'transplanted' to the consumer contract Directives and accordingly to Directive 93/13. A different solution would have dramatic consequences on legal certainty as it would result in an inconsistency of interpretation between Regulation 44/2001 on the one hand and the consumer contract directives on the other. If, for example, the same person was to be considered as a consumer under the Unfair Terms Directive but not under the Regulation a claimant would find himself in a situation where a jurisdiction clause may be held to be unfair under Directive 93/13 but would be not be subject to article 13 of the Regulation, hence it would be perfectly valid.

Finally, the Directive does not say anything on the burden of proof. This suggests that the usual rules apply, that is, it is for the person wishing to rely on the protection offered by the Directive to show that he is acting as a consumer.[22]

private use but with the intention of occasionally use for business. Accordingly, the Law Commission recommended that the consumer is defined as 'an individual who enters into it (the contract) wholly or mainly for purposes unrelated to a business of his'. This means that a party who enters into a contract for purposes that are merely incidental to its business but nevertheless related to it (such as *R&B*), should not be treated as acting as a consumer. It is not clear why the report does not simply adopt the terminology of the directive but uses a totally new one.

[21] In C–541/99 *Idealservice* [2001] ECR I–9049, for example, Mischo AG referred several times to *Di Pinto* in the context of the definition of 'consumer' for the purposes of Dir 93/13.

[22] This is confirmed by para 46 of the *Bay Wa* decision.

NATIONAL TRADITIONS

The notion of consumer in domestic law: comparative remarks

The issue of defining the exact limits of the notion of consumer has arisen in some national legal systems much before this was introduced by the Community legislator.

It is interesting to note, in this respect, that the *Di Pinto* case arose out of a reference made by a French court. French courts had often (but not consistently) adopted, in the application of the *loi Scrivener*, a notion of consumer that is broader than the one in EC law.[23] In 1987, for example, the Cour de Cassation held that a legal person could benefit from the application of the *loi Scrivener* whenever acting in an area outside its business or competence. In that specific case, concerning the installation of an alarm system, the company was 'in the same state of ignorance as any other consumer', in spite of the fact that it was a legal person acting for the purpose of further producing goods and service.[24]

This broad, competence-based reading was facilitated by the fact that the *loi Scrivener* affords protection to 'consumers' (without defining them) and *non-professionnels*, and the ambiguity of this formula contributes to the confusion surrounding the scope of the protection.[25]

In line with the *Di Pinto* ruling, however, two decisions of the French Cour de Cassation in 1996 have later refused to extend the benefit of the protection afforded by the 1978 law to a factory in relation to a contract concluded for the supply of water and to a company in relation to a credit agreement set up to finance the purchase of its IT system. It held that the law does not apply to contracts 'that have a direct link with the professional activity exercised by one of the parties'.[26]

In England, UCTA lays down special rules for cases in which one of the parties deals as consumer. The definition of consumer is given *a contrario*, in the sense that a consumer is someone who does not make the contract 'in the course of a business' (s 12): this has required judicial clarification.

In the case of *R & B Customs Brokers v United Dominion Trust*,[27] the Court of Appeal drew the guidelines for the adoption of a wide notion of consumer that

[23] Unsurprisingly, Mischo AG advocated a broad understanding of 'consumer' in *Di Pinto* [1990] ECR I–1189.

[24] Cour de Cassation 1ère Civile (Cass 1ère civ), 28 April 1987, 1987 Revue Trimestrielle de Droit Civil 1987, 537 (with a comment by J Mestre).

[25] In truth, the additional reference to *non professionels* was due to a disagreement between the *senateurs*, keen to use the word 'consumers', and the *deputés*, who thought that the word non-professional would be clearer. The resulting compromise was the use of both formulas, both meaning consumer. See also J Calais Auloy and F Steinmetz, *Droit de la Consommation* (Paris, Dalloz, 2000) 188–89.

[26] Cass 1ère civ 3 January 1996 and Cass 1ère civ 30 January 1996, both discussed by L Leveneur, 'Contrats entre professionels et législation des clauses abusives' in *Droit de la Consommation 10 ans de jurisprudence commentée 1990–2000* (Paris, Juris Classeur, 2000). See also A Cathelineau, 'La notion de consommateur en droit interne: à propos d'une dérive', *ibid* 63–65.

[27] [1988] 1 WLR 321.

would cover all transactions that do not form part of the buyer's business nor are incidental, unless regularly made, to it.

The plaintiff, a shipping and freight forwarding company, bought from the defendant finance company a car supplied by a third party. The agreement contained a term potentially covered by UCTA provided that the transaction was not done 'in the course of a business'. The car was the second or third acquired on credit terms and had been bought for both company and personal use. The Court of Appeal not only disregarded the fact that the plaintiff was not a natural person, but also ruled that the purchase was only incidental to the plaintiff's business activity and that, in such circumstances, a degree of regularity was required before the transaction could be said to be an integral part of the business and, hence, entered in the course of business. Since the car was at most the third bought on credit terms, there was no sufficient degree of regularity.[28] In this context, it is probably more correct to talk about 'frequency' rather than 'regularity'.

This decision seems to draw the line between who is regarded as a consumer and who is not, but the rationale of the distinction is debatable. On the one hand, equating the buying company with a consumer may be a good policy, because a firm of shipping brokers may be just as unqualified to assess a car and the value of the bargain as is the man in the street. If the firm regularly buys a car for its directors, however, it is no longer to be equated with a consumer; but certainly, a consumer who regularly buys a car would still be treated as such on grounds that the frequency of the bargain would not place him in a better position in terms, for example, of bargaining power. Accordingly, it is unclear why the frequency of a transaction should be the distinguishing criterion for enlarging protection to purchasers buying otherwise than for private consumption.

In other legal systems, such as the German and the Italian ones, the notion of consumer does not appear to be a criterion commonly used to justify the existence of a specific set of rules.

In German law the AGB-G did not use the concept of consumer in determining its sphere of application *ratione personae.* The AGB-G was in principle applicable to all standard contract terms (in the sense of § 1), whether used in consumer or business contracts, with the exception of specific types of contracts (eg. labour). § 24 excluded the application of certain protective provisions of the AGB-G (§§ 2, 10 and 11) to standard business terms which were proffered as against a businessperson (*unternehmer*); this meant that persons exercising a professional activity (not an entrepreneurial activity) such as lawyers or doctors came under the specific protective ambit of the AGB-G.[29]

The new rules of the BGB still aim to protect all parties to a contract made on standard terms, in the belief that 'the member states may, under the minimum

[28] For a similar, but more briefly justified conclusion see *Peter Symmons & Co v Cook* (1981) NLJ 758. A comparable reasoning is also contained in the decision under the Trade Description Act 1968 of *Davies v Sumner* [1984] 3 All ER 831.

[29] N Reich 'The Implementation of Directive 93/13/EEC on Unfair Terms in Consumer Contracts in Germany' (1997) *European Review of Private Law* 165, 169

protection clause, extend its ambit to contracts entered into with smaller traders'.[30] Whether this is a correct interpretation of the minimum harmonisation formula will be discussed below.[31]

Further away from the Community policy is the Italian example: prior to the intervention of the Community legislator, the *persona* consumer did not exist in Italian private law.

The reason for the absence of any direct means of protection, both in contract and in tort, is to be found in the aforementioned[32] idea, underlying the Italian civil code, of neutrality of the law towards the social status of the parties. The common opinion among lawyers was that the consumer was indirectly protected by the civil code as *aderente* (counterparty, arts 1341–42, 1370 cc), *acquirente* (buyer, art 1470 cc) *terzo* (third party, art 1494 cc), *danneggiato* (injured party, art 2043 cc) and by the laws on trademarks, enterprises and unfair competition.[33] It was clear, however, that the protection enjoyed by the consumer was only a mediated and indirect protection: it is significant in this respect that the Italian Constitutional Court (Corte Costituzionale) denied *locus standi* to consumers' associations in actions concerning unfair competition[34] on grounds that they are representatives of interests which have nothing to do with the fairness of commercial relationships.

It true that that some provision of the Italian Constitution could be understood as referring to consumers.[35] In particular, the combined provisions of Article 41 paragraphs 2 and 3 of the Constitution,[36] which entitle the law to regulate and limit economic activities for the purpose of protecting the interest of the society, have been understood as ensuring that consumers' security, freedom and dignity and are preserved against any economic activity that might endanger them.

However, rather than serving as a foundation for the elaboration of a consumer policy, the provision has been used as a yardstick for the evaluation of constitutionality of laws having the potential to restrict private economic activities or to

[30] *Ibid* 169. In truth, this is possible not by virtue of the minimum harmonisation formula, but by the fact that in the areas not covered by the directive states remain free to adopt or maintain their legislation.

[31] See below p 88.

[32] See Ch 3, p 38.

[33] G Sannia, 'Commento all'article 1469-bis comma 2' in E Cesaro (ed) *Clausole vessatorie e contratto del consumatore* (Padova, Cedam, 1998) 83.

[34] In 1980, the Tribunale di Milano made a reference to the Corte Costituzionale (Corte Cost) concerning the compatibility between Art 3 of the Constitution and the failure to confer *locus standi* to consumers' associations in actions brought under art 2601 cc (unfair competition), but the Corte Costituzionale (ord 59 of 21 January 1988 in Foro Italiano 1988, I, 2158) rejected the reference as 'manifestly inadmissible'.

[35] According to G Alpa, 'Consumatore (protezione del) nel diritto civile' in *Digest. Discipline Privatistiche* III, (Torino, Giappichelli, 1988), 547 it is possible to identify a 'constitutional backbone to consumer interests'.

[36] Art 41.1. Private economic initiative is free.

Art 41.2. Private economic initiative cannot be carried out so as to be contrary to public utility or so as to be detrimental to security, freedom and human dignity.

Art 41.3. The law shall establish programmes and controls which are appropriate to guide and coordinate public and private economic activity for social purposes.

allow a penetrating State control on them.[37] Although the notion of 'social utility' and 'interests of the society' has not found a clear and consistent application in the case-law of the Constitutional Court, it is possible to identify a relevant number of decisions where, in the name of 'social utility', the court 'saved' several laws which it considered aimed at protecting citizens and consumers' interests (but very often also national production)[38]: so, for example, the court declared compatible with Article 41 of the Constitution the obligation imposed by a law to produce pasta with durum wheat flour only: the aim of such restriction being, the court reasoned, the protection of the consumers and of public heath, as well as the support to specialised wheat cultivation. The notion of consumer in this context has obviously very little to do with the creation of a set of rules aimed at re-establishing the lost bargaining equality (if ever there was one) between consumers and traders.

The elaboration and adoption of a consumer code that systematises and simplifies the legislation adopted to implement the consumer directive represents an immense step forward. The acceptance of the idea of 'consumer', however, has been far from smooth, as the following paragraphs will show.

The impact of domestic legal traditions on the implementation of Directive 93/13

England: too many notions of consumer

The definition of 'in the course of a business' given in *R & B Customs Brokers* is not commonly considered to be a satisfactory one. First, it may end up unduly restricting the scope of application of UCTA if applied to the business party of a contract: a business that makes a contract which is not an integral party of its activity may

[37] A Maltoni, *Tutela dei consumatori e libera circolazione delle merci nella giurisprudenza della Corte di Giustizia* (Milano, Giuffrè, 1999) 22–33.

[38] Corte Costituzionale Sentenza (Corte Cost Sent) no 137 of 15 October 1971 in Giustizia Costituzionale 1971, I, 1577. The case is particularly interesting if compared to case 407/85 *Drei Glocken v USL Centro-Sud* [1988] ECR–4233, where the ECJ held the obligation to make pasta with durum wheat only as incompatible with art 28. In other, similar, decisions the Constitutional Court declared compatible with art 41 laws aimed at: price-fixing of medicines as a measure aimed at preserving public health, threatened by the danger of a free competition market (Corte Cost Sent no 29 of 1957 in Giurisprudenza Costituzionale 1957, I, 404); legal regulation of prices of beef for the purposes of preserving social wellbeing (Corte Cost Sent no 47 of 1958 in Giurisprudenza Costituzionale 1958, I, 527). Later on, in the seventies, the Court introduced the criteria of reasonableness/proportionality and demanded for itself the task of

> assessing the adequacy of the means to the ends in order to preserve the guaranteed freedom against interventions which are arbitrarily restrictive . . . or against interventions which in practice nullify the basic rights attached to such freedoms. (Corte Cost Sent no 78 of 1970 in Giurisprudenza Costituzionale 1970, I, 1052)

This brought to a drastic reduction in the number of laws that could pass the constitutionality test: for example, the Court declared unconstitutional the law that prohibited patenting of medicines as it was 'disproportionate to the end of protecting the right to health', which could be achieved by means that were less restrictive of private economic initiative (Corte Cost Sent no 20 of 1978 in Giurisprudenza Costituzionale I, 454).

be considered as not having acted 'in the course of a business', with the consequence that the consumer who makes a contract with it will not be protected by the UCTA. Section 1(3) limits the scope of the Act to 'business liability', that is, liability for breach of obligations and duties arising 'in the course of a business'. So, for example, if *R & B* had sold their car to a consumer, the contract would not be subject to UCTA since *R & B* would be considered not to be acting 'in the course of business'.[39] It can be argued that when faced with such a case a court could decide that a different approach should be taken to the interpretation of 'in the course of a business' so as to ensure to the maximum possible extent protection for the consumer. Nevertheless, it would appear odd if the same formula in the same piece of legislation was subject to two different interpretations.

Secondly, the later decision of *Stevenson v Rogers*[40] gives rise to inconsistencies with the definition of 'in the course of a business' in section 14(2) of the Sale of Goods Act 1979. According to this section, in contracts where the seller sells 'in the course of a business' there is an implied term that the goods supplied are of satisfactory quality. The Court of Appeal had to decide whether a fisherman, in selling his own boat to another fisherman, was acting 'in the course of a business'. The Court of Appeal analysed the legislative history of the section to conclude that the sale had been made 'in the course of a business' and accordingly a condition as to the satisfactory quality of the boat was implied. This decision focused on the capacity of the seller at the time of the sale and, accordingly, so long as it could be established that the seller was involved in a business then he would be caught by section 14(2) even though the goods sold were not of the type he may specifically deal with. The court insisted that there was no contradiction with *R & B Customs Brokers* since the ratio of the latter was limited to section 12 UCTA[41] and concerned the definition of consumer, while this case concerned the definition of seller. The court added that the two cases were not inconsistent as they were both aimed at ensuring the maximum level of consumer protection.

In spite of the court's desire to avoid contradictory interpretations, it must be regretted that a uniform understanding of 'in the course of a business' was not attempted in view of the fact that the two Acts are strictly related to each other.[42] If, as already mentioned, *R & B* were to sell the car bought, they would probably not be acting 'in the course of a business', thus depriving the buyer of the protection afforded by UCTA; on the other hand, they would be acting 'in the course of a business' for the purpose of the Sale of Goods Act and thus there would be in the

[39] E MacDonald, '"In the course of a business": a fresh examination' (1999) *Web Journal of Current Legal Issues* available at http://webjcli.ncl.ac.uk/1999/issue3/macdonald3.html

[40] [1999] 1 All ER 613.

[41] This was confirmed by the Court of Appeal in *Feldarol Foundry plc v Hermes Leasing Ltd* [2004] EWCA civ 747. The court held that the words 'deals as a consumer' in the 1977 Act, which conferred increased protection on consumer purchasers, were consistent with the wider meaning which the court gave to the words 'selling in the course of a business' in the Sale of Goods Act 1979. See a comment by C Twigg-Flesner 'Companies Dealing as Consumers: a Missed Opportunity' (2005) LQR 41, 42.

[42] For wider comments see J De Lacy, 'Selling in the Course of a Business under the Sale of Goods Act 1979' (1999) MLR 776; A Brown, 'Business and Consumer Contracts' (1988) JBL 386.

sale an implied term as to satisfactory quality. Such term, however, could be freely excluded since section 6, like the whole UCTA, is inapplicable to the transaction due to the fact that the seller is not acting 'in the course of business'.

The level of confusion is now increased by the UTCCR. The definition of consumer in the UTCCR follows that of the Directive, and accordingly the following discrepancies may be identified:[43]

—under UCTA (and its case-law), a company may deal as a consumer if it enters a transaction which is incidental to its business, that is, not made with a degree of regularity, while under UTCCR only a natural person can be a consumer;

—the notion of consumer as someone who does not 'act in the course of a business' (UCTA) is different from the notion of consumer as someone who 'acts outside trade of profession' (UTCCR). It would seem, for example, that a fisherman buying a boat (thus making a contract incidental to his profession) would be regarded as a consumer under UCTA but not under the UTCCR. Following *Stevenson v Rogers*, however, he would be considered as acting in the course of his business if he was selling his boat.

—UCTTR (and the Directive) says nothing about the burden of proof, while UCTA introduces a rebuttable presumption that the customer acts as a consumer.

The interpretation of UTCCR and of UCTA seems to be running on parallel tracks.

The Court of Appeal confirmed its decision in *R & B Customs Brokers* in relation to UCTA in the recent case of *Feldarol Foundry plc v Hermes Leasing Ltd*, thus missing a chance of bringing the interpretation of UCTA in line not only with the Sale of Goods Act 1979, but also with the notion of consumer in European law. On the other hand, in a couple of cases concerning UTCCR English courts appear to be willing to define the 'consumer' exclusively in the light and spirit of the EC law.

In *R (Khatun and others) v Newham London Borough Council*,[44] the Court of Appeal decided that the answer to the question whether tenants were 'consumers' for the purposes of UTCCR was, after examining the Directive 93/13 and its *travaux préparatoires* 'so plainly in the affirmative as to require no further reasoning'.

In *Standard Bank London Ltd v Dimitrios and Styliani Apostolakis*[45] the Queen's Bench Division dealt with the question of whether the defendants, a couple who had made substantial investments in foreign exchange transactions through the plaintiff bank, fell within the notion of consumer in the Brussels Convention as well as in the Unfair Contract Terms Regulations 1994 and 1999.

Even though the purpose of the contract with the bank was not to further produce or sell any goods or services, it could not be denied that Mr and Mrs

[43] Also note the different treatment for those who holds themselves out as consumers, see Law Commission and Scottish Law Commission, *Unfair Terms in Contracts* Law Com Report no 292 Cm 6464 (2005) (hereinafter Law Commission Report no 292, Cm 6464) para 3.25.

[44] [2005] QB 37.

[45] [2000] ILPr 766.

Apostolakis had made the contract for profit. The bank sought to rely on *Benincasa v Dentalkit*[46] where the ECJ stated that, for the purpose of identifying consumers, enquiry should focus on whether contracts were concluded for the purposes of satisfying an individual's own need in terms of private consumption. At first, the Court of Appeal seems to adopt a competence-based approach and states: 'it is certainly not part of a person's trade as a civil engineer or as a lawyer to enter into foreign exchange contracts. The only question is whether Mr. and Mrs. Apostolakis were engaging in the trade of foreign exchange contracts as such. I do not consider that they were'.

However, the English court continues, 'private consumption' cannot be taken as meaning that 'consuming' ought to be literally understood as 'destroying' rather than using or enjoying the relevant product. Accordingly, even though the contract made was aimed at profit-making, the court considers that merely to use the money in a way one hopes would be profitable is not enough to be engaging in trade.

The solution given by the English court is consistent with the framework of European legislation in terms of understanding 'private needs': the recent Financial Services Directive,[47] which is applicable only to consumer contracts, covers all types of financial services, including investment funds and pension and insurance plans: accordingly, it is self-evident that even transactions aimed at profit making can be consumer contracts.

Against this background, the Law Commission in its Report recommends that 'the definition of 'consumer' should refer to a person acting for purposes unrelated to his or her business'.[48] Compared to the formula used in UCTA, this one is closer to the wording of the Directive 93/13 but it is not entirely clear why it does not reproduce it more faithfully.

Italy: the problem of equal treatment

In Italy, where courts and lawyers are still unfamiliar with the idea of a law that applies *ad personam*, the limitation to physical persons has been perceived in terms of possible violation of the principle of equality embedded in Article 3 of the Italian Constitution.

In 1999 a reference was made by an Italian court to the Constitutional Court asking whether the choice to limit the scope of protection against unfair terms to consumers was contrary to the Constitution: their doubts concerned the compatibility of the new rules with, inter alia, Article 3 (principle of equality) of the

[46] C–269/95 [1997] ECR–I 3767.

[47] Dir 2002/65/EC Concerning the Distance Marketing of Consumer Financial Services ([2002] OJ L271/16).

[48] See Law Commission Report no 292, Cm 6464, above n 43, at para 3.21. It must also be noted that the draft Bill does not reproduce s 12(1)(c) UCTA whereby a contract for the sale of hire purchase of goods is not a consumer contract unless the goods are of a type ordinarily supplied for private use or consumption.

Constitution: the fact that they excluded from protection craftsmen and small businesses allegedly gave rise to an unjustifiable different treatment.[49]

The Constitutional Court dismissed the question by stating that the choice to limit protection to consumers also features in other Member States' laws and in EC law, and the simplification and uniformity of the means of protection for the EU citizens brought by the Directive is a good reason for limiting protection to consumers. In addition, the court stated, consumers are more likely to be unable to negotiate than the other categories of economic agents: as a matter of 'statistics' (*id quod plerumque accidit*) traders have, in most cases, enough information to be able to protect themselves.

The reasoning of the court appears to be rather shallow, but it is clear that if the court had opted for a different solution the consequences in terms of the relationship between national and EC law would be dramatic: while, in general, it can be excluded that Community law of secondary level can be subject to the domestic systems of hierarchy of rules and accordingly to the review of constitutionality, the Italian Constitutional Court has made it clear that they intend to retain the possibility of reviewing the constitutionality of an EC measure in the case of a conflict between the latter and the fundamental rights of the person and the fundamental principles of the constitutional order.[50] Rather, the relationship of trust and co-operation developed between the European Court of Justice and national courts would suggest that domestic courts put forward their doubts on the validity of a directive before the European Court in the form of a possible violation of the principle of equal treatment.[51]

The adoption of the Consumer Code, however, has now fully legitimised the entry of the consumer into the Italian legal system: article 1 of the Consumer Code refers, as well as to the EC Treaty in general and to article 153 EC, to the Italian Constitution. The sense of the reference is considered to be quite obscure: the Constitution is meant to operate as tool of interpretation and as a parameter for the validity of all secondary legislation, independently of any reference to it.[52] It is here submitted that the reference is made in order to highlight the new role of the Constitution in respect of consumers: this should no longer be read as a mere tool to assess the constitutionality of laws that restrict private economic activities, but must now be perceived as the cornerstone of a system of rules specifically targeted at re-balancing inequalities between consumers and traders.

The notion of consumer that is now found in article 3(a) of the Consumer Code reflects the one which is commonly found in the consumer contract directives: a

[49] Corte Cost 22 November 2002, no 469 in Corriere Giuridico 7/2003, 653–55. A similar question was referred in 1997 but was rejected on procedural grounds, see Corte Cost 30 June 1999 Foro Italiano 1999, 3118.

[50] Corte Cost 27 December 1973 no 183 Foro Italiano 1974, I, 314 and Corte Cost 8 June 1984 no 170 Foro Italiano 1984, I, 2062 with a useful comment by A Tizzano, 'La Corte Costituzionale e il diritto comunitario: vent'anni dopo . . .'

[51] See below, pp 84–86.

[52] A Gentili, 'Codice del Consumo ed "Esprit de geometrie" ' (2006) *I Contratti* 159, 160.

consumer (or user) is 'a natural person who acts for purposes which are outside the business or professional activity that he may carry out'.

Italian courts (in particular the Corte di Cassazione) have in general followed the case-law of the ECJ and adopted a function-based approach to this definition.[53]

AREAS OF CONFLICT BETWEEN THE DOMESTIC AND THE EUROPEAN DEFINITIONS

Extending protection to businesses

The text of Directive 93/13 itself and the fact that it is formally included in the Community programme of consumer protection make it clear that protection against unfair terms is reserved to consumers only.

The ECJ has confirmed upon a reference by an Italian court that 'the term "consumer", as defined in Article 2(b) of Directive 93/13 must be interpreted as referring solely to natural persons', thus expressly excluding legal persons from any protection.[54]

In *Idealservice*,[55] Mischo AG noted that the system of protection introduced by the Directive is based on the idea that

> the consumer is in a weak position vis-à-vis the seller or supplier, as regards both his bargaining power and his level of knowledge. This leads to the consumer agreeing to terms drawn up in advance by the seller or supplier without being able to influence the content of the terms. The intention to protect a category of persons in a weak position, and only that category of persons, is confirmed in the twelfth recital and article 3 of the Directive, under which only contractual terms which have not been individually negotiated are covered by the Directive . . . Legal persons and companies do not generally find themselves in that weaker position and there is therefore no reason to grant them protection which, as an exception to contractual freedom, must, moreover, be strictly interpreted.

The case-law of the ECJ itself in other areas of law, however, suggests that a presumption that businesses (at least individual businesses) are not comparable to consumers does not hold.

In the recent case of *Courage v Crehan*[56] the ECJ decided that the full effectiveness of article 81 of the Treaty requires that even an individual party to a

[53] Cass 10 August 2004 no 15475 available at http://www.ambientediritto.it/Giurisprudenza/consumatori.htm; Cass 25 July 2001 no 10127 I Contratti, 2002, 338. See also Cass 14 April 2000 no 4843 Corriere Giuridico 2001, 524. It is interesting to note that lower courts have been more inclined to follow a competence-based approach: see, eg, Tribunale Roma 20 October 1999 Foro Italiano, 2000, I, 646, concerning a professional sculptor who sued the courier company for the recovery of damages due to the loss by the company of one of his sculptures. See also Tribunale di Ivrea 5 October 1999 and Tribunale di Terni 13 July 1999 both in Foro Italiano Repertorio 2000, Item *Contratto in genere*.

[54] C–541 and 542/99 *Idealservice Srl and Idealservice MN RE Sas v OMAI Srl* [2001] ECR I–9049.

[55] *Ibid.*

[56] C–453/99 [2001] ECR I–6297. Note in particular the comment by G Monti, 'Competition Law. Anti Competitive Agreements: The Innocent Party's Right to Damages' (2002) ELR 284.

contract that, as part of a network of similar contracts, restricts or distorts competition is entitled to claim damages for loss caused to him by the contract. The possibility to claim damages is not unqualified, but account must be taken of the 'significant responsibility' of the claimant co-contractor for the breach, which will be assessed by taking into account the economic and legal context within which the parties found themselves, their respective bargaining power and the conduct of the parties. This suggests that both the bargaining position of the claimant and its conduct in negotiating the contract will be relevant to the determination of whether the claimant bears significant responsibility for the breach. In considering the relative bargaining position of the parties a national court should consider whether the claimant was in a markedly weaker position than the other, such as seriously to compromise or even eliminate his freedom to negotiate the terms of the contract and his capacity to avoid the loss or reduce its extent, in particular by availing himself in good time of all the legal remedies available to him. The court also dismissed as 'formalistic' the view that being a party to an agreement automatically constitutes a wrong on grounds that one party may be too small to resist the economic pressure imposed on it by the more powerful undertaking.

Although it cannot be denied that the aim of article 81 is to ensure the maintenance of a fully competitive market rather than protecting individual businesses or undertakings, by enabling the latter to recover damages the ECJ admitted that a business party can be the victim of the stronger bargaining power of its counterpart. The same court, however, firmly rejected in *Idealservice* the proposition that a business can be entitled to any form of protection against unfair terms.[57]

One may therefore wonder whether the question referred by the Italian court to the Constitutional Court could not be re-proposed to the ECJ in a more European perspective: has the Community legislator, in deciding to limit the protection offered by Directive 93/13 to natural persons, infringed the principles of equal treatment in cases where other categories of economic agents can be proven to be in the same situation as consumers?

To the extent that protection is limited to consumers who act outside their business or profession, there seems no discrimination against legal persons since these always pursue their institutional, thus *lato sensu* professional purpose. It may be argued, however, that the limitation itself to consumers who act outside their business or profession is discriminatory, and that protection should be extended as against contracts (or, more correctly, terms) which have not been individually negotiated, independently of the *status* of the parties.

If the reasons provided by the Italian Constitutional Court in support of the validity of Directive 93/13 (or, more precisely, of its implementing measure) were not sufficient, another line of defence could be built by taking into account the nature of the Community process of harmonisation of national laws.

[57] Additionally, it is illusory to think that arts 81 and 82 can provide a level of protection for business comparable to the one provided by Dir 93/13, see, eg, C–215–216/96 *Bagnasco and Others v Banca Popolare di Novara soc. coop. arl and Cassa di Risparmio di Genova e Imperia SpA* [1999] ECR I–135.

In EC law, the principle of equality operates within the limits imposed by the context within which harmonisation is being pursued:

> An interesting issue is to what extent the principle of equality imposes limitations on the Community legislature with regard to the choice of harmonisation areas. The application of this principle in this context encounters certain fundamental obstacles. In co-ordinating national laws, partial, step-by-step, harmonisation is the preferred, indeed the only feasible, Community policy. Incremental harmonisation may lead to differences in treatment since certain legal relations may be subject to Community rules whereas other comparable relations remain subject to national laws.[58]

In other words, difficulties surrounding harmonisation may be an objective justification for a difference in treatment.

In *Francovich*,[59] for example, it was argued that Directive 80/978 was in breach of the principle of equal treatment as it made certain rights available only to a certain category of employees and not to others, depending on the employer. The ECJ first recalled the principle that equal treatment requires that similar situations should not be treated differently and that different situations should not be treated identically unless such differentiation is objectively justified;[60] it then emphasised that the Directive had been adopted on the basis of Article 100 (now 95) Treaty and its aim was therefore to promote the approximation of national laws. It argued, however, that in the exercise of the powers conferred on them by Article 100 Treaty, the Community institutions have a discretion in particular with regard to the possibility of proceeding towards harmonisation only in stages, given the specific nature of the field in which co-ordination is sought and the fact that the implementation of harmonising provisions of that kind is generally difficult because it requires the competent Community institutions to draw up, on the basis of divergent, complex national provisions, common rules which conform to the objectives laid down by the Treaty.[61] In the light of such difficulties, a difference in treatment between different categories of employees was justified.

As far as Directive 93/13 is concerned, up to a certain point in the process of drafting of the Directive, some proposals envisaged a wider control and the Legal Affairs Committee of the Parliament suggested that the Directive should not be confined to the protection of consumers.[62] The Commission itself acknowledged that

> standard contract terms play an important part, not only in consumer contracts, but also in those between traders . . . It should be borne in mind that many of the arguments put forward apply equally to other contracts, particularly those between small traders and their suppliers.[63]

[58] T Tridimas, *The General Principles of EC Law* (Oxford, OUP, 2000) 63.

[59] C–479/93 *Francovich v Repubblica Italiana* [1995] ECR I–3843.

[60] C–306/93 *Winzersekt v Land Rheinland-Pfalz* [1994] ECR I–5555, para 30.

[61] Case 37/83 *Rewe-Zentrale v Landwirtschaftskammer Rheinland* [1984] ECR 1229 and Case C–63/89 *Assurances du Credit v Council and Commission* [1991] ECR I–1799.

[62] HOON Report in PE1000.931/fin. This was also the opinion expressed by the European Social Committee in ESC 598/91 OJ (17 June 1991) no 159, 34 ff.

[63] Commission Communication of 14 February 1984, COM (84) 55 final.

The 1990 Memorandum[64] explains that

> given the extreme difficulties which would be involved in obtaining acceptance of common rules applicable to (literally) all contracts, the Commission has decided that for the present its work should be confined to consumer contracts.[65]

This is confirmed by Recital 12 of the Directive explicitly stating that 'where they now stand, national laws allow only partial harmonisation to be envisaged': in the light of such difficulties, limiting the scope of protection to consumers appears to be justified.

Several Member States, however, have decided to adopt or maintain measures that extend protection to wider categories of weak parties than the 'consumer', as defined in EC law. It has already been mentioned that the German BGB applies, in principle, to all contracts made on standard terms; and that French law, in spite of the recent restrictive decisions of the Cour de Cassation, traditionally adopts a broader definition of 'consumer'. The Italian legislator has also partially enlarged protection in favour of retailers: pursuant to article 36 paragraph 4 of the Consumer Code the retailer has the right to claim compensation from the supplier for the damages he may have suffered where terms in the retailer's contract have been declared unfair (the unspoken assumption of this badly formulated rule being, of course, that the retailer applies the standard terms imposed to him by the supplier -as in franchising contracts).[66]

The most interesting example of extended protection is the Bill drafted by the Law Commission in the UK. The Law Commission has indicated that, although they are willing to follow the European approach to the notion of consumer in their reform,[67] they intend to extend protection, at least partially, to businesses. This is done for two reasons: first, a large number of provision of UCTA were applicable to all contracts, and the Law Commission has explicitly set as one of its target that of maintaining the level of protection already afforded by existing legislation. The second reason, logically related to the first one, is that in several cases decided under UCTA exemption clauses in business-to-business contracts on standard terms were found to be unreasonable.

In its Consultation Paper the Law Commission had originally proposed that the protection against unfair terms should be extended to business-to-business contracts along the lines of the protection afforded to consumer contracts by the UTCCR. The proposal proved to be controversial as a substantial majority of consultees argued that any expansion in the ability of businesses to challenge the terms as unfair would have undesirable consequences in terms of legal certainty.[68] In relation to business-to-business contracts the Law Commission therefore decided

[64] Explanatory Memorandum to the 1990 Proposal, COM (90) 322 final, 12.

[65] *Ibid*, 12.

[66] A Di Marzio, 'Clausole vessatorie nel contratto tra professionista e consumatore' (1996) *Giustizia Civile* 518.

[67] Law Commission Consultation Paper no 166, above n 17 at para 5.12.

[68] *Ibid* para 4.10.

to limit its intervention to broadly replicating the existing controls imposed by UCTA,[69] and accordingly:

—clauses which purport to exempt business from liability for death or personal injury caused by negligence continue to be of no effect;
—in contracts that involve the transfer of property in goods, terms that exclude or restrict implied undertakings as to title continue to be of no effect;
—business liability for other loss or damage caused by negligence continues to be subject to a judicially administered test.

Following complaints received by the Department of Trade and Industry (DTI), the Law Commission has nevertheless decided to consider extending protection to small enterprises. Many of the complaints appeared to be about exemption clauses which already fell within the controls imposed by UCTA on all business contract (and control therefore needed to be maintained in order not to fall below the existing threshold of protection); some other terms, however, were outside the UCTA controls, such as terms allowing the supplier to terminate the contract forthwith if the small-business commits any default, while the small-business cannot terminate for breach by the supplier without giving the supplier the opportunity to cure the default (para 5.8).

Using arguments that run close to those used by the supporters of a competence-based approach, the Law Commission recognised that when a small business contracts as a customer for goods or services which are outside its field of expertise it is in a position that is very similar to that of a consumer: in particular, many small businesses are unlikely to have a full understanding of the standard terms used by the other party.[70] The Law Commission, however, went even further and argued that, even when contracting in areas which are within its expertise, there is still a risk that a small business will not have understood the terms or (more often) would be met by a blanket refusal to negotiate them: accordingly, the unfairness produced when a small businesses deals on the other party's standard terms should be addressed in the new regime. This consideration led the Law Commission to propose that contracts with small businesses, the terms of which have not been negotiated, should be subject to control in order to avoid 'unfair surprise' terms.

Faced with the question of deciding what a 'small business' is, the Law Commission has decided to limit protection to businesses commonly called

[69] This is subject to two exceptions. First, the UCTA reasonableness test applies to both standard and negotiated terms that attempt to exclude or restrict liability for non-compliance with the implied undertakings of correspondence and quality. The proposed reform intends to limit challenges to standard terms only, recognising the reality that very few negotiated clauses dealing with implied terms will ever be the subject of dispute. In this respect, *ibid* paras 4.25 to 4.29. The same reasoning applies to negotiated terms in hire contracts relating to implied undertakings of a right to transfer possession, *ibid* paras 4.30 to 4.35.

[70] Beale highlights, however, that the issue whether a contract is made regularly would be relevant to whether the clause is fair or not: see H Beale, 'Unfair Terms in Contracts: Proposals for Reform in the UK' (2004) *Journal of Consumer Policy* 309

'micro' businesses, that is, those with nine or fewer employees,[71] as long as they do not form part of a larger group. Small business will no longer be considered as such when they make contracts with a value of more than £500,000 or when they make contracts which are 'part of a series, scheme or arrangement'[72] the value of which exceeds £500,000.

The fragmentation in the scope of protection that results from different national choices begs the question of the extent to which national legislators (or courts) are free to depart from the criterion used in the Directive. In particular, it may be unclear whether Member States are entitled to adopt a broader notion of consumer, based on 'competence' rather than 'function', and/or to extend protection to legal persons.

Should the subjective scope of protection be uniform throughout the EC?

Prima facie, the solution to the question posed in the previous paragraph seems to lie in the minimum harmonisation formula contained in article 8, 'expressly authorising the Member States to adopt or to maintain more stringent provisions in matters in respect of which it can make provision, in order to secure a higher level of consumer protection'.[73]

This solution is plainly wrong.[74] The minimum harmonisation formula allows states to adopt or maintain 'more stringent provisions' for the protection of consumers only within areas *already* covered by the Directive: but the extent to which Member States are allowed to subject contracts *other than consumer contracts* (within the meaning of 'consumer' established by the ECJ) to control mechanisms cannot be determined by reference to the minimum harmonisation formula.

Once affirmed that expanding the notion of consumer does not fall under the minimum harmonisation formula, it remains to be established to what extent Member States' action can depart from Community action; viz, whether the enactment of Directive 93/13 pre-empts national legislation in the field. The extent to which the exercise of Community powers via the adoption of acts of

[71] Law Commission Report no 292, Cm 6464, above n 43, at paras 5.34– 5.40. There is here a discrepancy between the Report and the more recent Commission definition of micro, small and medium enterprises (Commission Recommendation of 6 May 2003 OJ L124/36). The Recommendation defines as 'small business' enterprises which employ fewer than 50 persons and whose annual turnover and/or balance sheet does not exceed 10 million Euros; 'microenterprises' are those which employ fewer than 10 persons and whose annual turnover and/or balance sheet does not exceed 2 million Euros.

[72] Law Commission Report no 292, Cm 6464, above n 43, explanatory note to clause 29.

[73] N Reich, 'The Implementation of Directive 93/13EC on Unfair Terms in Consumer Contracts in Germany' (1997) *European Review of Private Law* 165, 169.

[74] See *Di Pinto* above n 14 paras 21–22:

> It should be recalled in this regard that Article 8 of the directive provides that it 'shall not prevent Member States from adopting or maintaining more favourable provisions to protect consumers in the field which it covers'. The object of that provision is to determine the freedom left to Member States in the area covered by the directive, namely that of consumer protection. It cannot therefore be interpreted as precluding States from adopting measures in an area with which it is not concerned, such as that of the protection of traders.

secondary law can determine the removal of Member States' regulatory jurisdiction is to be assessed by reference to whether Community regulation in the field is comprehensive and exhaustive:[75] the question is therefore to decide what the relevant 'field' is.[76]

In the recent case of *Skov v Bilka*[77], for example, the ECJ has held that Directive 85/374 on liability for defective products must be interpreted as precluding a national rule under which the supplier is answerable, beyond the cases listed exhaustively in article 3(3) of the Directive, for the no-fault liability which the Directive established and imposed on the producer. This is because any extension to suppliers of the liability established by the Directive falls within the competence of the Community legislature:[78] in other words, this field had already been occupied by Community action.

Determining the 'field' occupied by the Directive is not easy due to its ambiguous nature: being the result of an uneasy compromise between different (and somehow incompatible) systems of protection against unfair terms already in place in several Member States,[79] the Directive does not follow a clear rationale.

As discussed in Chapter 3,[80] that there are two possible theories that justify intervention against unfair terms, the 'transaction costs' theory, aiming to protect customers against the use of standard form contracts, and the 'abuse of power' theory, based on the idea of protecting consumers. The Directive follows neither of the two approaches clearly. The 1990 Explanatory Memorandum[81] in recognising the existence of some terms in contracts that are unfair because they unreasonably impose a certain obligation on the consumer, points out that those terms are often contained in the seller's or supplier's standard terms of contract. Accordingly, the Memorandum seems to consider that standard term contracts are nothing but the most common case where consumers, due to their *per definitionem* weak position, are unable to assert their interests and make sure that they are reflected in the terms of the contract. This, together with the fact that the 1990 and 1992 Draft Directives do not explicitly specify that the terms subject to the

[75] Case 222/82 *Apple and Pear Development Council* [1983] ECR 4121; Case 159/73 *Hannoversche Zucker* [1974] ECR 129. See also A Goucha Soares, 'Pre-emption, Conflict of Powers and Subsidiarity' (1998) ELR 132; ED Cross, 'Pre-emption of Member State Law in the European Economic Community: A Framework for Analysis' (1992) 29 CML Rev 447.

[76] So, eg, in case 16/83 *Criminal proceedings against Prantl* [1985] 2 CMLR 238 the Court held that the common organisation of the market in wine forms a complete system and thus excludes independent national legislation on matters covered by it. This did not, however, cover the shape of wine bottles, which remained within the competence of the Member States; in C–169/89 *Criminal Proceedings against Gourmetterie Van de Bourg* [1990] ECR I–2143 the Court held that Dir 79/409 had regulated exhaustively the Member States' powers with regard to the conservation of wild birds.

[77] C–402/03 judgment of 10 January 2006, nyr available at www.curia.eu.int. See also C–52/00 *Commission v France* [2002] ECR I–3827; C–154/00 *Commission v Greece* [2002] ECR I–3879.

[78] *Skov v Bilka ibid* para 44.

[79] see M Tenreiro and J Karsten, 'Unfair Terms in Consumer Contracts: Uncertainties, Contradictions and Novelties of a Directive' in *Rechsangleichung und nationale Privatrechte,* (Baden Baden, Nomos, 1999) 279.

[80] See p 34.

[81] Explanatory Memorandum to the 1990 Proposal, COM (90) 322 final, 2.

control are to be standard terms, thus limiting their application to consumer contracts only, perhaps brings the Directive closer to the 'abuse of power' theory,[82] but uncertainty between the two options is heavily reflected in the Directive which ends up limiting its application to both consumer contracts *and* standard term contracts,[83] thus 'firing two shots at the same target: . . . if we, for example, understand the philosophy of the Directive primarily to offer protection to the party who has been deprived of his/her right to influence the contract, and therefore focus only on non-negotiated terms, then we would not need to have the scope strictly limited to consumers. And, on the other hand, if the *ratio* is to protect the *per definitionem* weaker consumer, then the lack of protection against individual terms seems illogical'.[84]

In any case, it appears that the field occupied by the Directive results from the combination of the 'consumer contracts' criterion and the 'standard form contracts' (or, more precisely, contracts on terms which have not been individually negotiated) criterion: in terms of Member States' competence, this allows wide room to introduce or retain different provisions in all areas which do not fall within the Community competence as above determined.

An alternative doctrine suggests that domestic action should be precluded to the extent that it may constitute an obstacle to the achievement of the objectives affirmed via adoption of Community rules: this happens when the application of national measures would create a situation that would prevent the full achievement of the objectives stipulated by the Community measure. It does not seem, however, that expanding the scope of the Directive can be detrimental to the achievement of its objectives: in the best case, it would help reduce differences among domestic laws -thus reinforcing the internal market—and indirectly benefit consumers.[85]

[82] As confirmed by K Weil and S Puis 'Le droit allemand des conditions générales revu et corrigé per la directive communautaire relative aux clauses abusives' (1994) *Revue Internationale de Droit Comparé* 139–40.

[83] More exactly, the scope is limited to terms or aspects of terms which have not been individually negotiated. In practice, those are commonly standard form contracts.

[84] T Wilhelmsson, Final Report of Workshop 1 in *The Unfair Terms Directive: Five Years On* Acts of the Brussels Conference, 1–3 July 1999 (Luxembourg, Office for Official Publications of the European Communities, 2000) 99.

[85] It has actually been argued (V Roppo, 'La nuova disciplina delle clausole abusive nei contratti tra imprese e consumatori' (1994) I *Rivista di Diritto Civile* 282–83; see also E Hondius, 'The Reception of the Directive on Unfair Terms in Consumer Contracts by Member States' (1995) *European Review of Private Law* 243) that limiting the scope of the Directive to consumer contracts may be detrimental to consumers: if the retailer is not protected in his relationship with the manufacturer or the distributor, he will have to bear the burden of unfair terms imposed on him, which he will not be able to impose on the consumer. For example, a guarantee provision in the sale of a car may fail the fairness control at the retail level and therefore give rise to claims on the part of the consumer against the dealer; the latter, however, will have no possibility of recourse against the manufacturer or other intermediate suppliers because there will be no corresponding control at those higher levels, unless his contract with them expressly provides for a possibility of recourse. With regard to consumer guarantees, this is now partially remedied by Dir 1999/44 on Certain Aspects of the Sale of Consumer Goods and Associated Guarantees ([1999] OJ L171/12) which specifically avoids this type of problem by giving to the final seller remedies against the person or persons liable in the contractual chain (art 4).

It therefore appears that states that wish to take a broader approach to unfair terms control are free to do so; so, for example, a domestic court would be able to adopt a broader understanding of 'consumer' than the one adopted by the ECJ.

The practical significance of this lies in the fact that the more recent moves from the European Commission show some hostility towards the partial harmonisation ensured by means of minimum harmonisation: the most recent measures of consumer protection, such as Directive 2005/29 on Unfair Commercial Practices or Directive 2002/65 on the Distance Marketing of Financial Services, aim to achieve 'total harmonisation' (ie. they do not contain a minimum harmonisation formula) and the 2003 Commission Communication on 'A More Coherent European Contract Law'[86] explicitly states that 'the principle of minimum harmonisation in consumer protection legislation was criticised as not achieving the uniformity of solutions for similar situations that the internal market would require'. It is not unlikely that, should the Commission review the consumer *acquis* (including Directive 93/13) in the future, the minimum harmonisation formula will be removed.

Should this happen, the choice of the Law Commission and of other Member States to extend protection to businesses is, according to the above reasoning, a perfectly valid one: even in the absence of a minimum harmonisation formula, the states' competence to adopt or maintain legislation that protects business as well as consumers would not be pre-empted by Community action, as the latter would be covering a limited field that only includes consumer contracts (as defined in the EC legislation *and* case-law), the terms of which have not been individually negotiated.[87]

Against this background, it must be noted that Directive 2005/65 on the distance marketing of financial services presents an oddity. Recital (29) states that 'This Directive is without prejudice to extension by Member States, in accordance with Community law, of the protection provided by the Directive to non-profit organisations and persons making use of financial services in order to become entrepreneurs'. The oddity is in the fact that the field covered by the directive is, once more, that of 'consumer contracts': outside this sphere, Member States remain free to enact or maintain any other measures: there is therefore no need to overtly provide for such a possibility, unless one reads Recital 29 *a contrario* as meaning that the field covered by the directive is that of *all* contracts for the distance marketing of financial services, and not just that of consumer contracts.

THE BUSINESS PARTY

As highlighted in the Commission Communication on a More Coherent Contract Law, one problematic aspect of the current *acquis* is 'the absence of common

[86] COM (2003) 68 final.

[87] A corollary of this would be, on the other hand, that in the field covered by the Directive no Member State could adopt more stringent measures.

definitions',[88] which may lead to inconsistencies in the application of the Directive to similar cases, and of the introduction by directives of concepts which are alien to the existing national legislation.

Examples of both types of difficulty can be found in the definition of the party with whom the consumer deals. First, there is little coherence in the way that EC directives define this party. This is partly justified by the need to include each time different categories of economic agents, ranging from the producer, to the credit institution to the supplier. Other times, however, it is difficult to find a reason that may justify the different terms used in each directive: the Doorstep Sales Directive uses the word 'trader' to include 'a natural or legal person who, for the transaction in question, acts in his commercial or professional capacity'; the Distance Sales Directive applies to a 'supplier' (term which is usually associated with the provision of a service), that is, 'any natural or legal person who . . . is acting in his commercial or professional capacity'; and Directive 93/13 uses the words 'seller or supplier' to include 'any natural or legal person who, in contracts covered by this Directive, is acting for purposes relating to his trade, business or profession, whether publicly owned or privately owned'. It is hoped that the planned revision of the contract *acquis* will bring some uniformity in this respect.

In addition to generating confusion, the terminology used is not always the most appropriate: there is, in fact, a lack of conformity between the different language versions in the description of the business used in article 1 of Directive 93/13.

The French version uses the word *un professionel* and the German the word *Gewerbetreibende*, but the English version speaks about 'seller' or 'supplier': however, it is clear that the scope of the Directive should not be limited to the provision of goods or services: the definition of seller or supplier in the Directive does not make any reference to selling goods or supplying services. Accordingly, a seller or supplier will be the person who, as opposed to the consumer, is acting for purposes related to his trade, business or profession even if, for example, he is buying goods instead of selling (eg a garage that buys a car from an individual with a view to reselling it): in this case, words have to be interpreted on their own merits even though their prima facie understanding may be different.[89]

This terminological problem did not arise under UCTA, as section 1(3)(a) defined any 'business liability' in contract or tort as 'liability arising from things done or to be done by a person in the course of a business'.[90]

On the other hand, as previously discussed, there was some ambiguity on the exact contours of 'in the course of a business': *R & B Customs Brokers*[91] seemed to

[88] 'Communication from the Commission to the European Parliament and Council. A More Coherent European Contract Law. An Action Plan' COM (2003) 68 final, 8

[89] C–283/81 *Srl CILFIT and Lanificio di Gavardo v Ministero Italiano della Sanita*, [1982] ECR 3415. For a broad meaning of 'seller or supplier' see the English case *Kathun & Others v Newham LBC* [2004] EWCA Civ 55.

[90] 'Business' is further defined as including 'a profession and the activities of any government department or local or public authority', UCTA s 14.

[91] Above n 27

suggest that activities merely incidental to the business and not carried out regularly may be not be carried out 'in the course of a business': on the other hand, this interpretation was given in relation to the definition of 'consumer' and with the declared intent of widening the scope of protection of UCTA as much as possible. Accordingly, 'in the course of a business' may be subject to a different reading (along the lines of *Stevenson and Rogers*)[92] when relating to the definition of the other party.

The incoherence of the English version of the Directive is replicated in other languages: the French and Italian versions of the Doorstep Sales Directive use respectively the word *commerçant* and *commerciante* (terms which in both languages are commonly understood as excluding liberal professions);[93] and the word *fournisseur* and *fornitore* for the distance sales directive.

The underlying problem is that EC law sometimes introduces alien concepts in domestic legal systems. Italian private law, for example, lacks a general category of economic agents that could include anyone who deals in the course of a business. The Italian version of the Directive therefore borrows the French terminology of the *loi Scrivener* (*un professionel*) and uses the word *professionista.* This formulation in then kept in article 3 of the Consumer Code[94] although it is 'inconsistent with the terminology of the Italian legal system'.[95]

The reasons for such inconsistency are easy to explain. Although the word *professionale* can be used to designate any type of activity which is run in an organised, non-occasional way,[96] several articles of the civil code, by using the word *professionista,* only refer to intellectual activities: accordingly, a trader would not commonly be understood as being a *professionista.* In this respect, the notion of *professionista* (meaning someone who acts within his business) is a concept which is totally alien to Italian law.

[92] Above n 40.

[93] ie 'occupations requiring special training in the liberal arts or sciences' Report on Competition in Professional Services Communication from the Commission COM (2004) 83 final.

[94] According to this provision, *a professionista* is a natural or legal person who acts outside his business or professional activity (*attivita' imprenditoriale or professionale*), or his intermediary'.

[95] Commissione Giustizia della Camera in Atti Parlamentari CdD XII leg 1882–A, 91.

[96] See art 2060 cc.

6

Application to Public Services

ACCORDING TO ARTICLE 2(c), Directive 93/13 (the Directive) applies between a consumer and a seller or supplier, defined as 'any natural or legal person who, in contracts covered by this Directive, is acting for purposes relating to his trade, business or profession, whether publicly owned or privately owned'. Recital 14 further specifies that the Directive also applies to 'trades, business or professions of a public nature', thus making it clear that the Directive is meant to be applied to public services.

By referring to the 'public nature' of the seller or supplier the Directive uses the broadest possible formula and avoids the terminological ambiguities and the semantic confusion that would arise, had terms such as 'public services'[1] or 'services of general interest (SGIs)' been used.

A report compiled in 1997 for the Commission by a French/English 'task force' on public services has revealed that a good number of terms and conditions under which public services are provided (whether or not within a contractual framework) may be unfair under the Directive.[2]

Accordingly, the Directive could have a significant impact on the protection of consumers, if it was not for two limitations: first, the Directive only applies to relationships of a contractual nature; second, according to article 1(2) of the Directive 'contractual terms which reflect mandatory statutory or regulatory provisions and

[1] According to the European Commission, 'public service' is a rather imprecise term that can have different meanings and can therefore lead to confusion. The term sometimes refers to the fact that a service is offered to the general public, it sometimes highlights that a service has been assigned a specific role in the public interest, and it sometimes refers to the ownership or status of the entity providing the service. On the other hand, 'services of general economic interest' refers to services of an economic nature which the Member States or the Community subject to specific public service obligations by virtue of a general interest criterion. The concept of services of general economic interest thus covers in particular certain services provided by the big network industries such as transport, postal services, energy and communications However, the term also extends to any other economic activity subject to public service obligations. Finally, the term 'services of general interest', being broader than the previous one, covers both market and non-market services which the public authorities class as being of general interest and subject to specific public service obligations See 'Communication from the Commission to the European Parliament, the Council, the European Economic and Social Committee and the Committee of the Regions: White Paper on Services of General Interest' COM (2004) 374 final, 9.

[2] Institut National de la Consommation and National Consumer Council, Application de la Directive 93/13 aux prestations de service publique. Rapport final, 1997 (hereinafter INN/NCC report), available only in French at http://www.europa.eu.int/comm/consumers/policy/developments/unfa_cont_term/uct02_fr.html. See in particular Pt III, 124 ff.

the provisions or principles of international conventions' are not subject to control under the Directive.

The scope and implications of such limitations are unclear. First, there is uncertainty as to what constitutes a 'contractual' provision of a service, given that there is, at present, no common understanding at European level as to what a 'contract' is;[3] it is, however, a common view that the provision of a public service should not be excluded from the Directive by reasons of the simple fact that in a certain Member State the relation with the client is governed by regulations and not by a contract. This is supported by the Annex to the *procès verbal* to the Directive regarding article 2: 'The Commission states that the concept "contract" as referred to in article 2 also covers transactions by which supplies or services are provided in a regulatory framework'.[4] No further indications, however, have been given by the Commission, nor have Member States encouraged any discussion on the matter.[5]

Second, the meaning of the formula 'mandatory statutory or regulatory provisions' is ambiguous. It is commonly thought that article 1(2) aims to cover rules which, according to the law, apply between the contracting parties provided that no other arrangements have been established.[6] The main argument for this is based on the fact that Recital 13 states that 'the wording "mandatory statutory or regulatory provisions" in article 1(2) also covers rules which, according to the law, shall apply between the contracting parties provided that no other arrangements have been established'. It is therefore commonly thought that 'mandatory' is specifically meant to include 'default' rules.

The effect of these two limitations is dramatic as they could act as a Trojan horse to (re)introduce a means to shelter public services from the fairness control embedded in the Directive, especially if one takes into account the fact that before the EC measure was adopted national courts were 'reluctant to review the terms under which public services are provided on the grounds that basically these

[3] On the reasons why a Member State's classification as to whether there is a contract should not be conclusive see S Whittaker, 'Unfair Terms, Public Services and the Construction of a European Conception of Contract' (2000) 116 LQR 99–107.

[4] See also point A1(b)(ii) of the UK Government Response of 22 February 2001 to the Commission Review of Directive 93/13 available at http://www.dti.gov.uk/CACP/ca/consultation/uct.htm

[5] Only S Whittaker (above n 3, at 101–7) argues that the ECJ should take an autonomous view of 'contract' for the purposes of the Directive.

[6] There are at least three possible interpretations of this formula. The European Commission argues that to escape scrutiny under the Directive it is not sufficient that a contract term reflects any national legal provisions: these provisions must be required by legislation (ie be 'mandatory') to be included in the contract. It follows that under this narrow interpretation contract terms which are expressly allowed by law or which are authorised or approved by a person acting under statutory authority cannot evade scrutiny under the Directive. This narrow interpretation is clearly more protective of consumers but perhaps unfairly disadvantageous for traders. A second interpretation is that the exemption applies to all terms whose use is required or expressly permitted by law; a third and yet broader interpretation is that all terms which ultimately derive from a provision in statute fall within the exclusion. This would comprise terms drawn up by traders but which require approval by an administrative body acting under statutory authority; terms reflecting rules established by self-regulatory organisations, the authority of which is to be found in a provision of statute.

services are governed not by contract but by regulation. In practice, therefore, whole swathes of the economy are not subject to control in respect of unfair contract terms'.[7]

This chapter investigates the possible interpretations that may be given to the above limitations so as to ensure that the effectiveness of Directive 93/13 and of other relevant Treaty provisions is fully achieved.

THE NATIONAL TRADITIONS

Unfair Terms control and public services before Directive 93/13: comparative remarks

In the UK, relationships concerning water, electricity, post and health services were excluded from any contractual control since they were considered to be of non-contractual nature; they were therefore excluded from all the UCTA provisions that apply to contracts.

As long as other public services are concerned, s 29(1)(a) of UCTA exempts from control terms which are authorised, required or anyway permitted by the law by providing that (1) UCTA does not remove or restrict the effect of, or prevent reliance upon, provisions which are authorised or required by the express terms or necessary implication of any enactment,[8] and provisions which are made with a view to compliance with an international agreement to which the UK is party; (2) the reasonableness test will be taken to be satisfied where the relevant term is incorporated or approved by, or incorporated pursuant to a decision or ruling of, a competent authority acting in the exercise of any statutory jurisdiction or function, provided that that authority is not itself a party to the contract. The only relevant legal application of this principle seems to be *Timeload v British Telecommunications plc*,[9] where the Court of Appeal expressed 'grave doubts' as to whether the Director General of Telecommunications, who had seen and approved a contract used by BT, could be said to have approved the terms in the exercise of any statutory function or jurisdiction: the Director General had, in fact, no statutory jurisdiction or function to approve terms and conditions as such and had given no formal approval. On the other hand, approval of standard terms is

[7] Commission Report on the Implementation of Council Directive 93/13/EC/EEC of 5 April 1993 on Unfair Terms in Consumer Contracts COM (2000) 248 final, 27.

[8] This seems to cover both terms which are compulsory and those which are allowed even though not compulsory. The Law Commission brings the example of a contract for the sale of a used car to a car dealer, where it was stated that time for payment by the dealer was not of the essence: see Sale of Goods Act 1979, s 10: Law Commission and Scottish Law Commission, *Unfair Terms in Contracts. A Joint Consultation Paper* Law Commission Consultation Paper no 166/Scottish Law Commission Discussion Paper no 119 (2002) (hereinafter Law Commission Consultation Paper no 166) 33 fn 81.

[9] (1995) *European Market Law Review* 459. Bingham MR also noted the possibility that some of the terms contained in the licence granted to BT, such as the duty to provide a universal service, could be considered as terms implied in the contracts that BT makes with its the customers (see 466).

given by a competent authority in relation to gas and transport (train) services,[10] thus leaving only conditions relating to bus transport (and telecommunications) fall within the scope of control of UCTA.

In Italy, terms included in contracts for the supply of public services (where those are provided on a contractual basis, such as water, electricity, gas)[11] are often contained in *leggi* (for example in the fields of transport or post services) or in *regolamenti.* The latter form a rather heterogeneous group made up, inter alia, of governmental regulations, ministerial regulations which approve the so-called 'regolamenti di servizio',[12] and *regolamenti* issued by local authorities. Those rules are then reproduced in the contracts which are signed by the customers.

At a theoretical level, the answer to the question whether article 1341 cc was applicable to such contracts was positive in all cases where contract terms had a 'truly contractual nature'.[13] In other words, in contracts containing terms that merely reflected norms that had general application, article 1341 cc would not bite; where, on the other hand, contract terms were determined or simply authorised by provisions of administrative rather than normative nature, such terms would still be subject to article 1341cc. In practice, however, the distinction was difficult to draw and the rule was inconsistently applied: so, for example, in a case concerning the alleged unfair nature of some rules regulating a lottery run by CONI (the Italian National Olympic Committee), the Corte di Cassazione held that participation in the lottery created between the participant and CONI a relationship of contractual nature, in spite of the fact that the rules of the game (ie the standard terms of such contract) had been approved by a ministerial decree;[14] on the other hand, in a case concerning standard terms in an air transport contract with Alitalia, the Tribunale

[10] Gas services are provided on a contractual basis on terms drafted by British Gas. These are then approved by the Secretary of State (as required by Sch 5 of the Gas Act 1995) and the contract therefore falls within the exception under s 29 of UCTA. As to trains, contracts follow the National Conditions of Carriage and are applied by all operators; being approved by the Minister of Transport, the Condition falls outside the scope of UCTA. For bus transport, responsibility for the management of bus services is in the hands of London Transport but the lines are operated by private companies following competitive tenders. The tenders specify service standards but this cannot be considered as an approval by a regulator. There are no uniform conditions of contract and each operator is free to draft its own, although the bus companies are bound to respect the terms of the London Bus Passengers Charter.

[11] Contract for the supply of water, electricity, gas and bus travel are ordinary contracts of private law, drafted by the providers themselves. Postal services are also provided under a contract which is not subject to private law but to the 1973 Postal Code. Telecommunication services are provided on a contractual basis, but the contract form is approved by Minister of Post and Telecommunications. For rail transport, there is a contract but this is not regulated by private law but by conditions of carriage approved by a royal decree in 1934.

[12] The general conditions under which goods or services are supplied, adopted by the managing board of the seller or supplier.

[13] M Nuzzo, 'Contratto e servizi pubblici' in E Cesaro (ed) *Clausole abusive e direttiva comunitaria* (Padova, Cedam, 1994) 147.

[14] Cass Civ 12 July 1991 no 7763 Giurisprudenza Italiana 1992, I, 496.

di Cagliari[15] held that the mere fact that the contract had been approved by an administrative authority made article 1341 cc inapplicable.[16]

In France, the most formidable obstacle to an effective control of unfair terms in public services derived from the doctrine of separation of powers. It is a common practice that terms of contracts for the provision of public services are to be found in the *cahiers des charges*, regulatory measures established by the administrative authority that delegates to the relevant (private or public) body the provision of a certain public service;[17] the provisions contained in the *cahiers* are then directly reproduced in the contracts with the users. The doctrine of separation of powers entails that if in the course of a civil process a term is pleaded unfair the civil judge must declare himself incompetent to adjudicate on the issue:[18] the control of *règlements* is reserved to the administrative judge, who carries out such examination according to the rules of public law.[19] In 1994, however, the Conseil d'Etat held that a clause contained in the *cahier des charges* was invalid as it conferred 'excessive advantage' to one of the parties:[20] it did not clarify, however, whether the source of control was to be found in the *loi Scrivener* or elsewhere. In 2001 the Conseil d'Etat eventually established that 'terms of regulatory origin contained in a contract for the supply of water are subject to the law on unfair terms

[15] Tribunale di Cagliari 9 January 1991 Rivista Giuridirica Sarda 1993, 347.

[16] Rather than the contract terms, the rules themselves, as reproduced in the contracts, have often come under the Corte Constituzionale scrutiny: in a long series of judgments that started in 1988, the Corte Constituzionale declared unconstitutional several rules contained in Decree 29 March 1973 on post, banking and telecommunications services which introduced restrictions and exemptions of liability in all contracts made with the customers of such services (at the time entirely run by the state): while these could be historically explained as privileges awarded at the beginning of the seventeenth century by the king to those who were supplying such services to him and who were then entitled to supply the same services to the people, such justification could no longer stand in the current scenario, where relationships with the customers are to be considered as ordinary contracts subject to private law. The only acceptable exceptions should be justified by 'the objective nature of the service concerning the particular features of that service' (Corte Costituzionale (Corte Cost) 21 January 1999 no 4 in Giustizia Civile 1999, 640). See Corte Cost 17 March 1988 no 303 Foro Italiano 1989, I, 56 which declared unconstitutional some exemptions of liability for the loss or interference with registered letters containing certain items; Corte Cost 20 December 1988 no 1104 Foro Italiano 1989, I, 1 which declared unconstitutional the exclusion of any liability by SIP (at the time the state telecommunications services provider) for interruptions to the telephone service due to their own fault; Corte Cost 30 December1994 no 456 Giustizia Civile 1995, I, 1157 which declared unconstitutional the exemption of liability of SIP for providing wrong information in their phone book; Corte Cost 30 December 1997 no 463 Giustizia Civile 1997, 4050 which declared unconstitutional some exemptions of liability for incorrect performance by the Post of some tasks related to the provision of banking services.

[17] This does not entail that a relationship with the user is not be contractual: see S Whittaker, 'Contractual Control and Contractual Review in England and France' (2005) *European Review of Private Law* 757, 761.

[18] See the (in)famous *arrêt Septfonds* (Tribunal des Conflits 16 June 1923 Recueil Dalloz 1924, 3, 41).

[19] 'The provisions of the *cahier des charges*... have a regulatory nature, so that courts cannot, without contravening the principle of separation of powers, declare that the terms contained in a decree or reflected in a *règlement de service* for water are unfair according to art 35 of loi no 78-23 of 10 January 1978'. (Cour Cass 1ère 31 May 1988 Recueil Dalloz 1988, *sommaires commentés*, 406).

[20] Conseil d'Etat 29 June 1994 *Cainaud*, no 128.313 Lexis.

as it results from article L.132-1 of the *code la consommation*'.[21] The judgment seems to limit the scope of the decision to public services of industrial and commercial nature, thus leaving out the administrative services.[22] In addition, the Conseil d' Etat did not take into account, in carrying out the fairness assessment, the criteria used by civil judges, but built its own notion of 'unfairness', as if to emphasize the autonomy of the administrative system from the civil one.

In Germany, two specific exclusions were contemplated by the (now repealed) AGB-G. § 8 established that standard business conditions that reflect legislative provisions ('Rechtsvorschriften'; these include mandatory and non-mandatory provisions) were not subject to control; § 24(2) equally excluded from its scope public services. It is in these two provisions that the origins of the corresponding exclusions in the Directive are to be found.

Even though public authorities are considered to be as bad as private bodies in unfairly allocating risks towards customers, German civil courts have maintained that the regulations containing contract terms (*Satzungen* or *Rechtsverordnungen*) are still laws, and are therefore subject to a test of legality (*Normenkontrolle*), but not to a test of fairness (*Inhaltskontrolle*):[23] even administrative courts can only test such norms as against principles of public law or the enabling legislation (*Ermachtigungsnorm*), but cannot apply the AGB-G.

The application of Directive 93/13 to public services: the current situation

The exclusion from control of 'terms that reflect mandatory statutory or regulatory provisions' has not been transposed in French law, with the result that all term are potentially subject to the fairness control; in practice, however, the '*Septfond*' problem remains, with obvious consequences in terms of costs and delays for the consumers.

At the other end of the spectrum is the case of Germany, which has kept the exclusion that already existed in the AGB-G in what is now the corresponding (and intricate) provision in the BGB, § 307 (3). In addition, contracts for the supply of electricity, gas, heating or water that reflect regulatory provisions are subject to the general fairness test but the grey and black lists under §§ 308 and 309 do not apply.

Between these two 'extreme' choices stand those of the Italian and the English legislators, which implemented partially or with perceptible hesitation the article 1(2) exclusion.

[21] Conseil d'Etat 11 July 2001 *Société des Eaux du Nord* available at http://www.conseil-etat.fr/ and commented by J Amar, 'De l'application de la règlementation des clauses abusives aux services publiques: à propos de l'arrêt Société des Eaux du Nord rendu par le Conseil d'Etat le 11 Juillet 2001' Recueil Dalloz 2001, *chroniques* 2810.

[22] On the difference between 'administrative public services' and 'commercial or industrial public services' see S Whittaker, 'Unfair Contract Terms, Public Services and the Construction of a European Conception of Contract' (2000) LQR 96, 113.

[23] BHG 28 January 1987, BGHZ 100, 1, 9. See also I Tilmann, 'Die Kontrolle missbräulicher Klauseln bei der Erbringung von Services publics' (2003) *Zeitschrift für Europäisches Privatrecht* 129.

Article 34(3) of the Italian Consumer Code omits any reference to 'mandatory' provisions.[24] The Italian legal tradition, like the French one, relies on a distinction between rules which are *imperative* and *suppletive.* Even thought *imperative* (which is also the term used by the Italian version of the Directive) is the literal translation of 'mandatory', it was considered to be pretty clear from the text of Recitals 13 and 14 to the Directive that 'mandatory' also included default rules (*suppletive*). Accordingly, the Italian legislator did not refer to 'mandatory' provision, since by using the literal translation *imperative* they would exclude default rules; on the other hand, the current formulation makes it clear to any Italian reader that both *imperative* and *suppletive* rules are included.

Nor did the Italian legislator transpose the formula 'regulatory' provisions'[25] within the exclusions, which are then limited to 'provisions of law' (*disposizioni di legge*).[26] The word *legge* has in Italian a broad meaning, comparable to the English word 'law', and a narrower, technical meaning that indicates primary sources of law such as *leggi* (statutes) and legislation of comparable status (*decreti legge* and *decreti legislativi*).[27] It is unclear which of the two meanings is envisaged in article 34(3) of the Consumer Code.

Some of the academic commentators understand *disposizioni di legge* as referring only to primary sources of law, thus implying that terms which reflect secondary sources of law (*regolamenti*) are subject to the test of fairness;[28] according to some others,[29] article 34(3) excludes from the fairness test all forms of law, including secondary sources of law, as long as they have normative character. Secondary sources of law constitute an extremely wide and varied category of norms, with different characteristics, different effect and different nature according to the body that issues them and to the status conferred on them by the law: included are also regulations that have no normative character but that are mere administrative acts or which have the limited aim of approving the conditions under which a public body supplies goods or services to the public. Accordingly, adoption of this view entails a case-by-case investigation as to the nature of the *regolamento* at issue, in order to understand whether it has normative or rather administrative nature.

This unclear implementation has generated some divergence at the level of application: so, for example, one court has held that terms contained in a contract of transport by sea and approved by a specific ministerial order were subject to

[24] Article 34(3) reads: 'Terms which reflect provisions of law are not unfair'.

[25] *Disposizioni regolamentari* in the Italian version of the Directive.

[26] The exclusion under art 1(2) of the Directive is therefore reduced to the following text: 'Terms which reflect statutory provisions or the provisions or principles of international conventions to which all Member States or the EU are part are not unfair.'

[27] For a description of the different sources of law and their position within the hierarchy of norms see G Zagrebelsky, *Manuale di diritto costituzionale, vol I: Il sistema delle fonti del diritto* (Torino, UTET, 1984).

[28] M Sannia, 'Commento all' articolo 1469-bis comma 2' in E Cesaro (ed) *Clausole vessatorie e contratto del consumatore* (Padova, Cedam, 1998) 126–39.

[29] Supported for example by M Nuzzo, 'Contratto e servizi pubblici' above n 13, at 152–54.

control since article 34(3) only excludes terms which reflect *disposizioni di legge* 'while there is no reference, as opposed to the Directive, to terms that reflect *disposizioni regolamentari* (understood as secondary sources of law)';[30] one other court[31] has held that *disposizioni di legge* is a broad term that includes *regolamenti.*[32]

In England, the 1994 Regulation did not transpose the word 'mandatory' due to the concern that this would imply that default rules would not be covered by the exclusion. Once clarified that this was not what was meant under the Directive, the Government re-introduced the word 'mandatory' in 1999 via Regulation 1(2), but in its response to the Commission's recent consultation, the UK Government expressed the view that the scope of the exclusion is not clear.

The view of the Government[33] is that the exclusion should be kept but redrafted in order to make it clear that it applies to all terms which (1) are required, expressly permitted by law or applicable where there is no express clause on the subject, but only to the extent that they do not go beyond what is required/permitted, and in this sense they 'reflect' such provisions; (2) are approved in advance by an independent regulator who has a duty to protect the interests of the consumers. It remains to be established what criteria need to be taken into consideration to decide whether a regulator is required to approve such terms or not.

The Department of Trade and Industry (DTI) takes the view[34] that Regulation 1(2) should be given a wide interpretation to encompass practices permitted by specific industry regulators, whose knowledge and experience of the industries concerned should put them in the best position to consider the fairness of particular terms in the round.

While the interpretation proposed both by the DTI and the Government would reproduce quite faithfully the exclusions provided for by UCTA, the Law Commission takes a narrower approach to the scope of the exclusion. Terms that are not substantially different from a 'default rule' of common law or a statute should continue to be exempt;[35] and so are terms which are required, but not merely approved, by a regulator.[36] The reason for the latter distinction is not clear: if terms which a regulatory agency has required to be inserted in a consumer

[30] Tribunale di Palermo 3 February 1999 Foro Italiano 1999, I, 2085. See also Tribunale di Torino 12 April 2000 Giurisprudenza Italiana 2001, I, 505.

[31] Tribunale di Roma 2 August 1997 in Foro Italiano 1997, I, 3010.

[32] In the specific case, the court held that the *regolamenti* concerning conditions to participate in a lottery, even though issued through ministerial decrees of the Ministry of Finance, could not enjoy a different status from any other common contract terms because the lottery was being run and controlled by the Minstry itself, the court introduced the requirement that a *regolamento* is issued by a body which is different from the one that applies it in its contracts if it is to fall within the article 34(3) exclusion.

[33] See the UK Response to the European Commission Review of Directive 93/13/EEC on Unfair Terms in Consumer Contracts', DTI, 21 February 2001.

[34] DTI, *The Unfair Terms in Consumer Contracts Regulation 1994: Guidance Notes* (London, DTI, 1995).

[35] But only in so far as they are in plain language: Report, 3.69.

[36] Law Commission and Scottish Law Commission, *Unfair Terms in Contracts* Law Com Report no 292 Cm 6464 (2005) para 3.67.

contract are exempt on the ground that they 'reflect' the statutory provision empowering the terms to be set, then terms which have been merely approved by a regulator should also be exempted on the ground that they reflect the statutory provision requiring that the terms are approved. In addition, there is no specific discussion on how terms that reflect 'secondary' (ie delegated) legislation' would in general be treated.[37]

A 'EUROPEAN' APPROACH TO PUBLIC SERVICES IN DIRECTIVE 93/13

The inadequacy of the current scenario to take into due account the process of liberalisation and privatisation of public services

The scenario resulting from the brief overview given above is rather chaotic: not only does the obscurity of article 1(2) allow wide differences between Member States in interpreting the 'mandatory statutory or regulatory' exception (and consequently in determining the extent to which public services escape control), but the scope of the exception is sometimes unclear *within* an individual state. The ambiguous exclusion under article 1(2), in combination with the requirement that public services are provided within a 'contractual framework', may easily act as a means to frustrate the good intentions of the Directive to introduce some control on the fairness of terms relating to the provisions of public services.

It is here submitted that, in the light of the twofold aim pursued by the Directive (ie facilitating the establishment of the internal market and ensuring effective consumer protection) and of the recent changes in the way that public services are managed and provided, the definition of the scope of application of the Directive to public services should not be left to the Member States but should be guided by common, EC-based criteria[38] and be narrowly determined.

As a consequence of the establishment of the internal market,[39] the process of liberalisation and privatisation of public services (usually referred to, in this context, as 'services of general interest, 'SGIs') has gained momentum in the last decades and the provision of public services has increasingly been organised in co-operation with the private sector or entrusted to private or public undertakings, while the definition of public service obligations and missions has remained a task

[37] See Law Commission Consultation Paper no 166, above n 8, at para 3.40.

[38] S Whittaker ('Unfair Contract Terms' above n 22, at 102–3) argues that the ECJ should, for this purpose, contribute to the creation of a 'European' notion of contract and brings, as an example of how ECJ can contribute to the accomplishment of such a task, the ECJ decision interpreting the notion of 'contract' under art5(1) of the Brussels Convention (now Reg 44/2001 [2001] OJ L12/1), such as cases 34/82 *Martin Peeters Bauunternehmung GmbH v Zuid Nederlandse Aannemers Vereniging* [1983] ECR 987; case 9/87 *Arcado SPRL v Haviland SA* [1988] ECR 1539; C–26/91 *Jakob Handte v Traitements Mechano-chimiques des Surfaces SA* [1992] ECR I–3967.

[39] K Van Miert, 'Liberalization of the Economy of the European Union: The Game is Not (Yet) Over' in D Geradin (ed) *The Liberalization of State Monopolies in the European Union and Beyond* (The Hague, Kluwer, 2002) 1.

for the public authorities;[40] following this process, the provision of public service takes now place, in many cases, on a competitive basis and according to the free-market rules.

As a matter of internal market, it would be quite pointless to enable a Member State

> to be in the position to protect the provision of a particular type of service (whether or not its provider is publicly owned) from the requirements of the Directive simply according to whether or not it chose to classify the relationship under which they are provided as 'contractual' . . . For this would allow a Member State to distort competition and in particular to protect its own offshoots in a discriminatory manner from competition from other suppliers who might wish to supply services in that State, for a considerable number of public services are provided in areas where private persons offer (or would wish to offer) similar services, which may indeed be competing with them (for example, in relation to delivery of parcels by post or the provision of higher education).[41]

As a matter of consumer protection, it must be noted that European action in the area of public services has, until Amsterdam, mainly focused on competition and access to the market, without taking into much account the position of the individual users. Just as with the early stages of the internal market, consumers/users were supposed to indirectly benefit from the fact that public services would be rendered by private companies within the framework of the market dynamics. In practice, privatisation and liberalisation have often resulted in an increase in prices, which, in combination with a substantial decrease in quality in some key sectors like local public transport and railways,[42] has shown the limits of an approach to SGIs which is based mainly on articles 82, 86 and article 49 EC.[43]

This has required some reconsideration of the original focus and has ultimately resulted, inter alia, in the introduction of article 16 in the EU Treaty, as well as article 36 in the Charter of Fundamental Rights (and of Article III–122 in the European Constitutional Treaty), with the clear intention of requiring, on behalf of both the EU and the Member States, some form of commitment to protect the interest of consumers/users.[44]

[40] 'Communication from the Commission to the European Parliament, the Council, the European Economic and Social Committee and the Committee of the Regions: White Paper on Services of General Interest' above n 1, at 5.

[41] S Whittaker 'Unfair Contract Terms' above n 22 at 104.

[42] According to the most recent survey (*Eurobarometer* No 219—Consumers' Opinions on Service of General Interest, October 2005; see in particular p 14), available at <http://europa.eu.int/comm/consumers/publicationshtm?kk> the overall level of consumer dissatisfaction with rail services between towns/cities and with transport services within towns/cities stands at 28% and 24% respectively.

[43] D Hall, 'Services of General Interest in Europe: An Evidence-based Approach', Written Submission to the European Parliament Committee on Economic and Monetary Affairs, Public Services International Research Unit, February 2001, available at http://www.psiru.org/reportsindex.htm

[44] It is currently unclear what the exact effect and status of art 16 EC are. While it is commonly accepted that the provision cannot give rise to any right for individuals that can be invoked in national courts, some argue that the provision nevertheless obliges Member States and the EU to ensure the achievement of the objectives it sets and that the violation of this commitment can give rise to liability

Against this background, an important role can be played by the occupation by private law of the public law domain.[45] If, in the era of privatisation and deregulation, public services can increasingly be provided in a 'private' law environment, the providers of such services should nevertheless assume the responsibilities involved in operating within such a system, since within a liberalised framework there seems to be no reason why they should in principle not be subject to the same legal requirements as enterprises within other sectors.

In addition, the expectations of citizens are that those services that used to be provided within a public framework law will remain subject to public law principles[46] such as universality, equality, affordability, continuity and high quality:[47] and, once public services are placed out of the reach of public law, such principles can usefully be enforced by means of private law, such as unfair terms control. So, for example, 'access to services' also implies that a contract guaranteeing access cannot be easily terminated, particularly where the termination of a contract exposes the consumer to significant risks, such as health risks (eg. cutting off the heating in winter); quality requirements come into play when service providers seek to exempt liability for not keeping the quality standards that was promised or that is required by law; continuity means that the provider is obliged to ensure that the service is provided without interruption.[48] In this respect, article 4(1) of the Directive offers some flexibility in providing that the unfairness has to be assessed taking inter account, inter alia, the nature of the goods and services for which the contract was concluded and by referring to all circumstances attending the conclusion of the contract.

In conclusion, if public services are to be increasingly delivered through markets that are removed from Member States' regulatory powers, it is then difficult to see that these should nevertheless remain subject to a special regime in relation to contract law: the provision of a public service within a liberalised framework

in damages (M Maresca, 'The Access to the Services of General Interest (SGI's), Fundamental Right of European Law, and the Growing Role of Users' Rights' paper delivered at the 10th Conference of International Consumer Law, Lima, 4–6 May 2005) or that at least it 'represents a critical step in the concretizing of non-market (or post-market) concerns in both the psyche and legal hierarchy of legal development' (M Ross, 'Article 16 EC and Services of General Interest: From Derogation to Obligation?' (2000) ELR 34), and that it reinforces 'a growing recognition that the values associated with public services do have an important role as limits on the scope of competition law values' (T Prosser, *The Limits of Competition Law. Market and Public Services* (Oxford, OUP, 2005) 140); some others suggested that its importance lies in its support for the provision of public services through competitive markets rather than outside them (E Szyszczak, 'Public Service Provision in Competitive Markets' (2001) *Yearbook of European Law* 63–64).

[45] For a recent example of the shift from public to private enforcement at EC level see Commission Green Paper 'Damages Actions for Breach of the EC Antitrust Rules' COM (2005) 672 final.

[46] T Wilhelmsson, 'Services of General Interest and European Private Law' in C Rickett and T Telfer (eds) *International Perspectives on Consumers' Access to Justice* (Cambridge, CUP, 2003) 156.

[47] P Rott, 'A New Social Contract Law for Public Services? Consequences from Regulation of Services of General Economic Interest in the EC' (2005) *European Review of Contract Law* 323, 331.

[48] Many other interesting examples of the interaction between unfair terms and public service obligations are given by P Rott (*ibid*) 332–42.

should trigger the application of all rules that govern such market, including rules relating to contract (and hence rules relating to unfair terms control). Holding otherwise would entail that undertakings entrusted with the provisions of a public service would be able to reap the fruits of operating within a liberalised, competitive market (such as profit-making) without assuming the corresponding responsibilities, to the detriment of both market integration and consumers.[49]

In relation to unfair terms, this means that Member States should be able to rely neither on the fact that the relationship is non-contractual, nor on the 'mandatory statutory or regulatory provisions' exception to shelter undertakings of private or public nature acting within competitive markets from the requirements of the Directive: liberalisation requires that state and non-state actors operate on one level playing field in all respects.

Although the EC is meant to be taking, under article 295 EC, a neutral approach to public services, it is under its pressure and support that the process of deregulation and liberalisation described above has taken place. The ECJ in particular has played a key role in identifying the extent to which state activities should be subject to market rules or should rather retain special privileges.

Accordingly, it is here suggested that the process by which the ECJ has decided whether to place public services out of the reach of competition law or not could provide useful criteria for understanding whether the same services should be subject to contract law rules; in other words, the guidelines used to determine whether state activities should be submitted or not to the free market rules can enhance our ability to draft EC-based criteria that could guide our understanding of whether and to what extent the provision of public services should be subject to unfair terms control, the underlying idea being, as discussed, that an undertaking subject to competition law rules should also be subject to ordinary rules of contract law.

The next few pages will therefore present a review of the criteria employed by the court to identify the scope of competition law in relation to public services; at the same time, they will also present an analysis of the extent to which, and how, these criteria can be 'transplanted' in the field of contract law to determine the scope of unfair terms control. It is submitted that, in order to do so, it will simply be necessary to adopt a novel reading of the limitations to the Directive's scope of application: first, whether the relationship between the provider and the consumer is a contractual one or not should not depend on how each Member State classifies it, but on the extent to which the provision of a certain public service within that state is considered as 'economic', that is, provided within a competitive market. In practice, this means that the ECJ case-law on whether an undertaking providing a certain service is to be subject to competition law would also determine the extent to which such a service is provided within a 'contractual' framework; second, the exact meaning of the term 'mandatory' should be determined with reference to the ECJ case-law establishing derogations to the Treaty provisions in the case where interests higher than market integration are involved.

[49] T Wilhelmsson, 'Services of General Interest and European Private Law' above n 46, at 160.

The application of competition law criteria to determine whether the provision of the service is 'contractual'

In order for an entity to be subject to Community competition law, it must be classified as an 'undertaking'. Although the EC Treaty makes frequent reference to this concept, it does not define it and it has instead been clarified by the case-law according to 'functional' criteria: an entity is an undertaking for the purposes of Community competition law if, irrespective of its legal status and the way in which it is financed, it is engaged in an economic activity.

The core question therefore revolves on what an 'economic activity' is.

First, if private organisations and public bodies carry on the same activity, competition, even of a limited and circumscribed nature, may have a role to play between them. The fact that the two kinds of entity carry on the same activity means that the services provided are similar and that they respond to the same demand on the market. In this case, the ECJ seeks to avoid a situation where public bodies may act in competition with undertakings while at the same time claiming immunity from competition law.[50]

Second, the ECJ has established a clear link between participation in a market and the carrying on of an economic activity. In holding that Italian customs agents are undertakings, the court described their activities as follows:

> they offer, for payment, services consisting in the carrying out of customs formalities, relating in particular to the importation, exportation and transit of goods, as well as other complementary services such as services in monetary, commercial and fiscal areas.[51]

In subsequent judgments, the court directly assimilated participation in a market with the economic nature of the activity carried on. Thus, it stated in *Pavlov and Others* and *Ambulanz Glöckner* that 'any activity consisting in offering goods and services on a given market is an economic activity'.[52] This may well be so even when the state has reserved to itself a statutory monopoly for the carrying on of an activity: still the activity can be carried out under 'market conditions'. The fact that an activity may be exercised by a private undertaking amounts to further evidence that the activity in question may be described as a business activity.[53]

[50] C–41/90 *Höfner and Elser* [1991] ECR I–1979.

[51] C–35/96 *Commission* v *Italy* [1998] ECR I–3851, para 37.

[52] More specifically in C–180/98 *Pavlov and Others v Stichting Pensioenfonds Medische Specialisten* [2000] ECR I–6451 it was held that given the fact that self-employed medical specialists receive remuneration for their medical services and also bear the financial risks of exercising their profession, they must be considered to be undertakings A similar reasoning was followed in C–475/99 *Ambulanz Glöckner* [2001] ECR I–8089 in respect of emergency and standard transport of sick and injured persons: these services are provided for remuneration and therefore do not necessarily have to be provided by public bodies. See also C–35/96 *Commission v Italy* [1998] ECR I–3851, para 36, and T–513/93 *Consiglio Nazionale degli Spedizionieri Doganali v Commission* [2000] ECR II–1807. This approach was summarised in the 2003 Commission Green Paper on Services of General Interest as: 'any activity consisting in offering goods and services on a given market is an economic activity' COM (2003) 20 final, para 44.

[53] C–82/01 *Aéroport de Paris v Commission* [2002] ECR I–9296 para 82.

Accordingly, any undertaking, whatever its nature and funding, that carries out an activity 'consisting in offering goods and services on a given market' carries out an 'economic activity' and should be subject, it is argued, not only to competition law, but also to contract law rules, including unfair terms control; and this will be so even when the state has reserved to itself a statutory monopoly, if the activity can still be carried out under 'market conditions'.

The 'economic activity' test is too vague and broad to be easily applicable; it is therefore easier to establish when it is that an activity is not carried out under 'market conditions'. In the first place, tasks which are matters of vital national interest and the prerogative of the state (such as security, justice, diplomacy or the registry of births, deaths and marriages)[54] are excluded from competition law: this also includes, for example, the maintenance of air navigation safety[55] and the protection of the environment,[56] as well as all activities that are considered to form part of the essential functions of the state[57] or which involve the exercise of official authority (*imperium*) for the purpose of regulating the market and not with a view to participating in it.[58] In this case, it would make sense to maintain that rules of contract law and unfair terms control should also not be applicable.

In other areas, the ECJ has considered whether the activity is organised in such a way that the requirements of solidarity are satisfied in all material respects or whether, on the contrary, the undertaking concerned pursues an objective of capitalisation. Basically, whether conduct is undertaken with the objective of capitalisation or in accordance with solidarity allows it to be determined whether a market exists or not (even if legislation in force prevents genuine competition from arising).

Where it is a question of measuring the degree of solidarity involved in the provision of a service, a guarantee of universal access to users, whether in the field of health, telecommunications or energy, implies solidarity in so far as any differences in actual costs are eliminated in favour of a uniform price. Nevertheless, the constraints imposed by universality of access are not, by themselves, capable of rendering the activity concerned non-economic in nature: 'activities such as postal services or the distribution of electricity have always been considered to be economic activities in Community law, even where their tariffs are largely based on the principle of solidarity'.[59] It remains open to the state to combine market conditions in a certain sector with restrictions, such as an obligation to provide a universal service.[60] A similar principle can also be found in Recital 16 of Directive 93/13, where it states that the different interests involved must be considered when making the fairness assessment, 'in particular in sale or supply activities of a

[54] Commission Communication 'Services of General Interest in Europe' [1996] OJ C 281/3, para 18.

[55] C–364/92 *Eurocontrol* [1994] ECR I–1520.

[56] C–343/95 *Calì & Figli Srl v Servici Ecologici Porto di Genova Spa* [1997] ECR I–1547.

[57] *Ibid*, para 22.

[58] E Szyszczak, 'State Intervention and the Internal Market' in T Tridimas and P Nebbia (eds) *EU Law for the Twenty-first Century* (Oxford, Hart, 2004) vol II pp 225–26.

[59] JL Buendia Sierra, *Exclusive Rights and State Monopolies under EC Law* (Oxford, OUP, 1999) 58.

[60] C–393/92 *Almelo* [1994] ECR I–1477

public nature providing collective services which take account of solidarity among users':[61] this seems to suggest that a degree of solidarity does not necessarily exclude the application of the Directive. On the other hand, a higher level of solidarity is achieved where the service in question is available free of charge, as there is then no connection between the cost of providing the service and the price paid by the user.

The distinction between an economic and a non-economic activity has been particularly problematic in fields such as pension and social insurance schemes;[62] for these cases, the ECJ has developed a more elaborate and concrete[63] set of criteria to assist in the assessment in these areas. In particular, the court has held that schemes where affiliation was compulsory, where there was no link between the level of contributions made and benefits received, where the level of contributions and benefits was fixed by law, and where benefits were paid directly out of current contributions rather than on the basis of income from a capital fund entailed such an element of redistribution in the interest of social solidarity that little remained for the various actuarial, investment and intermediary services which private pensions and insurers can and do supply on the market: they therefore cannot be considered as carrying out an economic activity.[64] Again, there seems to be no good reason why pension and social insurance schemes which are subject to competition law should not equally fall within the scope of application of the Directive as far as the conditions applied to the customers are concerned.

While there is no pre-determined list of what activities are to be considered 'economic', the state is nonetheless under a duty to act consistently: it is free to withdraw certain activities from the market only on the condition that it effectively implements the principle of solidarity and gives effect to redistribution policies.[65]

[61] See Recital 16:

> Whereas the assessment, according to the general criteria chosen, of the unfair character of terms, in particular in sale or supply activities of a public nature providing collective services which take account of solidarity among users.

[62] Jacobs AG in C–264/01 *AOK Bundesverband* [2004] ECR I–2493, para 28.

[63] J Van de Gronden 'Purchasing Care: Economic Activity or Service of General (Economic) Interest?' (2004) ECLR, 87- 88. As a result of this approach health care providers such as doctors, hospitals and the like have to observe competition law but health insurers, who are the natural business partners of these providers, do not seem to have this obligation (see also S Belhaj and J Van de Gronden, 'Some Room for Competition Does Not Make a Sickness Fund an Undertaking. Is EC Competition Law Applicable to the Health Care Sector?' (2004) ECLR 685)

[64] C–160/91 *Poucet and Pistre* [1993] ECR I–637. By contrast, pension schemes which are funded through the administration of a capital fund into which contributions are paid and in which benefits are directly related to contributions are subject to EC competition rules, despite the existence of some elements of solidarity see C–244/94 *FFSA* [1995] ECR I–4013 and C–67/96 *Albany* [1999] ECR I–5751. It is impossible to identify any specific point at which the redistributive component of a pension of insurance will be sufficiently pronounced as to eclipse the economic activities of such undertakings: classification will necessarily be a matter of degree. However, the introduction of an element of competition in order to encourage operation in accordance with the principles of sound management (ie the most effective and least costly manner) does not change the nature of an activity from non-economic to economic, C–264/01 *AOK Bundesverband* above n 62 and a comment by K Lasok, 'When is an Undertaking not an Undertaking?' (2004) ECLR 383.

[65] Poiares Maduro AG in C–205/03 *FENIN*, nyr, para 27.

Some hints that this is the direction that national court are going to take comes from the English case of *Kathun and Others v Newham LBC.*[66] The Court of Appeal had to decide, inter alia, whether a Council whose responsibility was to provide housing to the homeless was a 'seller or supplier' under the UTCCR, and in deciding this point uncertainty arose as to whether the Council was pursuing 'a trade, business or profession'. In coming to the conclusion that it was, the Court of Appeal referred to the decision of the Appeals Tribunal of the Competition Commission in the *Bettercare* case,[67] in which the Tribunal undertook a detailed review of the ECJ case-law of the definition of 'undertaking' in order to decide whether a statutory entity was subject or not to competition law. As the activity which *Bettercare* was carrying out was one which could be carried on by a private undertaking in order to make profits,[68] there was no doubt the it could be considered as a 'trade, business or profession' within the meaning of article 2(c) of Directive 93/13. The ECJ did not even consider whether, under these circumstances, there actually was a contract: this point seems to be adsorbed by the wider issue about the nature of the activity carried out. In truth, the two issues are, from the viewpoint here presented, entirely overlapping since when activity can be classified as 'economic' (within the meaning explained above) it should be subject to Directive 93/13 independently of any other requirements that domestic law may impose to recognise the existence of a contract.

Application of other competition-based criteria to interpret the 'mandatory provisions' exemption

If the 'economic activity' criterion can contribute to the construction of a European notion of 'contract' for the purposes of the Directive, it must be recalled that, even if a relationship is classified as 'contractual', the terms that regulate it may be exempted under the 'mandatory provisions' exemption.

It will be recalled that the formula 'mandatory or statutory provisions' is understood as covering rules which apply to the parties provided that no other arrangements have been made (ie 'default rules'). This reading is based on the assumption that 'mandatory' is a clumsy attempt to specifically include default rules, and the main argument for this is that Recital 13 of the Directive states that 'the wording "mandatory statutory or regulatory provisions" also covers rules "which, according to the law, shall apply between the contracting parties provided that no other arrangements have been established"'.

It is possible, however, that the reference to default rules could be read in the entire formula 'mandatory statutory or regulatory provisions', and that 'mandatory' must therefore be given a different meaning: after all, the exclusion is

[66] [2004] EWCA Civ 55.

[67] [2002] CAT 7.

[68] C–41/90 *Höfner and Elser v Macrotron GmbH* [1991] ECR I–1979.

borrowed from § 8 of the German AGB-G, and there the relevant word *Rechtsvorschriften* (ie 'provisions of law') already included 'default rules' (and could have therefore have be translated in the Directive as 'statutory or regulatory provisions'). This opens the question of what additional meaning, if any, could be given to the word 'mandatory'.

It has been argued that 'mandatory' could be understood within the meaning given in the *Cassis de Dijon*[69] decision on article 28 EC, thus indicating a rule which pursues an aim which is in the general interest of the market and of its users,[70] such as consumer protection, effectiveness of fiscal supervision, or protection of the environment.

Alternatively, it has been argued that 'mandatory' provisions should be held to be the ones which have been adopted to ensure the accomplishment of a task of public service.[71] This suggestion is drawn from the formula used in article 86(2) EC, according to which undertakings entrusted with the operation of services of general economic interest or having the character of revenue-producing monopolies are subject to the competition rules of the Treaty only to the extent that this would not 'obstruct the performance, in law or in fact, of the particular tasks assigned to them'.[72]

The scope of this exemption has been subject to different interpretations over the years: an originally narrow approach held that the notion of 'obstructing performance' should trigger a stringent economic analysis aimed at identifying whether full compliance with the Treaty would make it impossible for the entrusted undertaking to carry out its functions, the underlying central concerns being the risk of detriment to the market and ensuring the priority of market values over non-market values.[73] From the *Corbeau*[74] case, however, the ECJ has taken a looser appraisal of how the undertaking is located in its specific environment and has replaced the notion of 'obstructing performance' with the notion of 'economic equilibrium ' or 'economically acceptable conditions'.

So, for example, the uninterrupted supply of electricity throughout a certain territory to all consumers in sufficient quantities to meet demand at any given time, at uniform tariff rates and on terms which may not vary save in accordance with objective criteria applicable to all customers, is a task of general economic

[69] 120/78 *Rewe-Zentral v Bundesmonopolverwaltung für Branntwein* [1979] ECR 649.

[70] 'Application de la Directive 93/13/EC aux prestations de service public. Rapport final' in *The Unfair Terms Directive, Five Years On* Acts of the Brussels Conference, 1–3 July 1999 (Luxembourg, Office for Official Publications of the European Communities, 2000) 117.

[71] *Ibid* 112.

[72] The operation of art 86(2) depends on whether the activity can classified as one of 'general economic interests'. Both the Court and the Commission have, however, accepted as such a wide range of activities, such as postal services, electricity, telecommunications, employment procurement, sectoral pension scheme: see E Szyszczak, 'Public Service Provision in Competitive Markets' above n 44, at 47 fn 52.

[73] Case 155/73 *Sacchi* [1974] ECR 409; C–18/88 *RTT* [1991] ECR I–5941. See L Moral Soriano, 'How Proportionate Should Anti-Competitive State Intervention Be?' (2003) ELR 121; M Ross, 'Article 16 EC and Services of General Interest: from Derogation to Obligation?' (2000) ELR 24.

[74] C–320/91 [1993] ECR I–2523.

interest within the meaning of article 86(2) EC;[75] the reliable and efficient operation of the national public electricity supply at costs which are as low as possible and in a socially responsible fashion provides services of general economic interest within the meaning of article 86(2) EC:[76] and, accordingly, it is sufficient that the application of competition rules obstruct the performance, in law or in fact, of the special obligations incumbent upon that provider for article 86(2) EC to be triggered. It is not necessary that the survival of the undertaking itself be threatened, but it may be sufficient to 'to take into consideration the economic conditions in which the undertaking operates, in particular the costs which it has to bear, and the legislation . . . to which it is subject'.[77]

> This seems to suggest that the availability of a derogation is to be measured by a balancing exercise based upon competing priorities rather than inhibiting that choice by insisting upon narrow economic tests to be satisfied before normal market rules can be disapplied

and that

> the crucial methodological switch is from economic measurement to value judgment in the application of the derogation. . . . Such approach would be strongly reminiscent of, consistent with, the development of a rule reason elsewhere in the Treaty. As seen most clearly in the free movement cases stretching back to *Cassis de Dijon*, the overt disapplication of normal rules in favour of higher interests recognized by Community law has been a cornerstone in balancing Community and national regulation of markets.[78]

Although the interpretation of the 'mandatory requirements' under *Cassis* and article 86(2) EC may appear likewise based on an idea of 'overriding requirement of general interest', two main differences seems to persist: first, considerations under article 86(2) EC are mainly (and originally solely) economic-based, while those under the mandatory requirements are not, since a 'mandatory requirement' can only be a general interest of a non-economic nature;[79] second, the derogation under article 86(2) EC refers to reasons that are inherent to the provision of a service of general economic interest itself: in other words, what justify the exemption from competition rules are the characteristics themselves of the service to be provided (eg. providing universal access to a reliable and efficient system; providing a service in a socially responsible fashion, ie at affordable prices). On the other hand, the mandatory requirements act as justifications for rules that do not serve a purpose inherent in the provision of the service itself but, so to say, an 'external' purpose.[80]

[75] C–393/92 *Almelo* [1994] ECR I–1477. See also C–157/94 *Commission v The Netherlands* [1997] ECR I–5699 para 40.

[76] Commission Decision 91/50 *Ijsselcentrale and others* [1991] OJ L28, p 32.

[77] C–393/92 *Almelo* above n 75, para 49.

[78] M Ross, 'Article 16 EC and Services of General Interest: from Derogation to Obligation?' above n 73, at 25.

[79] Case C–347/88 *Commission v Greece* [1990] ECR I–4747. Note, however, case C–120/95 *Decker* [1998] ECR I–1831 and C–158/96 *Kohll* [1998] ECR I–1673. See also E Szyszczak, 'Public Service Provision in Competitive Markets' above n 44, at 50.

[80] There is, however a certain degree of overlap between the two types of derogation: compare for example Cosmas AG and the Court in C–157/94 *Commission v Netherlands* above n 75.

In order to understand whether any of the above criteria can be applied to article 1(2) of the Directive, it is necessary to consider how the 'mandatory' exception could in practice operate. The third part of INC/NCC Report on unfair terms in public services identifies a number of unfair terms (mostly of regulatory origin and therefore potentially covered by article 1(2) of the Directive) currently used in the provision of public services in several European countries. In reviewing such terms, the INC/NCC also assess whether such terms can in practice be justified by *exigences impératives.* So, for example, in contracts for the supply of electricity or gas the provider is often entitled, by contract terms that reflect statutory provisions, to cut off supply to customers who do not pay their bill. While a broad power to cut off supplies is unacceptable, the need to maintain affordable prices can justify terms that allow such a possibility (while at the same time setting out in detail the measures that the suppliers must take before this happens). In this case, statutory terms that entitle suppliers to cut off supplies within very limited circumstances can be held to be 'mandatory'. Or, to give another example, terms (of statutory origin) that impose penalties for passengers boarding a train without a ticket may also be justified by the need to keep costs down (and maintain the service at affordable prices), provided such terms differentiate between passengers who do so fraudulently and those who were unable to buy a ticket because, for example, the opportunity to buy tickets is too restricted. Finally, terms that put users in charge of maintaining the security of meters on their premises or make them responsible for damages caused by their acts or omissions may be justified by the need to ensure the safety and uninterrupted operation of the network.

It appears that most of these reasons have to do with the need to guarantee that the public service can be provided in accordance with the criteria that inspire the provision of service itself (including affordability) and for this reason an article 86(2)-based reading of the 'mandatory' exception seems to be more appropriate. Accordingly, a term that reflects a mandatory statutory or regulatory provision escapes the fairness control if it can be demonstrated that this is necessary to ensure that the provision of the public service is not obstructed.[81]

This leaves, however, a last difficulty to overcome. While the above reasoning makes sense in the context of the provision of public services, one has to remember that article 1(2) refers to all 'mandatory statutory or regulatory provisions', including those that have nothing to do with the provision of a public service.[82] The interpretation of the word 'mandatory' suggested above would certainly be inapplicable with reference, for example, to the 'statutory provisions' of the Sale of Goods Act 1979. It could be argued that, in this case, the provisions of the Act are 'mandatory' in the sense that they pursue an aim which is in the general interest of

[81] In this sense see J Huet, in INC, *Hebdo* no 1015 of 12 December 1997 p 40.

[82] S Whittaker, 'Unfair Contract Terms', above n 22, at 118. It must also be noted that the word *bindende* contained in the German version (but not in the implementing measure) can hardly correspond to the interpretation here suggested, as *bindende* means 'binding', rather than 'mandatory'. On the other hand, if *bindenden Rechtsvorschriften* was understood as meaning 'binding legal provision', it would not make any sense to a German lawyer: *Rechtsvorschriften* are always binding.

the market and of its users, thus resorting to the first of our possible interpretations of the word 'mandatory'. In the case of the Sale of Goods Act, as with contract law rules in general, it can be easily argued that such measures pursue an aim in the general interest of the market and its users as they, for example, ensure a fair allocation of the risk between the parties.[83]

This would mean that, in practice, the possibility that terms reflecting mandatory statutory or regulatory provisions are subject to judicial review depends on whether the case at issue relates to public services: if this is so, then the likelihood that the term is subject to courts' scrutiny is greater since in order to escape control one will have to prove that the 'mandatory' provision was adopted to ensure the fulfilment of a public mission.

In the light of the importance of public services for consumers and of the fact that rules relating to the provision of such services tend to be more biased in favour of the provider than ordinary rules of contract, it appears that such a difference in the standard of review could perhaps be acceptable.

[83] In fact, domestic rules of contract law are often used by courts as a yardstick to assess whether a contract term is unfair. Courts do so on the assumption that the closer contract terms come to the default rule, the fairer they are: see, eg, Tribunale di Roma 21 January 2000 in Foro Italiano 2000, I, 2045.

7

Objective Scope of Application

THE OBJECTIVE SCOPE of application of Directive 93/13 (the Directive) is determined by three limitations.

First, the fairness control does not apply to terms which have not been individually negotiated. The notion of 'terms which have not been individually negotiated' is comparable, but broader than, the notion of 'standard form contracts': while the latter are generally drafted for general use, the Directive only requires that a term is not negotiated, that is, that it is imposed on the customer, even if it is used only in one transaction.

Second, terms that relate to the definition of the main subject matter of the contract or the adequacy of the price or remuneration as against the goods or services supplied in exchange are excluded from control, provided they are expressed in plain, intelligible language.

Third, terms that reflect mandatory statutory or regulatory provisions or the provisions of international conventions are not subject to control, as already discussed in Chapter 6. 'Mandatory statutory or regulatory provisions' also covers rules which, according to the law, shall apply between the contracting parties provided that no other arrangements have been established, that is, default rules: the expression 'mandatory' in this context does not reflect the traditional civil law distinction between 'binding' (imperative) and 'opt-out' (or default) provisions and covers both meanings, but it has earlier been argued that to include such provisions there is no need to add 'mandatory' and that this term rather concerns the special nature of such provisions. The rationale for this provision is that statutory or regulatory provisions usually establish solutions which the legislator has considered to be the most equitable ones. The most problematic question raised by this provision concerns the effects it has on the application of the Directive to public services: this issue has been discussed in Chapter 6.

This chapter therefore deals with the first two limitations. The peculiarity of the English system in relation to land has also prompted the idea of carrying out a brief analysis of another possible limitation of Directive 93/13, that is, whether it applies to contract relating to land. This is discussed in the last part of this chapter.

INDIVIDUALLY NEGOTIATED TERMS

National traditions

Both the English and the Italian law are familiar, rather than with the notion of 'non-negotiated term', with that of 'standard form contract', which defines the scope of application of section 3 UCTA and of articles 1341–42 cc.

Section 3 UCTA imposes a test of reasonableness for certain contractual exclusions in contracts with consumers or on the other party's written standard terms of business. Those are intended to be the ones that are used with some regularity,[1] but a number of other grey areas surround the scope of the provision. In general, contracts have been considered to be on standard terms even though they have been altered in part,[2] or even though the recipient of those terms negotiated and agreed certain matters and details: if

> the section is designed to prevent one party to a contract from having his contractual rights, against a party who is in breach of contract, excluded or restricted by a term or condition, which is one of a number of fixed terms or conditions invariably incorporated in contracts of the kind in question by the party in breach, and which have been incorporated in the particular contract in circumstances in which it would be unfair and unreasonable for the other party to have his rights so excluded or restricted—then—the phrase 'standard form contract' cannot be confined to written contracts in which both parties use standard forms. It is . . . wide enough to include any contract, whether wholly written or partly oral, which includes a set of fixed terms or conditions which the proponer applies, without material variation, to contracts of the kind in question.[3]

In *Salvage Association v CAP Financial Services Ltd*[4] Thayne Forbes J, while reminding that in this respect the nature of the contract 'will be a question of fact and degree to be decided in all the circumstances of the particular case', lists a set of facts to be taken into account in coming to a decision and which focus on the actual extent to which terms have been imposed by one party, or rather negotiated and established by common agreement. In this sense, the judicial refusal to embed the notion of 'standard terms contract' in a rigid formula is fully consistent with, and somehow explained by, the argument of the Law Commission that 'courts are well able to recognise standard terms used by persons, in the course of their busi-

[1] See eg *Hadley Design Associates Ltd v Westminster* [2003] EWHC 1617 QBD (TCC), *McCrone v Boots Farm Sales Ltd* [1981] SC 68; see also *British Fermentation Products v Compare Reavell* [1999] 2 All ER Com 389 and the discussion in Law Commission and Scottish Law Commission, *Unfair Terms in Contract: A Joint Consultation Paper* Law Commission Consultation Paper no 166/Scottish Law Commission Disussion Paper no 119 (2002) (hereinafter Law Commission Consultation Paper no 166) para 5.53.

[2] See, eg, *St Albans City and District Council v International Computers Ltd.* [1996] 4 All ER 481 with a comment by E MacDonald, 'The Council, the Computer and the Unfair Contract Terms Act 1977' (1995) MLR 585; *Chester Grosvenor Hotel Ltd v Alfred McAlpine Management Ltd* (1993) BLR 115.

[3] *British Fermentation Products Ltd v Compair Reavell Ltd*, above n 1, at 391. See also *Pegler Ltd v Wang Ltd* [2000] EWHC Technology 127.

[4] [1995] FSR 654.

ness, and that any attempt to lay down a precise definition of 'standard form contract' would leave open the possibility that terms that were clearly contained in a standard form might fall outside the definition. In our view this would be unfortunate. We have not, therefore, attempted to formulate a statutory description of a standard form contract'.[5] This reasoning has been applied, for example, in *Hadley Design Associates Ltd v Westminster*, where the High Court stated

> if the only agreed contract terms are those of 'written standard terms of business' the conclusion that the parties dealt on the 'written standard terms of business' of the relevant party may be obvious. It is unlikely to be enough to avoid that conclusion that, apart from the 'written standard terms of business', some term was specially negotiated for the purposes of the particular contract. However, the role in the context of possibly voluminous documentation of a pre-prepared document setting out 'written standard terms of business' may be so small in relation to the whole, or the modifications to a pre-prepared document setting out 'written standard terms of business' may be so significant, that it may be an abuse of language to describe the resulting contract as a deal on the 'written standard terms of business' of one or other of the parties.[6]

In Italy, the case-law on standard form contract mainly restates the requirement that contracts subject to article 1341 cc are be made up for a indefinite number of transactions, not just for a single one, that is, there must be a 'standardisation' of the terms so that the same text is meant to regulate a plurality of similar contracts; additionally, the contract must be unilaterally drafted.

In one case, for example,[7] the plaintiff received from the defendant a letter stating the terms of a certain contract. The terms had been entirely prepared by the defendant who then invited the plaintiff to sign the contract and send it back to him. It was obvious that no negotiation had taken place as the plaintiff simply adhered to the terms presented to him. He later claimed that one of the terms was *vessatorio* and needed specific approval. The Court declared that article 1341cc did not apply as the document at issue did not fulfil the requirement of 'generality:

> the rationale underlying the rules concerning contracts of adhesion (economic imbalance of the parties) cannot be referred to individual cases. On the contrary, one should look at cases of substantial, even though limited, monopoly (revealed by the fact that the contract has been pre-determined for an indefinite number of transactions); the text itself of article 1341 by referring to '*condizioni generali di contratto*' ... is in favour of such interpretation.

The mere fact that a contract has been formulated in advance by one party, so that the other has no option other than taking it or leaving it without participating in

[5] Law Commission, *The Law Commissions' 1975 Report: Exemption Clauses: Second Report*, Law Com Report no 69, para 157.

[6] *Hadley Design Associates Ltd v Westminster*, above n 1, at para 83.

[7] Tribunale di Messina 17 May 1962 reported in E Cesaro *Le condizioni generali di contratto nella giurisprudenza*, vol II (Padova, Cedam, 1993) 33; see also Corte di Cassazione (Cass) 6 December 1999 no 13605 in Giustizia Civile Massimario 1988, 2451; Cass 14 May 1977, no 1952 in Giustizia Civile Repertorio 1997, item *Obbligazioni e contratti* no 86; see also Cass 21 April 1988 no 3091 in Giustizia Civile Massimario 1998, issue 4.

its formation, is not enough to trigger the application of article 1341cc so far as the form and the terms are not meant to regulate an indefinite number of contracts.

The Directive

According to article 3(1), application of the Directive is limited to terms which have not been individually negotiated.

The fundamental criterion established by the Directive is the impossibility for the consumer to influence the substance of the term: hence, the notion of 'not individually negotiated terms' covers not only standard terms but all terms where there has been no preliminary negotiation:[8] this means that the control of the Directive will be triggered every time a contract (or some of its terms) has been unilaterally drafted by one party, no matter whether it has been drafted ad hoc in relation to a certain transaction or for general use.

This limitation is one of the most criticised points of the Directive, for both its formulation and its substance.[9] In practice, however, the Commission has noted that

> the CLAB database . . . shows that this exclusion has not had any practical effect in the Member States which transposed it, because none of the cases in the database concerns an individually negotiated contractual term. Indeed it is fanciful to think that contracts of adherence could truly contain individually negotiated terms other than those relating to the characteristics of the product (colour, model, etc.), the price or the date of deliv-

[8] T Wilhelmsson, 'Clauses contractuelles abusives' in Acts of the Conference 'Consumer Protection in the European Community, session d'été', Louvain La Neuve, 3–12 July 1996.

[9] The 1990 Proposal for a Directive on Unfair Terms was to be applied to all types of consumer contracts, independently of whether they were on standard or individually negotiated terms. Nevertheless, the first year of discussion in the Council exhibited a major division between the delegations which wanted to see the directive encompass all contracts (this was, eg, the position of the Scandinavian countries and of France, where such limitations are still not included in the implementing measures), and those which considered that only standard contractual terms should be covered because the control of the unfair nature of individually negotiated terms was perceived as contrary to private autonomy and to the proper functioning of market economies (the German delegation was particularly adamant on this point and enjoyed full support by the German legal doctrine, see, eg, H Bradner and P Ulmer, 'The Community Directive on Unfair Terms: Some Critical Remarks on the Proposal Submitted by the EC Commission' (1991) CML Rev 652 ff.). The Parliament discussed the question at length and adopted an amendment that only excluded application to contracts in which all the terms were individually negotiated. The Commission decided in its amended proposal of March 1992 to divide art 2(1) of the original proposal into two articles: art 3(1), relating to contractual terms which had not been individually negotiated, and art 4(1), which was applicable to all types of terms (see the Explanatory Memorandum of the amended proposal, COM (92) 66 final, 2). In practice, the basic difference would be that an extra condition would be required for a negotiated term to be considered as unfair: it would be necessary that the terms had been imposed on the consumer 'as a result of the economic power of the seller or supplier and/or the consumer's economic and/or intellectual weakness'. However, the Commission failed to convince the Council to accept the control of negotiated terms, even in more restricted circumstances, and the article disappeared in the final text (a detail report on the travaux préparatoires of the Directive in this respect can be found in M Tenreiro, 'The Community Directive on Unfair Terms and National Legal Systems' (1995) 3 *European Review of Private Law* 273).

ery of the good or provision of the service–all terms which rarely give rise to problems concerning their potential unfairness.[10]

This provision has its origin in German law. § 1 AGB-G (now § 305 BGB) originally limited the scope of protection to standard business terms (*Allgemeine Geschäftsbedingungen*) that are pre-established for a multitude of contracts which one party to the contract (the user) presents to the other party upon the conclusion of the contract. Contractual terms do not constitute standard business terms where they have been individually negotiated between the parties.

In practice, German law required (it no longer does so)[11] that the general conditions were to be used for a plurality of contracts, although courts have held that the mere intention to use them for a plurality of contracts was sufficient.[12] As to negotiation, courts have been generous in holding that a contract where only some of the terms were negotiated was not entirely removed from control, but the non-negotiated terms were still subject to control.[13]

The concept of non-negotiated term under the Directive is broader than its parent concept of 'standard business contract term' in two respects: first, under the Directive a term which is presented by the business party but which has been drafted by a third would still be a 'standard term': this was a debated question in German law, and § 310 now introduces a presumption that standard business terms have been presented by the business party even when they have been formulated by a third; second, the scope of control under the Directive extends to pre-established conditions of contract even if drafted for use only once. Again, § 310 has made the necessary amendments.

After stating the criterion upon which the exclusion is based, article 3 continues in paragraph (2), but only generates confusion. It provides that a term has not been individually negotiated when it has been drafted in advance, and the consumer has therefore not been able to influence the substance of the term; the following paragraph, however, states that the fact that certain aspects of a term or one specific term have been individually negotiated shall not exclude the application of the Directive if an overall assessment of the contract indicates that it is nevertheless a pre-formulated standard contract. This provision would have made sense in the context of the AGB-G, the scope of which is defined by reference to standard business contracts: in this case, there would be a risk that, if several terms of a standard contract have been, in a particular case, individually negotiated, the contract would lose his character of being a 'standard contract' and would therefore be subject to no control; on the other hand, the scope of the Directive is

[10] Report from the Commission on the Implementation of Council Directive 93/13/EEC of 5 April 1993 on Unfair Contract Terms in Consumer Contract, Brussels, (27 April 2000) COM (2000) 248 final.

[11] In order to implement Dir 93/13 § 310 BGB now specifies that, as far consumer contracts are concerned, the fairness test under §§ 305c (2) and §§ 306, 307–9 applies to pre-established conditions of contract even if they are intended for use only once and in so far as, because they are pre-established, the consumer could not influence their content.

[12] BGH NJW 1991, 843.

[13] BGH ZIP 1986, 698, 699.

defined not by reference to standard contracts, but to consumer contracts, whether they are standard or not. The only limitation is that the Directive will not apply to the 'individually negotiated terms'. The provision in 3(2) second paragraph may give another impression, because it would imply *a contrario* that in some cases the Directive would not be applicable to some non-negotiated terms in consumer contracts. That was obviously not the intention of the legislator and therefore the article must be interpreted taking into account the other provisions and the rationale of the Directive.[14]

Article 3(2) also states that a seller or supplier who claims that a standard term has been individually negotiated has the burden of proving negotiation. This statement is borrowed from German legal doctrine, where it was controversial whether a standard term that had been negotiated but had been left unchanged could really be considered as 'negotiated'. Article 3(2) seems to suggest that the solution to this problem would be that, if the seller or supplier is able to prove negotiation, an (unchanged) standard term could be considered as negotiated. This contradicts article 3(2) itself, where it states that terms drafted in advance shall *always* be regarded as not individually negotiated. The last paragraph of article 3(2) must therefore be understood as referring to standard terms that have been modified (eg in handwriting): even in such a case, the burden of the proof rests on the trader.[15]

One may wonder what type of activity should there be for a term to be individually negotiated. Article 3(2) of the Directive appears to suggest that it is necessary to check whether the consumer has actually had the opportunity to influence the content of the term or not: this does not clarify whether, for example, effective amendments to the original contract are necessary in order to have 'negotiation'.[16] The answer to this question can partly be found, at domestic level, in the courts' case law.

National traditions and implementation

In Italy, the formula adopted by the Consumer Code is less ambiguous than the one used in the Directive: article 34(4) simply states that 'terms or parts of terms

[14] M Tenreiro and J Karsten, 'Unfair Terms in Consumer Contracts: Uncertainties, Contradictions and Novelties of a Directive' in H Schulte-Nölke and R Schulze (ed) *Europäische Rechtsangleichung und nationale Privatrechte* (Baden-Baden, Nomos, 1999) 223, 234.

[15] Tenreiro and Karsten 'Unfair Terms in Consumer Contracts' previous n, at 235.

[16] See, eg, V Roppo 'La nuova disciplina delle clausole abusive nei contratti fra imprese e consumatori' (1994) I *Rivista di Diritto Civile* 281; E Scarano 'Commento sub article 1469-ter, comma 4' in G Alpa and S Patti (eds) *Le clausole vessatorie nei contratti con i consumatori* (Milano, Giuffrè, 1997) 612. Attention has also been devoted in Italy to the question whether contracts negotiated collectively by trade unions can be considered as 'individually negotiated': according to S Troiano ('L'ambito oggettivo di applicazione della Direttiva Cee del 5/4/199; la nozione di "clausola non oggetto di negoziato individuale"' in G Alpa and M Bianca (eds) *Le clausole abusive nei contratti stipulati con i consumatori* (Padova, Cedam, 1996) 647), for example, a collective contract ensures adequate protection of the weak party's interests and is therefore comparable to an individually negotiated contract; contra, F Casola 'Commento sub article 1469-ter' in A Barenghi (ed) *La nuova disciplina delle clausole vessatorie nel codice civile* (Napoli, Jovene, 1996) 111.

which have been individually negotiated are not unfair', thus making it possible to control all clauses which have not been individually negotiated even when the contract appears to have been in general negotiated.

In the UK, Regulation 5(2) contains a definition of a non-negotiated term which is almost identical to the one in the Directive; hence, it does not remedy the ambiguity generated by article 3(2) of the Directive which appeared to exclude control on terms which had not been individually negotiated where the contract had been in general negotiated. As with the Directive, the correct reading of the Regulation seems to be that it applies to any term which has not been individually negotiated, regardless of whether the overall contract could be described as a 'pre-formulated standard contract',[17] the reason supporting this view being that the rationale of the rule—the inability of consumer to influence the terms—can be invoked against all terms which have not been individually negotiated and not only against standard form contracts.

In this respect, the scope of application of the Regulations is broader than UCTA, in that it takes, following the Directive, a 'term-by-term approach'[18] under which each term (whether in a standard form contract or not) is assessed independently.

In *Bryen & Langley Ltd v Martin Boyston*[19] the High Court commented obiter that where a consumer had selected the standard form of contract on which he wished the construction work to be carried out, it was 'at least arguable' that the consumer had been able to influence the substance of a term and that accordingly this term could be regarded as having been 'individually negotiated'. This interpretation cannot be correct, as

> the Regulations talk about having been able 'to influence the substance of a term', and the fact that a consumer has chosen one set of standard terms over another set does not mean that the consumer has had any influence over the substance of the term in question.[20]

The obiter is later doubted by Court of Appeal who, in the same case, suggests that the terms in circumstances such as those in the case may fall outside the scope of Regulation 5(1).[21]

An interesting point emerges from a comment made in the case of *Picardi v Cuniberti*,[22] which reveals that the guidance provided by the Royal Institute of British Architects (RIBA) to its members when concluding a contract with a consumer includes the following:

[17] R Brownsword and G Howells, 'The Implementation of the EC Directive on Unfair Terms in Consumer Contracts: Some Unresolved Questions' (1995) JBL 246.

[18] Law Commission and Scottish Law Commission, *Unfair Terms in Contracts* Law Com Report no 292 Cm 6464 (2005) (hereinafter Law Commission Report no 292, Cm 6464) para 4.52.

[19] [2004] EWHC 2450 (TCC).

[20] C Twigg-Flesner, 'The Implementation of the Unfair Contract Terms Directive in the United Kingdom' in H Collins, L Tichy and S Grundmann, *Standard Contract Terms in Europe* (The Hague, Kluwer, forthcoming).

[21] *Bryen & Langley Ltd v Martin Boston* [2005] EWCA Civ 973.

[22] [2002] EWHC 2923 para 51.

> As well as the commendable advice to explain the agreement and important clauses to the consumer, there is a recommended clause by which both parties to the contract would confirm that the clauses have been individually negotiated. Architects are also advised to give consumers an opportunity to raise any concerns and to record these.[23]

It has been noted[24] that this seems to assume that basic explanation and subsequent agreement to standard terms would amount to individual negotiation where the consumer has been given the opportunity to influence a term (by raising concerns), but has chosen not to do so. If this were sufficient for a term to be regarded as having been individually negotiated, then the Regulations could be displaced very easily: as earlier noted, however, English courts have taken a rather flexible approach when defining 'standard terms of business' under UCTA and have admitted that, where necessary, small amendments or some negotiation over the contract will not necessarily make the contract a 'negotiated' one. In the light of this, it is unlikely that the RIBA practice can successfully exclude, in principle, the application of the Regulations.

A similar issue was raised in an Italian case, where the Tribunale di Bologna,[25] had to decide whether application of articles 1469-bis ff (now arts 33 ff) could be excluded by a declaration that was included in the contract and signed by the consumer that the terms had been previously negotiated. The court replied that the

> effective protection of the weak party, together with a sound realism, . . . make it difficult to imagine that in mass contracts there is any room for any bargaining between the party who prepares the standard contract terms and the party who is called to accept them.[26]

The fact that inequality of bargaining power had played a significant role in the English system of unfair terms control under UCTA is reflected in the Law Commission's suggestion to abolish the limitation of individually negotiated terms in relation to consumer contracts. The choice is motivated partly by the desire to preserve the level of protection ensured by UCTA and by the concern that 'there are some obligations which business simply should not be able to evade or restrict, by whatever means'.[27] But, more importantly, the Law Commission believes that 'for a negotiation to be meaningful the customer must genuinely understand the proposed term and must be able to assess its possible impact',[28] which is not usually the case in consumer contracts.

The proposed English reform puts the finger on the underlying hypocrisy of the Directive: if its purpose is to protect the structurally weak party to the transaction,

[23] Twigg-Flesner, above n 20.

[24] Twigg-Flesner, above n 20.

[25] 14 June 2000 Corriere Giuridico 2000, 527.

[26] Similarly, the Tribunale di Milano (27 January 1997 I Contratti, 1998, 48) in a case concerning doorstep sales disregarded a term of the contract where the customer declared in writing that the good had been bought for a purpose which was related to the customer's business.

[27] Law Commission Consultation Paper no 166, above n 1, at para 4.49.

[28] *Ibid,* para 4.50.

it is contradictory to imagine that a negotiation process which is based on the disparity of the parties can ensure a fair result. In many instances negotiation may take place and still bring no significant advantage to the consumer: the trader may explain the meaning of the contract terms to the consumer and reassure him that the possibility that they apply to his case is very remote (actually a rather common problem with unfair terms is the tendency to think that the event envisaged by such terms will never occur), or that they are common usage in the trade, so that the consumer agrees not to have them changed;[29] the trader may agree to change the terms indicated by the consumer but their effect may still be unfair (eg accept to change an exemption clause into a limitation clause); the trader may change terms and re-draft them so that they have basically the same effect; the trader may finally agree to change terms and—why not?—make them more disadvantageous for the consumer.

On the other hand, the Law Commission intends not to subject to any control negotiated terms in business-to-business contracts as this would inject an additional element of uncertainty in business relations.[30]

Non-negotiated terms in business-to-business contracts remain nevertheless subject to some control. The Law Commission has emphasised that there has been a number of cases in which courts have found clauses in business-to-business contracts to be unreasonable under UCTA, while there has been only one case where a negotiated term has been held unreasonable.[31] For this reason, the Bill retains control ensured by s 3, s 6(1) and s 7(3A) UCTA through its clauses 9 and 10. It does not retain, on the other hand, control under s 6(3), s 7(3) and s 7(4) UCTA for the reason that, on the grounds of past experience, such terms are unlikely to be found unfair but their challenge may be used as a delaying tactic.

Finally, the similarity of small businesses with consumers persuaded the Law Commission to put forward another suggestion: in contracts with small businesses, a term is subject to the general fairness test if it (1) was put forward as one of the other party's standard term of business; and (2) the substance of the term was not, as a result of negotiation, changed in favour of the small business. This solution is aimed to allow a challenge of standard terms that were not negotiated, but it looks like an unduly complicated provision. Little enlightenment is provided by the Law Commission in this respect.[32]

In cases where it opts to control standard business terms, the Law Commission has considered two options: following the route of the Directive, that is, adopting a 'term by term approach', whereby the fact that some terms are negotiated does not exclude control on the others; or adopting the approach of UCTA, whereby

[29] In this respect Italian law is more consumer-friendly than the Directive since the Directive refers to the 'possibility' of changing the terms while the Consumer Code requires that terms are subject to individual negotiation, thus requiring effective intervention.

[30] The only exception is business liability for negligence, where the UCTA protection is preserved by making exclusion clauses void or subject to a fairness test depending on the liability they exclude.

[31] Law Commission Consultation Paper no 166, above n 1, at paras 5.28–5.29.

[32] Law Commission Report no 292, Cm 6464, above n 18, at para 4.46.

control is triggered only if the contract as a whole has not been negotiated. The Law Commission opted in favour of the latter solution, on grounds that a business party that has the time, expertise and power to negotiate substantial changes to some of the other party standard terms should not have the opportunity to be able to challenge the non-negotiated ones at a later stage.

'CORE' EXCLUSIONS

The provisions of the Directive

According to article 4(2) of the Directive, the main subject matter of the contract and the relationship between the good or service purchased and the price paid are outside the scope of the Directive provided that these parts of the contract are spelled out in 'plain, intelligible language'. This principle was introduced at the end of the preparatory stage and was justified by the Council as being due to the need to exclude from the scope of application of the Directive 'tout ce qui résulte directement de la liberté contractuelle des parties'.[33] In other words, the Directive does not aim to regulate the core of the contractual relationship, as long as this is expressed in clear and comprehensible language.

While a similar provision did not exist in the French *loi Scrivener*, it is likely that its inclusion was inspired by the German AGB-G, whose § 9 (now § 307(3) BGB) provides that the content of the main obligations under the contract is not subject to judicial control. German courts have taken a quite restrictive approach to this exclusion: so, for example, they still consider as subject to the fairness control 'secondary terms' relating to the price (*Preisnebenabreden*) such as those concerning the method of calculation,[34] or adjustment of the price,[35] as well as terms determining the price of ancillary obligations (*Preise von Nebenleistungen*) such as transport or installation.

Recital 19 of the Directive similarly suggests that article 4(2) has to be interpreted in a restrictive way and makes it clear that the exemption of the price/quality *ratio* from the fairness control is limited to the *ratio* itself and not to any other term related to the price. As a result, terms determining how the price is to be calculated or how it can be changed are submitted to the control of the Directive. In addition, still according to Recital 19, the main subject matter of the contract and the price/quality *ratio* may be taken into account in assessing the fairness of other terms. In that way, an indirect control of the price is admitted. So, for example, a clause fixing the price cannot be considered unfair just because the price is too high; but it cannot be excluded that a contract clause that gives rise to

[33] Common Position adopted on 22 September 1992. The document with the justifications of the Council was later published in (1992) *Journal des Politiques de Consommation* 483–87.

[34] BGH 1 January 1992 BGH NJW 1993, 1128.

[35] BGHZ 1981, 229, 232.

significant imbalance can in practice be held not to be unfair if the contract provides for a particularly advantageous price for the consumer. The same Recital gives an example of the restrictive interpretation that should be given to article 4(2) by explaining that in insurance contracts not all terms that define the insured risk should be considered as relating to the main subject matter: terms can escape control only if they define or circumscribe clearly the insured risk, and if the restriction of the insurance liability is taken into account in calculating the premium paid. If one is to apply this principle to all contracts, it would mean that deviations from the legitimate expectations of the consumer should be clearly stated and the price duly reduced.[36]

The exact scope of the 'subject matter' exclusion is slightly more difficult to determine than the price exclusion, since it requires in the first place defining what the 'main subject matter of the contract' is. This evokes the notorious legal puzzle of the distinction between terms defining the contractual obligations and terms excluding or restricting liability for breach of obligations. In both England and Italy, in cases concerning the alleged unfair nature of an exemption clause under UCTA or under article 1341 cc, the issue has arisen of whether such clause operates as a defence to breaches of the contractual obligations (exclusionary term) or it actually plays a role in defining those obligations in the first place (definitional term). For example, in the case of an insurance policy containing terms which exclude insurance cover whenever a certain event or certain circumstances occur, the question is whether, for the fact that they reduce the objective scope of the responsibility of the insurer as established in the contract or in law, these terms are to be considered as exemptions/limitations of liability; or whether they only define the subject matter of the contract by setting out the insurer's obligations.

Obviously, only a term that defines the parties' obligations can possibly be a 'core term': a term excluding liability does not define the subject matter of the contract but rather restricts liability for a pre-existing obligation.

Definitional and exclusionary terms in Italian and English law

In the English pre-UCTA case-law the question of the identification of the fundamental elements of the contract had acquired some importance as one of the techniques through which courts limited the effect of potentially unfair terms: the doctrines of fundamental breach and breach of a fundamental term relied on the identification of terms which, if not complied with, would render performance completely different from the one which the contract contemplated; since liability for the breach of such terms could not be excluded, the more protective of consumer interest courts were, the more broadly such terms were defined. In the context of UCTA, on the other hand, courts have often rejected the definitional

[36] Tenreiro and Karsten 'Unfair Terms in Consumer Contracts' above n 14, at 240.

approach as an attempted evasion of legal control over unfair terms and have accordingly tried to restrict the category of terms defining the parties' obligations as much as possible.[37]

These divergent approaches, both motivated by the desire to protect the weaker party, may provide an unstable background for the interpretation of the Regulations and there is potential for some difficulties to arise.[38]

A usual feature in the judicial response to the definitional argument in Italy (and in England too) is a remarkable discomfort in accepting that such a distinction can be used as an artifice to escape liability. In the English leading case on the matter, *Smith v Eric Bush*,[39] the House of Lords observed that applying the definitional argument to that case 'would not give effect to the manifest intention of the 1977 Act but would emasculate the Act'. Similarly, in deciding a seminal case on banks' liability for loss of items contained in a safe deposit box the Corte di Cassazione[40] expressed annoyance at the fact that the term at issue in the case was nothing but a clever re-formulation of a type of term which the Cassazione itself had previously declared to be a limitation of liability:[41] the fact that the term was carefully worded so as to appear as a determination of the subject matter of the contract did not prevent the court from examining its substance and effect to conclude that it was rather a limitation of liability.

Beyond this prima facie similarity, Italian and English courts have tackled the question of the definitional or exclusionary nature of contract terms from different angles.

In England, before UCTA, only a *dictum* by Lord Diplock in *Photo Production v Securicor Transport*[42] (unsuccessfully) adopted a definitional approach to exclusion clauses by acknowledging that primary obligations (the promises of the contract, the breach of which gives rise to the secondary obligation to pay damages) may be modified or recast by the terms of the contract no less than the secondary obligations to pay damages.

The provisions of UCTA itself appear to be drafted on the unquestioned premise that exception clauses operate as defences to accrued rights of action: the wide wording of s 13(1) seems to be intended to make it clear that even a clause which defines the obligations of the parties may be an exemption clause.[43] A

[37] See *Phillips Products v Hyland* [1987] 2 All ER 620 and *Smith v Eric S Bush* [1989] 2 All ER 691.

[38] See R Brownsword and G Howells, 'The Implementation of the EC Directive on Unfair Terms' above n 17; and E MacDonald, 'Mapping the Unfair Contract Terms Act 1977 and the Directive on Unfair Terms in Consumer Contracts' (1994) JBL 462.

[39] [1990] 1 AC 831.

[40] Cassazione Sezioni Unite (Cass Sez Un) 1 July 1994 no 6225 Giurisprudenza Italiana 1995, I, 206.

[41] Since 1976 the court had held that a term that states in advance the maximum value of the content to be kept in the safe deposit box amounts to a limitation of liability and may therefore be caught by art 1229. The court noted here that the term at issue was a simple re-formulation of the same exclusion: the only difference was that the formula previously used (pre-determining the maximum value of the items kept) has been replaced by a specific *prohibition* to keep in the safe deposit box items above a certain value.

[42] [1980] AC 827.

[43] See Ch 3, n 23.

seminal application of this principle in *Smith v Eric Bush*[44] reconfirmed the impression that courts are not prepared to accept the definitional argument: in order to determine whether a negligent surveyor could rely on a disclaimer of liability contained in his report, the House of Lords reasoned that it was necessary to disregard the term purporting to exclude liability, and ask whether, but for the existence of the term, there would have been a duty of care; if such a duty existed, then the purpose of the term was to exclude it, rather than defining the surveyor's obligations. This solution closes the leeway to excluding the application of the statutory control to a large number of cases where 'a party to a contract or a tortfeasor could opt out of the 1977 Act by declining to recognise their own answerability to the plaintiffs'.[45]

A solution similar to the English 'but for' approach was adopted by the Italian Corte di Cassazione when, in the 1994 judgment mentioned above,[46] it clarified the issue of the bank's liability for loss of items contained in a safe deposit box. A contract for the deposit of some items in the safe box of a bank prohibited the deposit of items of a value higher than 25 million lire. Due to the bank's negligence, a theft occurred and the content of the safe deposit box was stolen. One of the customers sued the bank for the recovery of the value of the items contained in his safe box, for a sum equal to 300 million lire and claimed that the prohibition concerning the value of the items deposited was in fact a limitation of liability, which prohibited by article 1229 in cases where the damage is due to gross negligence. The bank claimed that the term only aimed at defining the subject matter of the contract and not their liability.

The court observed that, according to the provisions of the Italian civil code on contracts of deposit, the obligation undertaken by the bank consisted merely in providing a suitable place for the items deposited, ensuring suitable surveillance and invigilating on the integrity of the box. The term at issue did not affect any of these elements. Accordingly, the determination of the content of the box or of its value was not a term defining the obligations of the bank, but was simply a way of putting a cap on the bank's liability in case of breach of one of its obligations.

The English and the Italian cases, apparently rather different, are comparable in that they both place emphasis on the set of obligations attached by the law to a certain contract. Those are the necessary point of reference to determine the obligations of each party.

There are, however, other possible routes to identifying the 'subject matter of the contract'. In England, for example, it has been suggested[47] that courts should determine whether a term in a contract 'excludes or restricts' liability by asking whether it deprives a contracting party of the contractual performance which it

[44] Above n 37, at 831.

[45] Nourse LJ in *Harris v Wyre Forest District Council* [1988] 1 All ER 691 at 697.

[46] Cass Sez Un 1 July 1994 no 6225 Giurisprudenza Italiana 1995, I, 206.

[47] E MacDonald, 'Exclusion Clauses: The Ambit of s 13(1) of the Unfair Contract Terms Act 1977' (1992) LS 277.

reasonably expected. However, while in England this suggestion remained at academic level, a similar idea was applied in a number of decision by the Cassazione where it invited lower courts to investigate, in case of doubt, whether, under the veil of a delimitation of the object, there hides an attempt to limit the allocation of the risk *normally* related to the performance owed or not.

A comparison of two apparently similar cases can provide an example of this reasoning. In one case,[48] a removal company had entered into an insurance contract that did not cover cases where damage occurred to the goods carried while the company's vehicles were unattended. During one of the journeys the driver of one of the lorries stopped to have lunch in a restaurant. The furniture was stolen and the insurance refused to pay. The insured claimed that, as an exclusion clause, the term was not enforceable as it had not been specifically approved. The Cassazione held that, as the clause had the purpose of defining the subject matter of the contract, it was not to be considered as an exclusion clause and was therefore not covered by article 1341(2).

In another case,[49] the owner of a yacht had insured his boat against theft. The insurance policy contained a clause that excluded the insurer's liability in cases where the owner did not take all suitable measures for the safety and surveillance of the yacht when on ground. When the yacht was stolen, the insurer tried to rely on the fact that the term only defined the insurer's obligations, but the insured claimed that, as an exclusion clause, it had not been specifically approved in writing. The Cassazione held that the term was an exclusion clause as it aimed to limit the insurer's liability rather than to define the subject matter of the contract; accordingly, it required specific approval.

The difference between the two cases does not lie in the nature and the position of the parties but rather in the extension of the exclusion of liability. As opposed to the first case, the second case identifies the situation justifying the exemption not on grounds of a simple lack of ordinary diligence: for the exemption not to apply, the insured should have undertaken an extremely burdensome and penetrating activity of surveillance—which is in practice very difficult to carry out unless the owner chooses not to leave the boat. The circumstances envisaged by the term at issue, that is, the owner leaving the boat and being unable to watch properly over the boat are bound to occur: and, because these events will necessarily occur, the term turns out to be an exemption to the commitment undertaken by the insurer. In other words, the event of the owner leaving the boat unattended was certainly one of those, in view of which the policy had been made: accordingly, a term that entails loss of the insurance cover when this occurs, is an exemption of liability rather than a determination of the subject matter of the contract.[50]

[48] Cass no 10947 of 16 June 1997 in *Danno e Resposabilità*, 1998, 384.

[49] Cass no 8643 of 21 October 1994 *Diritto ed Economia delle Assicurazioni*, 1995, 921.

[50] The distinction between exclusionary and definitional terms, however, is far from being clearly drawn and consolidated, and in some cases Italian courts resort to simply analysing the way terms are worded in the single contract, thus contributing to the creation of a huge and often contradictory amount of case-law: for some examples see F Bartolini (ed) *Il codice civile commentato con la giurisprudenza* (Piacenza, La Tribuna, 1996) under art 1341.

As a result, the English and, to some extent, the Italian case-law on definitional/exclusionary clauses seem to suggest two possible criteria for the identification of the 'subject matter of the contract': a term does not define the subject matter when it aims to exclude a liability that would otherwise arise under the law; or a term does not define the subject matter when it aims to exclude liability for rendering a performance which is different from the one which is normally expected under that type of contract.

The first approach is too rigid and narrow. It is too narrow because it can only be used in the case of exemption clauses stricto sensu, that is, those terms that seek to exclude liability for non-performance, but not the ones that allow different performance. At the same time, this criterion is too rigid as it does not allow any variations from the obligations prescribed by the law. One example in English law may suffice. In a contract to supply and fit a cowl to a chimney of a smoking fireplace, parties may act on the understanding that the cowl may or may not cure the fault. However, the customer would later have the possibility to argue that the builder's statement concerning the possibility that the fault is not cured as an exemption clause: the statement would be seen as an attempt to evade the quality warranties implied by law;[51] similarly, if used in the context of the Directive, one would come to the conclusion that the statement does not define the 'subject matter of the contract', as it entitles the business party to escape the duties imposed by law.

The second criterion appears to be more suitable for the purpose of defining the 'subject matter of the contract': it must be noted, however, that there are different understandings as to what parties' expectation might be, as the following paragraph will show.

Implementation

The 'core terms' exclusion is replicated in article 34(2) of the Italian Consumer Code and in Regulation 6(2) of the 1999 Regulations.

There are no reported cases on the Italian implementation. Yet, one can imagine that the task of determining the main obligations attached to a contract is somehow easier for a continental lawyer: in Italian law, as well as in other codified systems, once parties have agreed upon what type of contract they intend to conclude, the law itself attaches to it a number of primary and ancillary obligations

[51] See E Macdonald, *Exemption Clauses and Unfair Terms* (London, Butterworths, 1999) 92–93.

[52] This is the principle of *tipicità contrattuale*: most contracts fall within a 'type' which is regulated in some detail by the Consumer Code (eg *contratto di vendita, contratto di deposito, contratto di appalto*). Contracts which do not fall within the categories drawn by the code are still valid and enforceable (*contratti atipici*), as long as they serve a useful socio-economical function.

(*obbligazioni principali* and *secondarie*).[52] In the common law, on the other hand, the parties simply undertake all the liabilities which follow from the contract: it is therefore more difficult to justify a distinction between principal and subsidiary liabilities as all of them form an integral part of the bargain.[53]

The Law Commission proposes to determine the 'subject matter' by drawing inspiration from section 3(2)(b)(i) UCTA.[54] Under this provision, terms which allow the business to render a performance which is substantially different from the one that was reasonably expected are subject to the reasonableness test. The 'reasonable expectation' of the customer refers not to what is written in the contract (because this would not differ, of course, from what the business claims to be entitled to render) but to the other party's reasonable expectations derived from all the circumstances, including the way the contract was presented to him.[55] Applied in the context of the 'core' exemption of Directive 93/13, whether a term is part of the definition of the main subject matter would depend on what the consumer's expectations are in relation to the contract: a 'core term' is one that is central to how the consumer perceives the bargain. So, if a holidaymaker had been told that the hotel booked was still under construction and that, if completion was delayed, he would be put in a different hotel, this would be considered as being part of the definition of the main subject matter. Similarly, if a holiday was described as comprising travel by air, or in the event of strikes, by coach, this term would be considered as contributing to defining the subject matter. If, on the other hand, the holiday was described as providing travel by air, followed by some small print allowing the company to carry the customer by coach in the event of a strike, this not would be seen as determining the subject matter of contract, because this is not how the deal had been presented to the consumer.

Accordingly, the Law Commission Report suggests that the new legislation should 'exclude the main subject matter and the price from the scope of review, but only in so far as the term is not substantially different from what the consumer reasonably expected', and stated in plain language.

The Law Commission believes that their view that emphasis should be put on the way that the deal is presented to the consumer is supported by the Office of Fair Trading (OFT), where they declare that their approach is not to consider 'core provisions' terms which have not been brought to the consumer's attention: 'In our view, this exemption [regulation 6(2)] does not apply to terms which are hidden from the consumer's view or if he has no chance to get to know the terms.' The reason for this would be that 'a supplier would surely find it difficult to sustain the argument that a contract's main subject matter was defined by a term which a consumer had been given no real chance to see and read before signing'.[56]

[53] A De Moor, 'Common and Civil Law Conceptions of Contract and a European Law of Contract: the Case of the Directive on Unfair Terms in Consumer Contracts' (1995) *European Review of Private Law* 267.

[54] Law Commission Report no 292, Cm 6464, above n 18, at para 3.59.

[55] The *Zockoll Mercury Group* [1999] Entertainment and Media Law Reports, 385, 395.

[56] (1998) 4 *Unfair Terms Bulletin* (OFT) 16.

It is not self-evident, however, that one can draw from this statement the inference that a term which is adequately brought to the consumer's attention defines the subject matter: it merely says that a term which is *not* brought to the attention cannot be considered as defining the subject matter of the contract. In addition, it seems unfair that whether the exclusion operates or not should depend on how the 'deal' is presented to the consumer: if a consumer buys a 'luxury holiday', he should be able to expect that he will not be put in a budget hotel, even if the deal is described and presented as 'including accommodation in a luxury hotel or, if this not available, in a lower class hotel'. This is a matter that should be taken into account in the assessment of the fairness of the term,[57] and not excluded from control as part of the subject matter.

One alternative criterion could be to assess the consumer's 'reasonable expectations' *in abstracto*, that is, not by taking into account the way that the deal was presented but whether, in the ordinary course of things, one would expect a certain performance under a certain type of contract: agreeing to buy a 'luxury package holiday' creates, *in abstracto*, the expectation that accommodation will be of first class standard, even if the contract purports to alter such an expectation. This reflects the approach taken by Italian courts in the cases, earlier described, on exclusionary/definitional terms: a term does not define that subject matter of the contract when it aims to exclude liability for rendering a performance which is different from the one which is *normally* expected.

The Law Commission also noted that the 'reasonable expectation' (under either of the two interpretations given) criterion may be too broad: a consumer may 'reasonably expect' a certain term, but this may not be part of the main subject matter. This matter is addressed in *DGFT v First National Bank*,[58] where the House of Lords rejected the argument that in a loan agreement a term that the borrower in default with his payments should continue to pay interest at the contractual rate even after the judgment obtained against him had been discharged fell within the definition of the main subject matter. Along the same lines, the Court of Appeal noted that the provision was a 'subsidiary term', a default provision 'dealing with a situation where there is a breach of contract; it is not there that one finds defined the main subject matter of the contract'.[59] For the same reason, the term at issue could not fall within the definition of the remuneration: 'terms concerned with the adequacy of the price or remuneration are . . . those which define the parties' rights and obligations in the due performance of the contract'.[60]

[57] In this case, the fact that the consumer was aware of the possibility to be put in a lower standard accommodation should count in favour of the fairness of the term.

[58] In the High Court: [2000] 1 WLR 98; in the Court of Appeal: [2000] 2 WLR 1353; in the House of Lords: [2001] 3 WLR 1297. The argument was rejected at all three instances.

[59] [2001] 3 WLR 1297 1364. A different reasoning is required in case of insurance contracts: in *Bankers Insurance Company Ltd v South* [2003] EWHC 380 a travel insurance policy excluded from insurance cover accidents caused by the insured consumer whilst in possession of 'motorised waterborne craft'. It was accepted that the term specifying exclusions from the insurance policy was a 'core term' as it formed part of the specification of the risks covered by the policy.

[60] *Ibid* 1364.

One interesting case on this matter is the High Court's decision in *Bairstow Eves v Smith*.[61] A contract used by an estate agent provided that they were entitled to a standard rate of commission of 3 per cent, but also provided for an 'early payment discounted commission rate' of 1.5 per cent. The latter was available if payment was made within ten days after the sale of the property had been completed; after this, the standard rate would apply. As litigation arose, the estate agents argued that the term concerning the commission rate came within the 'core terms' exception. The High Court held that only the term providing for the 1.5 per cent rate was a core term, whereas the term specifying the standard commission rate was not. They came to this conclusion by noting that 1.5 per cent was the prevailing rate in the market and negotiation between the parties had focused mainly on that rate; in addition both parties seemed to have proceeded on the assumption that the payment was going to be made within the ten days period.

This decision confirms that the question of whether a particular term is a 'core term' turns

> on the construction of the particular contract. In this regard, it has long been the practice of the English courts to be guided not only by the wording of a contract itself, but also on the circumstances surrounding the conclusion of the contract.[62] If a particular term will not come into play during the ordinary performance of the contract, then it cannot be a core term, irrespective of how the term may be described in the contract.[63]

In this case, what mattered was not the way that the contract was physically presented to the consumer, but the way it was negotiated, as well as the common practice in that business: the reasoning takes into account both 'abstract expectations' and the way the contract had been negotiated.

The OFT has also taken the view that clauses related to the price agreed, such as price variations clauses, do not fall within the exclusion; in the case of a term providing for the rate of interest to be paid by a debtor to be increased on default, OFT considered that this could not be a core term

> regardless of how the term is drafted and whether the higher rate of interest is expressed to be the ordinary rate. The term providing for the higher rate of interest is in substance a term making provision for payment of compensation upon a breach of an obligation and not, therefore, a core term.[64]

CONTRACTS RELATING TO LAND

The fact that 'land' in English law is considered as neither goods nor services has raised the question of whether the new Regulations should also apply to contracts

[61] [2004] EWHC 263.

[62] 'Seminally, *Investors Compensation Scheme Ltd v West Bromwich Building Society* [1998] 1 WLR 896'.

[63] Twigg-Flesner, above n 20.

[64] See OFT, *Non Status Lending: Guidelines for lenders and Brokers* (London: OFT, 1997) 192. Further discussion on this issue can be found in the Law Commission Report no 292, Cm 6464, above n 18, paras 3.27–3.34.

relating to land. At the level of the Directive, the question was not clarified after the only reference to immovable property—a term concerning purchase of time-share interests in land in the annex to the 1990 proposal—disappeared in the subsequent texts; failure of the Department of Trade and Industry (DTI) to clearly address the issue[65] has perpetuated the problem. Accordingly, the answer to the question can be given only having regard to a wider range of considerations.

First, the corresponding Italian term *beni*, the French *biens*, and their Spanish and Portuguese cognates all include immovable property. Second, the Directive should not be interpreted as applying to goods and services as an English lawyer would understand those terms: the interpretation of Community law

> involves a comparison of the different language versions. . . . Furthermore, it must be emphasised that legal concepts do not necessarily have the same meaning in Community law and in the law of various Member States. Finally, every provisions of Community law must be interpreted in the light of the provisions of Community law as a whole, regard being had to the objectives therefore an to its state of evolution at the date on which the provisions in question is to be applied.[66]

Under EC law, the issue is not clear: 'goods' are not defined in the Treaty, but clarification can occasionally be found in the case law[67] and in a number of Directives that use that word:[68] the Sixth VAT Directive,[69] for example, defines the 'supply of goods' as meaning 'the transfer of the right to dispose of tangible property as owner, including, inter alia, '(a) certain interests in immoveable property, (b) *rights in rem* giving the holder thereof a right of user over immoveable property', thus making it clear that 'goods' is capable of a meaning going beyond the normal English language and usage; elsewhere, when the scope of a Directive applying to contracts for the supply of goods or services is meant not to extend to land-related contracts, a specific exclusion is normally set out.

In *Freiburger Kommunalbauten*[70] a reference was made in relation to the possible unfairness of a term contained in a contract for the sale of a parking space located in a multi-storey car park. Neither of the parties, nor the ECJ, raised the issue of the applicability of the Directive to that contract, thus implicitly confirming that the Directive applies to immovable property.

[65] These are complex matters which reflect the host State's underlying heritage and system of property ownership. The DTI doubted that transactions concerning land could be properly considered to be within the scope of the Directive, but following various consultations they were eventually persuaded by the views of a number of consultees that it would be prudent to assume that the Directive could extend to transactions in land (DTI, *The Unfair Term in Consumer Contracts Regulations 1994 Guidance Notes* (London, DTI, 1995) 7).

UCTA expressly excluded such contracts from its application.

[66] Case 283/81 *CILFIT Srl and Lanificio di Gavardo SpA v Ministry of Health* [1982] ECR 3430.

[67] See, eg, case 7/68 *Commission v Italy* [1968] ECR 423 where goods are defined as 'products which can be valued in money and which are capable, as such, of forming the subject of commercial transactions'.

[68] See the analysis carried out by S Bright and C Bright, 'Unfair Terms in Land Contracts: Copy In or Copy Out?' (1995) LQR 655.

[69] Dir 77/388 on the harmonisation of the laws of the Member States relating to turnover taxes OJ L145/1.

[70] C–237/02 [2004] 2 CMLR 13 ECJ.

Along the same lines, in the case of *Newham LB v Kathun*[71] the English Court of Appeal has held that the Directive (and the Regulations) apply to contract relating to land:

> in our domestic law, these distinctions [between movables and immovables] have a long history and a present utility. In the context of a Europe-wide scheme of consumer protection, they could be nothing but an embarrassing eccentricity.[72]

One issue which might be raised at this stage is the extent to which definitions provided in one context can be used to clarify the meaning of the same word in another context. The word 'good', for example, is also used in Directive 99/44 on Consumer Sales, in the Doorstep Sales Directive and in the Distance Sales Directive. The Directive on Consumer Sales defines goods as 'tangible movable items', thus automatically excluding that land can be a 'good' for the purposes of the Directive; on the other hand, the directives on distance and doorstep sales apply to 'contracts concerning goods or services', but not to 'contract concluded for the construction and sale of immovable property or relating to other immovable property rights': this can either mean that immovable property is not 'goods', or, by comparison with the definitional technique used for consumer sales, that immovable property is indeed 'goods' (so that a specific exclusion had to be included).

While it would be an attractive option to ensure, both at the level of law-making and at the level of interpretation, a certain level of uniformity in the terminology used, one needs to bear in mind that each Community measure must be interpreted on its own merits, and 'transplants' are not always possible.[73] It is to be hoped that the programme undertaken by the Commission to improve the quality of the EC *acquis* will enhance the consistency of EC terminology.

[71] [2004] EWCA Civ 55.

[72] *Ibid* para 78.

[73] See, eg, Tizzano AG in *TUI v Leitner* [2002] ECR I–2631 paras 34–35.

8

Formal and Substantive Controls

THE FAIRNESS CONTROL introduced by Directive 93/13 (the Directive) relies on two pillars: a formal requirement of transparency, in combination with a rule of interpretation, and a substantive test.

The Community *acquis* in the areas of consumer law and of free movement offers some tools that may enhance our understanding of the formal transparency requirement, although one needs to take into account that such tools have been elaborated in a context which is different from the one of the Directive and may therefore not be easy to 'transplant'.

The way that substantive controls have been applied by national courts and enforcement authorities such as the Office of Fair Trading (OFT) reveals that the different approaches noted in Chapter 3 may also affect the way that the Directive is interpreted and applied. The fairness test of the Directive does not provide clear guidelines as to how it should be applied, and this has left domestic courts rather free to build their own notion of 'unfair'.

FORMAL CONTROLS

Transparency

The transparency requirement in Directive 93/13

Article 5 of the Directive, by requiring that terms are drafted 'in plain, intelligible language' introduces a transparency requirement.[1] 'Plain and intelligible' are not

[1] The 1992 proposal specified that terms which had not been individually negotiated should be regarded as having been accepted by the consumer only where the latter had had a proper opportunity to examine the terms before the contract was concluded. In the legislative process, however, the Council chose to delete that provision because it thought that it went too far in the national rules about acceptance and conclusion of contract, which was not the subject matter of the Directive. Reference to this idea, however, remained in the 20th Recital of the Directive which states that

> whereas contracts should be drafted in plain, intelligible language, the consumer *should actually be given an opportunity to examine all the terms* and if in doubt, the interpretation most favourable to the consumer shall prevail.

Another reference is made by letter i of the Annex which considers as an example of unfair term one which has the object or effect of binding the consumer to terms with which he had no real opportunity of becoming acquainted before the conclusion of the contract.

tautological in that a term is in 'plain' language when it is not surprising, it cannot be misunderstood and it does not give rise to any doubts; 'intelligibility', on the other hand, encompasses both the style used and how a contract term is actually printed on paper.[2]

The transparency principle is deeply rooted in Community Law, both in secondary legislation and in the case-law of the European Court of Justice (ECJ). The importance of informing and protecting the consumer has been stressed since the first two programmes for consumer protection and information policy of the Community;[3] almost every consumer directive includes information duties: information should be given in a sufficient, precise and clear way;[4] 'when a brochure is made available to the consumer it shall indicate in a legible, comprehensible and accurate manner both the price and the adequate information';[5] it should respect ethical principles, human dignity as well as political beliefs;[6] it must be easily accessible and it is often demanded that it is confirmed in writing.[7]

These requirements allow the consumer to be 'conscious of his rights and responsibilities',[8] to be able to make a rational choice between competing products and services and to know what to do if he thinks that some of the regulations have not been complied with.[9] As later described, the case-law of the ECJ has often stressed the relationship between consumer protection and consumer information and has constantly considered the provision of full information to the consumer as the cornerstone of the consumer protection Community policy. The fact that consumer choice and consumer information have become leading elements in EC legislation and case-law, however, does not help to shed light on the practical application of transparency in the context of the Directive:[10] there are several issues that need clarification.

[2] See, among many, M Herington and S Brothers, 'Unfair Terms and Consumer Contract Regulations' (1995) *International Insurance Law Review* 263.

[3] See Ch 2, p 6.

[4] Art 3.2 of Dir 90/314/EEC of 13 June 1990 on Package Travel, Package Holidays and Package Tours ([1990] OJ L158/59); see also art 4.2 of Dir 97/7/EC on the Protection of Consumers in Respect of Distance Contracts ([1997] OJ L144/19), according to which 'information . . . shall be provided in a clear and comprehensible manner'.

[5] Art 3.2 of Dir 90/314 previous n.

[6] Annex, Commission Recommendation of 7 April 1992 on Codes of Practice for the Protection of Consumers in respect of Contracts Negotiated at a Distance ([1992]OJ L156/21).

[7] See, eg, art 6 of Dir 87/102/EEC for the Approximation of the Laws, Regulations and Administrative Provisions of the Member States concerning Consumer Credit ([1987] OJ L42/48); art 4 of Dir 85/577/EEC to Protect the Consumer in respect of Contracts Negotiated Away from Business Premises ([1985] OJ L372/31); art 5 of Dir 97/7 above n 4; art 3 of Dir 94/47 on the Protection of Purchasers in respect of Certain Aspects of Contracts relating to the Purchase of the Right to Use Immovable Properties on a Timeshare Basis ([1994] OJ L280/83).

[8] Council Resolution of 14 April 1975 OJ C92, 25 April 1975, 1

[9] Eg Dir 85/577/EEC, above n 7, requires at art 4 that the name and address of a person against whom a right may be exercised should be mentioned.

[10] A complete account of the problems raised by the transparency requirement is given by H Micklitz, 'Final Report from Workshop 4, Obligation of Clarity and Favourable Interpretation to the Consumer' *The Unfair Terms Directive: Five Years On* Acts of the Brussels Conference, 1–3 July 1999 (Luxembourg, Office for Official Publications of the European Communities, 2000) 147.

In the first place, it is not clear whether 'transparency' is limited to some sort of negative control which allows at most the elimination of unclear and incomprehensible contract terms or whether it might be understood as providing for positive information duties, that is, explaining and summarising the implication of certain contractual terms: the principle of transparency may also be seen as a form of substantive control if read in the light of the criteria enshrined in article 3 (substantive transparency): transparency would mean, in this case, not only a duty to provide information before the conclusion of the contract, but also to point out its effects, including an active explanation and education concerning the content of the contract.[11]

Second, the Directive fails to address the question of the language in which clauses should be presented to the consumer, problems which had been addressed at legislative level in matters of labelling,[12] time-share, insurance contracts,[13] in the recommendation on the payment systems[14] and at judicial level in a number of ECJ decisions.[15]

Third, the sanctions for infringement of the transparency requirement are not clearly stated: article 5 only deals with the case where more than one meaning can be attributed to a certain term: 'where there is doubt about the meaning of a term, the interpretation most favourable to the consumer shall prevail'; it does not indicate, however, what the sanction is if a contract term not only is recognised not to be written in plain and intelligible language but does not appear to have a meaning, or has only one (unclear) meaning.

Fourth, it is not clear what standard of transparency is required under the Directive, that is, by reference to what model of 'consumer' transparency would be assessed.

Only the last two questions have been discussed at domestic and European level.

The transparency requirement in domestic law

While the Italian implementing measure, article 35 of the Consumer Code, has remained rather faithful to the European formulation, Regulation 7 separates the transparency requirement and the rule of interpretation *contra proferentem* in two paragraphs, thus putting more emphasis on each single requirement.

[11] Commission of the European Communities, *Report from the Commission on the Implementation of Council Directive 93/13/EEC of 5 April 1993 on Unfair Terms in Consumer Contracts* COM (2000) 248 final, 155.

[12] So, eg, art 13a(2) of Dir 79/112 [1979] OJ L33/1 (now repealed by Dir 2000/13, [2000] OJ L129/29) prescribes that 'the Member State in which the product is marketed may . . . stipulate that those labelling particulars shall be given in one or more languages'.

[13] See art 38 Council Dir 92/96/EEC on the Coordination of Laws, Regulations and Administrative Provisions relating to Direct Life Assurance (Third Life Assurance Directive) [1992] OJ L360/1.

[14] Commission Recommendation 88/590 of 17 November 1988 concerning Payment Systems OJ L317 of 24 November 1988, 55–58.

[15] See, eg, C–369/89 *ASBL Piageme v BVBA Peeters* [1991] ECR I–2971; C–51/93 *Meyhui v Schott ZwieselGlaswerke* ECR [1994] I–3879.

English courts' traditional dislike of small print and unclear drafting in standard forms contract has led to imposing transparency requirements such as the one that onerous terms must be brought to the attention of the customer with reasonable steps; or that the nature, size and location of terms and of their clarity and prolixity is relevant to their reasonableness under UCTA. In respect of the Regulations, the OFT has already indicated that they consider Regulation 7 as capable of biting not only as regards vocabulary but also structure of contracts: long and complex sentences and cross references are likely to be considered unfair.[16]

In Italy, on the other hand, the requirement of *conoscenza* and *conoscibilità* under article 1341(1) cc has seldom been translated into a duty to draft terms in plain, intelligible language and basically only when terms were not physically available did courts declare the contract in violation of article 1341(1): as previously described, specific written approval of a term is sufficient to sweep away any doubt that the term was not *conosciuto* or *conoscibile* by the customer.

Interestingly, in determining what sanction should be applied for the violation of the transparency requirement, the Italian and English approach seem to converge in favour of solutions that most favour the consumer. In the Italian case *MFD c ABI*[17] the Tribunale di Roma held that a term which is not transparent can in itself be 'a source of unfairness by increasing the asymmetry of information which already exists in standard form contracts': in other words, lack of transparency can automatically trigger the unfairness of the relevant term. The view expressed by the OFT and by the Law Commission in England points in the same direction: the OFT believes that a term may be unfair simply by reason of not being in plain intelligible language,[18] since a violation of the transparency requirement can still in itself harm consumers by misleading or confusing them. The Law Commission goes even further by proposing that the transparency factor is expressly taken into account in assessing fairness:[19] clause 14 of the Unfair Contract Terms Bill provides that whether a term is fair and reasonable is to be determined by taking into account '(a) the extent to which the term is transparent'.

This solution must sound familiar to German lawyers: until 2002, the German legislator had not found it necessary to formally implement the transparency requirement as this was already being taken into account in the *Inhalteskontrolle* of § 9 AGB-G (now § 307 BGB). In a 1989 case,[20] for example, the *Bundesgerichtshof*

[16] P Edwards, *The Challenge of Unfair Contract Terms Regulation* Unfair Contract Terms Bulletin no 4/1997 (London, OFT, 1997) 18; see also (May 1996) *Unfair Contract Terms Bulletin* (OFT) 16.

[17] Tribunale di Roma 21 January 2000 Foro Italiano 2000, I, 2045; see also Tribunale di Roma 24 March 1998 in Foro Italiano I, c 3332 and Corte d'Appello di Roma 24 September 2002 in Foro Italiano 2003, I, c 331

[18] (1996) 1 *Unfair Contract Terms Bulletin* (OFT) 13.

[19] Law Commission and Scottish Law Commission, *Unfair Terms in Contract: A Joint Consultation Paper* Law Commission Consultation Paper no 166/Scottish Law Commission Discussion Paper no 119 (2002) (hereinafter Law Commission Consultation Paper no 166) para 4.106. On the notion of 'substantive transparency' see F Brunetta D'Usseaux, *Formal and Substantive Aspects of the Transparency Principle in European Private Law* (1998) Cons LJ 320–39.

[20] BGH 17 January 1989 NJW 1989 Westpapier Mitteilungen, 1989, 126; see also BHG 24 November 1988, Westpapier Mitteilingen 1988, 1780.

held that some terms can be unfair under para 9 AGB-G because of their lack of transparency, independently of their being actually unfair or not. In such cases, the lack of transparency prevents the client from comparing different offers, or from being clearly informed of his legal position, or from realising how much he is concretely paying for a certain service, even though the relevant terms in themselves cannot be criticised. When the true situation is not disclosed, this constitutes a violation of the principle of transparency which can be considered unreasonable, leading to the term being declared ineffective as it results in an unreasonable disadvantage for the consumer. With the 2002 reform, however, the German legislator decided to introduce an express reference to transparency[21] and § 307 BGB now explicitly states that 'an unreasonable disadvantage *may* also result from the fact that the provision is not clear and comprehensible' (although the word 'may' suggests this is not always so).

It appears that, at least to the extent that the legal systems here examined show, there is some convergence towards considering transparency as the 'third pillar' of the fairness test. This solution, probably provoked by the legislator's failure to provide a specific sanction for lack of transparency, certainly ensures the most effective means to guarantee the achievement of the objective of avoiding ambiguous terms in standard contracts.[22]

Transparency and the 'average consumer'

Whether there is transparency or not largely depends on the consumer image that guides the interpretation of article 5: what is transparent for an educated, well-informed consumer may be obscure to an illiterate, uninformed one. At ECJ level, the definition of the 'type' of consumer that should be protected within the EU has been a popular issue in the areas concerning misleading and unfair advertising.

For this purpose, the ECJ has developed the concept of 'informed consumer' or 'average consumer' in a number of cases referred by national courts (mainly German courts) under article 234 EC.[23]

In such cases, national courts were faced with the question whether a domestic measure aimed at protecting consumers against a certain unfair trade practice could be justified and therefore maintained although it may have been contrary to article 28 EC. In deciding whether the measure could be justified or not, it was essential to determine which parameter of consumer should be adopted: would,

[21] It is possible that the proceedings that the Commission started against the Netherlands for a comparable inaccuracy in implementation and resulting in a declaration of infringement (C–144/99 *Commission v The Netherlands* [2001] ECR I–3541) played a role in the German legislator's decision.

[22] A Orestano and A Di Majo, 'Trasparenza e squilibrio nelle clausole vessatorie' Corriere Giuridico 2000, 523 and 528.

[23] See, eg, C–220/98 *Estée Lauder v Lancaster* [2000] ECR I–117; C–470/93 *Verein Gegen Unwesen in Handel und Gewerbe Köln e V v Mars GmbH* [1995] ECR I–1923: C–315/92 *Verband Sozialer Wettbewerb e V v Clinique Laboratoires SNC and Estée Lauder Cosmetics GmbH* [1994] ECR I–317; C–313/94 *Fratelli Graffione v Ditta Fransa* [1996] ECR I–6039; C–210/96 *Gut Springenheide GmbH v Oberkreisdirektor des Kreises Steinfurt-Amt für Lebensmilleluberwachung* [1998] ECR I–4657.

for example, a domestic rule that prohibits the use of a certain misleading packaging be justified if it could be proven that it misleads only 10 to 15 per cent of consumers (ie the most vulnerable consumers only)? In other words, should the relationship between domestic measures of consumer protection and article 28 EC be assessed having in mind the vulnerable consumer or rather the mature and critical consumer? The rule developed by the ECJ is that such relationship is to be assessed on the grounds of the 'average consumer, reasonably well informed and reasonably well observant and circumspect'.[24]

If applied in the area of unfair terms, the notion of well-informed consumer, alert, keen in making use of better and greater choices, able to bring the necessary information together and difficult to deceive will entail that the standard of transparency required by the Directive will be to some extent brought down and the supplier would to some extent be released from his duty to provide clear and intelligible standards. On the other hand, reference to the weak consumer, unable to understand the law, needing information on his/her rights in simple and clear form would entail raising the transparency standards and placing the burden on the supplier.

The extent to which the 'average consumer' criterion would be followed by the ECJ in interpreting article 5 of the Directive is not, however, entirely clear. The case-law above referred to was aimed at striking down domestic measures which were incompatible with article 28 EC and was therefore primarily driven by the objective of market integration, in conjunction with the ambition to open national markets to new products and de-crystallise consumer habits.[25]

Similarly, in the *Nissan* case,[26] the ECJ established that a claim is 'misleading' according to Directive 84/450[27] if it can affect 'the decision to buy on the part of a significant number of consumers to whom the advertising in question is addressed': reference to a 'significant number' of consumers indicates that particularly vulnerable consumers would not enjoy protection under the Directive. It must be noted, however, that although Directive 84/450 is a measure of consumer protection, in that specific case the ECJ was once more not particularly concerned with defining a Community standard of consumer protection but rather with facilitating parallel imports: the assessment of the misleading nature of an advertisement was therefore strongly influenced by the desire to encourage cross-border competition.

Finally, in *Sektellerei*,[28] the ECJ had to interpret Regulation 2333/92[29] laying down general rules for the description and presentation of sparkling wines (in principle, a measure aimed at both market integration and consumer protection).

[24] Opinion of Fennelly AG in C–220/98 *Estée Lauder v Lancaster, ibid*, para28.

[25] See in particular case 788/79 *Italian State v Herbert Gilli and Paul Andres* [1981] 1 CMLR 146; case 178/84 *Commission v Germany (Beer purity)* [1987] ECR 1227.

[26] C–373/90 *Criminal Proceedings against X* [1992] ECR I–131.

[27] [1984] OJ L250/17.

[28] C–303/97 *Verbraucherschutzverein eV v Sektellerei GC Kesler GmbH* [1999] ECR I–513.

[29] [1992] OJ L231/9.

In deciding whether certain brands would be misleading for consumers, the ECJ referred to 'the presumed expectations . . . of an average consumer who is reasonably well informed and reasonably observant and circumspect'.

On the other hand, Directive 93/13 may need to be interpreted from a different perspective: being a measure primarily aimed at consumer protection, it may have to be read having in mind consumer protection rather than market integration.

The *Buet*[30] case on Directive 85/577[31] (the Doorstep Sales Directive) in fact suggests a different approach: the ECJ upheld a French measure totally forbidding doorstep sales of educational material although it provided a much higher level of protection compared to the directive, that only regulated the modalities of doorstep sales: according to the court, the potential purchaser of educational material would often belong to a category of people who, for one reason or another, are behind with their education and are 'particularly vulnerable'. Accordingly, the ECJ seemed prepared to accept that in some cases national courts adopt their own (higher) standard of consumer protection: in the context of Directive 93/13 national courts may therefore decide that 'particularly vulnerable' consumers should be entitled to 'particularly transparent' contract terms. On the other hand, the *Buet* decision seems to include, as part of its rationale, the fact that the French measure was not generally restrictive, but only applied to the sale of educational material for the reason that this was targeted at particularly vulnerable consumers. Accordingly, one may draw the inference that more restrictive measures are allowed only when aimed at protecting particularly vulnerable groups of consumers and not when they have general application.

Another point made in *Buet* was that the directive at issue contained, like Directive 93/13, a minimum harmonisation formula entitling Member States to take more stringent measures for the protection of consumers: an interpretation by a national court that aims a protecting particularly vulnerable consumer would therefore still be allowed even if the ECJ had indicated, in its case-law, a different parameter.

A similar solution must be adopted should a state wish to adopt a higher standard of protection: comments in England indicate that the standard of intelligibility should be set by reference to the naïve and inexperienced consumer[32] or, alternatively, that of the 'ordinary consumer without legal advice'.[33]

[30] Case 328/87 *Buet v Ministère Public* [1989] ECR 1235.
[31] [1985] OJ L372/31.
[32] H Collins, 'Good Faith in European Contract Law' (1994) OJLS 248.
[33] Edwards, above n 16.

Interpretatio contra proferentem

The principle stated in the second part of article 5 that an ambiguous term must be interpreted in favour of the consumer is known with small variations to several European legal systems as the *contra proferentem* rule.[34]

In Italy, as previously explained, the hierarchy of rules of interpretation envisaged by the Civil Code has privileged the use of subjective rules of interpretation to the detriment of article 1371cc. The *contra proferentem* rule is now re-stated in article 35 of the Consumer Code: the fact that the Consumer Code is defined as the 'general law for consumers' arouses hope that the principle, previously embedded in article 1371 cc, will now be given priority over the other criteria for interpretation of the civil code. Hence, it is hoped that its weight and importance in judicial decision-making will remarkably increase.

In England, the rule of *interpretatio contra proferentem* was widely used in the pre-UCTA case-law, where the lack of any other remedy forced judges into adapting and stretching the existing rules and techniques to provide fair solutions; and, although this practice had received some judicial disapproval after the enactment of UCTA, rules of interpretation continue playing a role in cases which did not fall within the scope of UCTA. The Law Commission, however, takes the view that the test under article 5, which imposes that the interpretation *most* favourable to the consumer be taken into account, is more comparable to 'the extreme way in which, before the advent of statutory controls over exemption clause, the courts sometimes applied the common law rule'.[35] It is evident, on the other hand, that such a rule alone is a weak weapon against clearly drafted terms, or terms which although capable of more than one meaning are still detrimental to the consumer.

In addition, an interpretation favourable to the consumer is not always desirable: in the interest of the best possible consumer protection, a disadvantageous interpretation of an individual clause may be, at the end of the day, more beneficial to the consumer if it renders the term unfair and therefore void: in that case, the remaining contract terms may put the consumer in a better position than with an unclear clause interpreted favourably. For this reason the rule does not apply to collective litigation (article 5 of Directive 93/13): while in individual cases it could generate positive results for the consumer who may have an interest in the survival of the term, in the case of collective action it would ultimately rebound on consumers by preventing the prohibition, via collective actions, of obscure terms which, in a normal interpretation, would be deemed unfair.

[34] Art 5, however, is formulated so as to always favour a specific party, the consumer. The interpretation *contra proferentem* known to other legal systems (including Italy) may operate so as work to the advantage of either contracting party, depending on who tries to rely on a certain term or on who drafted it.

[35] Law Commission Consultation Paper no 166, above n 19, at para 3.74.

SUBSTANTIVE CONTROLS

The fairness test in article 3 of Directive 93/13

According to article 3 of the Directive, a contract term is unfair if:

—it causes a significant imbalance in the parties' rights and obligations arising under the contract, to the detriment of the consumer;
—it is contrary to the requirement of good faith.

The 1990 proposal of the Commission[36] started from a very different approach to the definition of unfair terms: in an attempt to ensure that all the criteria already used in national systems are echoed in the Directive it contained four alternative criteria for the assessment of fairness of contractual terms; failure of a term to comply with just one of them could render it unfair and therefore unenforceable.[37]

The inclusion of the requirement of good faith among the proposed criteria must be seen in the light of two factors:[38] first, the importance of such a principle within the framework of continental systems, in particular Germany; second, the fact that one Member State had already used good faith alone as a general criterion for the assessment of unfairness: the Portuguese law of 1985 on contract terms established, at article 16, that 'general contractual terms which are contrary to good faith shall be prohibited'. In addition, § 9 AGB-G (now § 307 BGB) included the principle of good faith in the general criteria of control of unfair terms.

In the 1992 Proposal[39] the criteria of control were reduced to two; good faith lost its status as an independent criterion and was combined with the other two criteria. A term would then be considered as unfair when, contrary to the requirement of good faith,

—it causes to the detriment of the consumer a significant imbalance in the parties' rights and obligations arising under the contracts; or
—it causes the performance of the contract to be significantly different from what the consumer could legitimately expect.

[36] Proposal for a Council Directive on Unfair Terms in Consumer Contracts COM/90/322 final OJ C243, 28 September 1990, 2.

[37] A term could be unfair in the following cases: (1) it caused, to the detriment of the consumer, a significant imbalance in the parties' rights and obligations arising under the contract; or (2) it caused the performance of the contract to be unduly detrimental to the consumer; or (3) it caused the performance of the contract to be significantly different from what the consumer could legitimately expect; or (4) it was incompatible with the requirement of good faith.

[38] M Tenreiro, 'The Community Directive on Unfair Terms and National Legal Systems' (1995) 3 *European Review of Private Law* 275. Tenreiro (a Portuguese national) was Head of the Legal Matters Unit at the time when the Directive was drafted.

[39] Amended Proposal for a Council Directive on Unfair Terms in Consumer Contracts COM/92/66 final OJ C73, 24 March 1992, 7.

The reason why good faith as an independent criterion was removed seems to lie in the 'visceral aversion'[40] of the representatives of certain Member States, such as the UK, to this principle. Accordingly, in order to 'save' the principle, the Commission had to deprive it of its autonomy and to add a recital in order to clarify the values lying behind it. It therefore comes as no surprise that some of the guidelines on the meaning of good faith contained in Recital 16 of the Directive closely resemble the reasonableness criteria embedded in UCTA: 'the strength of the bargaining positions of the parties, whether the consumer had an inducement to agree to the term and whether the goods or services were sold or supplied to the special order of the consumer' all sound familiar to common lawyers. In addition to this, the Recital states that good faith involves 'an overall assessment of the interests involved' and that the seller or supplier must deal 'fairly and equitably with the other party whose legitimate interests he has to take into account'.

In spite of the Anglo-Saxon flavour, the continental origin of the fairness test under the Directive appears rather evident if we look at the German and French legislation: it will be recalled that the French *loi Scrivener* hinged the concept of unfairness upon the idea of 'avantage excessif' deriving from a term imposed on the consumer through an 'abus de puissance économique'[41] and in the *travaux préparatoires* explained this as meaning 'an evident imbalance in parties' rights and obligations'. The German AGB-G provided two lists of unfair terms, each of them having different effects, complemented by a general clause referring to the concepts of good faith (*Treu und Glauben*) and unreasonable disadvantage (*unangemessene Benachteiligung*).[42] The two criteria appear to be parallel: what matters in both cases is the objective imbalance which needs to be out of proportion, 'significant'; this equates to the criteria set out in the Directive.

Since the negotiations leading to the first proposal of the Directive, there has been concern that the notion of unfairness expressed by the general clause would lack sufficient accuracy and precision to be applied in a uniform way in all Member States. An Annex containing an indicative and non-exhaustive 'grey' list of terms that *may* be considered unfair was therefore added to the Directive with the purpose of providing a more detailed and practical elaboration of the notion of unfair term.[43]

[40] Tenreiro, above n 38, at 277–78.

[41] The French law seems to include a requirement of procedural fairness inherent in the exploitation of a stronger bargaining power. However, courts and doctrine have consistently held that the two criteria tend to overlap since the term conferring an excessive advantage is deemed to have been imposed through the abuse of one party's bargaining strength, see J Ghestin and I Marchessaux 'L'élimination des clauses abusives en droit français, à l'épreuve du droit communautaire' (1993) *Revue Européenne de Droit de la Consommation* 80.

[42] According to K Weil and F Puis ('Le droit allemand des conditions génèrales d'affaires revu et corrigé par la directive communautaire relative aux clauses abusives' (1994) 1 *Revue Internationale de Droit Comparé* 126) the Directive has been drafted 'en des termes de plus en plus allemands'.

[43] The content of the Annex varied remarkably from the first to the second proposal of the Commission. In 1990 the Commission not only wanted to add a list of unfair terms (the nature of which was not clear), but also wanted to force Member States to harmonise certain rules on contracts of sale by conferring certain rights on purchasers. This proposal required the achievement of a high level of harmonisation and therefore attracted criticism for 'its rather unusual method to pursue

Judges (or any other national competent authorities) have the possibility of assessing the fairness of a clause corresponding to a model clause in the Annex with full freedom: a contract term that corresponds to one of the models in the Annex is not automatically unfair just as a contract term not included in the list is not automatically fair.

The fairness test: implementation

The uncertainty and confusion that have surrounded the implementation of article 3 of the Directive in Italy are mainly due to the clumsy formulation of the corresponding article 33 Consumer Code (formerly article 1469-bis para 1 cc) According to this provision,

> terms in a contract between a consumer and a professional are regarded as unfair (*vessatorie*)[44] when, in spite of good faith, they cause a significant imbalance in the rights and obligations arising out of the contract to the detriment of the consumer.

This formula seems to be a servile reproduction of the text of the Directive but, in fact, it misinterprets the requirement envisaged by the Community legislator.

The version of the Directive in the other languages and Recital 16[45] make it clear that good faith must be understood in an objective and not a subjective sense. Untranslatable nuances of the Italian formula, on the other hand, suggest the adoption of a subjective meaning of good faith: a term will be considered as unfair if, in spite of the (good) intentions of the trader, it causes a significant imbalance in the rights and obligations arising out of the contract to the detriment of the consumer.[46] As a consequence, the question of the correct interpretation of article 1469-bis para 1 occupied the greatest part of academic comments and concerns: however, there is currently widespread agreement that reference should be to objective good faith.

private law harmonisation virtually through the backdoor of an Annex of a Directive that supposes to aim predominantly at controlling unfair contract terms' (M Tenreiro and J Karsten, 'Unfair Terms in Consumer Contracts: Uncertainties, Contradictions and Novelties of a Directive' in H Schulte-Nölke R Schulze (eds) *Europäische Rechtsangleichung und nationale Privatrechte* (Baden-Baden, Nomos, 1999, 284). In the 1992 version the Commission abandoned that proposal and presented a list similar to the one contained in the final text, but classified it as a 'black list'. Unfortunately, once adopted by the Council, the list no longer matched the expectations of the Commission and was defined 'indicative and non-exhaustive'.

[44] It must be noted that art 1469-bis used the word *vessatorio* (as in art 1341) rather than *abusivo*, which was the term employed by the Italian version of the Directive. The Consumer Code adopts the art 1341 terminology.

[45] According to Recital 16 good faith must be appreciated by reference to an 'overall evaluation of the interests involved', including 'the strength of the bargaining position of the parties . . . whether the consumer has received an inducement' and whether 'the seller or supplier . . . deals fairly and equitably with the other party whose legitimate interests he has to take into account'.

[46] For a history of the mistake see U Ruffolo, *Clausole 'vessatorie'e 'abusive'. Gli artt.1469-bis e seguenti del codice civile e i contratti del consumatore* (Milano, Giuffrè, 1997) 39–42.

The fact that the misinterpretation already existed in the Italian version of the Directive is a sign of the dangers inherent in the multi-linguistic law-making process at Community level; and the fact that the Italian Government, aware of the mistake, maintained the wrong text is a worrying sign of carelessness in the implementation process.[47] For the rest, the Italian implementation follows closely the wording of the fairness test in the Directive as far as the circumstances to be taken into account are concerned (article 34 consumer code).

In England, the fairness test has been faithfully reproduced in Regulation 5(1). Thus, a term is unfair 'if, contrary to the requirement of good faith, it causes a significant imbalance in the parties' rights and obligations under the contract, to the detriment of the consumer'. It is further provided that, in assessing whether a term is unfair, account should be taken of 'the nature of the goods or services for which the contract was concluded and by referring, at the time of conclusion of the contract, to all the circumstances attending the conclusion of the contract and to all the other terms of the contract or of another contract on which it is dependent.'[48] It should be noted that this is expressed to be without prejudice to Regulation 12, which deals with the public enforcement of the Regulations by the OFT and other bodies.

The introduction of a fairness test containing the 'good faith' criterion has revived the terms of the debate, started in the late 1950s, on whether a concept of good faith should be adopted in English contract law.[49] To sum up briefly the terms of the debate, a negative, a neutral and a positive view can currently be identified.[50] The negative view, represented by Lord Ackener's statement in *Walford v Miles*[51] is based on the argument that good faith is incompatible with

[47] Art 33 consumer code hides another ambiguity. '*Malgrado la buona fede*' is subject to two interpretations: first, *malgrado* may be interpreted as 'in spite of', meaning that the behaviour of the trader is irrelevant: no matter whether he was in good faith or not, a term that causes a significant imbalance will be held to be unfair: the only requirement to fulfil in order to prove that a term is unfair would be the 'significant imbalance', and one would therefore wonder why good faith is mentioned at all; second, *malgrado* may be understood as 'contrary', thus meaning that a term is unfair if it causes a significant imbalance and, in addition to this, is contrary to good faith, ie the professional did not deal fairly and equitably; this interpretation is less favourable to the consumer but seems more compliant with the spirit of the Directive and with the other linguistic versions of the Directive, including the English one, which in this respect leaves no room for doubt.

[48] Regulation 6(1).

[49] Various texts in English language have been written on good faith in general and on good faith in English law. For the purposes of this work, useful sources have been found in the following texts: C Willett (ed) *Aspects of Fairness in Contract* (London, Blackstone, 1996); R Brownsword, N Hird and G Howells (eds) *Good Faith in Contract* (Aldershot, Dartmouth, 1999); J Beatson and D Friedmann (eds) *Good Faith and Fault in Contract Law* (Oxford, Clarendon Press, 1995); R Brownsword, 'Contract Law, Co-operation and Good Faith: the Movement from Static to Dynamic Market Individualism' in S Deakin and J Michie (eds) *Contracts, Co-operation and Competition* (Oxford, OUP, 1997); JF O' Connor, *Good Faith in English Contract Law* (Aldershot, Dartmouth, 1989).

[50] For a useful overview of such doctrines see R Brownsword, 'Positive, Negative, Neutral: The Reception of Good Faith in English Contract Law' in Brownsword, Hird and Howells (eds) *Good Faith in Contract*, previous n, 13–40.

[51] 'The concept of a duty to carry on negotiations in good faith is inherently repugnant to the adversarial position of the parties when involved in negotiations. Each party to the negotiations is entitled to pursue his (or her) own interest, so long as he avoids making misrepresentations . . . a duty to negotiate in good faith is unworkable in practice as it is inherently inconsistent with the position of a negotiating party'. [1992] AC 138.

the adversarial ethic underpinning English contract law and that the moral standards imposed by good faith are unclear and vague, threatening to import uncertainty into English law. The neutral view holds that there is nothing objectionable about good faith but that English law already has its doctrinal tools to achieve the results which are achieved via a good-faith doctrine in other legal systems.[52] This view assumes that there is a strict equivalence between a general doctrine of good faith and the piecemeal provisions of English law. The positive view[53] argues that the adoption of a good faith doctrine would allow judges to give effect to their sense of justice and to avoid contortions and subterfuges.

The above views must be combined with a clarification of what exactly is meant by 'good faith': 'good faith' is, after all, an 'empty shell', a mere formula that needs to be fleshed out with a precise meaning.[54] In principle, different conceptions of good faith in the context of academic debates oscillate between two poles, one of 'procedural good faith' and one of 'substantive good faith'. Procedural good faith focuses on improprieties and defects in the negotiation and conclusion of the contract and would accordingly include, inter alia, all the techniques currently existing in English law to prevent dishonest and unfair behaviours. Substantive good faith, on the other hand, is independent from any procedural consideration and rather aims at imposing an abstract standard of contractual justice which is drawn from somewhere else.

Unsurprisingly for a country where good faith is considered 'mysterious and exciting',[55] the recent Unfair Terms Bill[56] proposes to rely merely on the 'fair and reasonable' criterion already existing under UCTA.[57] The Law Commission considered that it was neither necessary nor desirable to include an explicit reference to good faith: first because the question of forms and methods of implementation are a matter for Member States; second, because good faith is unfamiliar to English and Scots lawyers; third, because it is considered to be confusing and likely to mislead. None of those justifications would stand should the Commission bring infringement proceedings against the UK: the relevant point is that the UK should prove that the final outcome of the 'fairness and reasonable' test would be the same as that under article 3 Directive. The best reason for doing away with good faith seems to be that, as later discussed, it adds nothing to 'significant imbalance': however, since the exact meaning of the fairness test in the Directive itself is not clear

[52] This view is associated with Lord Bingham's statement that English law has arrived to the same position as other countries that have a good faith doctrine by developing 'piecemeal solutions in response to demonstrated problems of unfairness' *Interfoto Picture Library v Stiletto Visual Programmes Ltd.* [1989] QB 439.

[53] Expressed by R Powell in a seminal lecture on good faith, *Good Faith in Contracts* (1956) Current Legal Problems 16.

[54] An overview on how differently good faith operates in European countries that recognise this principle can be found in R Zimmermann and S Whittaker (eds) *Good Faith in European Contract Law* (Cambridge, CUP, 2000).

[55] Collins, above n 32, at 249.

[56] Law Commission and the Scottish Law Commission, *Unfair Terms in Contracts* Law Commission Report no 292 Cm 6464 (2005).

[57] S 11(1) UCTA.

it is difficult to determine whether the Bill reflects it faithfully enough, and only its practical application, hopefully combined with some clarification by the ECJ, will tell whether the intentions of the Directive are preserved, in which case there are no objections to couching the fairness test in different terms.[58]

The Bill also includes detailed guidelines on the application of the 'fair and reasonable' test, drawn in part from Directive 93/13 and in part from UCTA and the UCTA case-law.[59]

Although the formula 'indicative and non exhaustive' does not say anything concerning the obligation to transpose it,[60] both Italy and the UK have transposed the Annex and left it as a 'grey list'. While in England Schedule 2 to the Regulations literally 'copies' the Annex of the Directive, the Italian implementation has the originality of having split the terms there contained into two lists. The one in article 36(2) consumer code contains a list of terms that may be ineffective even when individually negotiated;[61] article 33(2) contains the remaining fourteen groups of terms, expanded to twenty, more detailed, sets of terms, which are 'presumed' to be unfair.[62] If a term falls within this list, the burden of proving that it is not unfair will lie on the trader, with an inversion of the general rules of civil procedure (whereby the burden of proof is on the plaintiff).

The fairness test: possible interpretations

Little assistance can be provided by the case-law of the Court of Justice as to the meaning of good faith: the few references to good faith in judgments of the Court of Justice concern subjective good faith, that is, a psychological condition, and not objective good faith, that is, a standard of fairness.[63]

[58] It may be argued that if among the tasks of the Directive one includes that of introducing the concept of 'good faith' in all legal systems so as to facilitate harmonisation, the fact that this is not mentioned in the Bill goes against the aim and spirit of the Directive. However, there is nothing in the Directive that suggests that this is its actual aim (while it may well be a side effect); moreover, the complexity of the issues involved in harmonisation of contract law deserves a more systematic and logical approach than sectoral intervention, see in this respect my discussion in the comment to *DGFT v FNB* (2003) CML Rev 983–95.

[59] Clause 14(4).

[60] On this point see C–478/99 *Commission v Sweden* [2002] ECR I–4147.

[61] These are terms which have the object or effect of (1) excluding or limiting trader's liability in the event of death or personal injury to the consumer resulting from an act or omission of the trader; (2) excluding or limiting the rights of the consumer against the trader or another party in the event of total or partial non-performance or inexact performance; (3) extending the consent of the consumer to terms which in the practice the consumer had no opportunity to be aware of.

[62] The word 'presumption' is used by the legislator in an a-technical manner. *Presunzione* in Italian law is a reasoning according to which from a fact which is known the interpreter can draw the inference that another (unknown) fact has occurred, and this unknown fact produces legal effects (so, for example, a child born in the course of a marriage is presumed—unless the contrary is proven—to be the child of the spouses, fact which produces legal effects). This is clearly not the meaning of 'presumption' in art 33(2), where it simply indicates a reversal of the burden of proof.

[63] See, eg, C–251/00 *Ilumitrónica-Iluminação e Electrónica Lda and Chefe da Divisão de Procedimentos Aduaneiros e Fiscais/Direção das Alfândegas de Lisboa* [2002] ECR I–10433.

As earlier mentioned, good faiith could be understood in a procedural sense, having to do with fair and open dealing:

> Openness requires that the terms should be expressed fully, clearly and legibly, containing no concealed pitfalls or traps. Appropriate prominence should be given to terms which might operate disadvantageously to the customer. Fair dealing requires that a supplier should not, whether deliberately or unconsciously, take advantage of the consumer's necessity, indigence, lack of experience, unfamiliarity with the subject matter of the contract, weak bargaining position.[64]

In other words, a term would be contrary to good faith (in a procedural sense) if the trader has dealt in any way unfairly or inequitably with the consumer: assessment of good faith would include verifying whether the consumer had an opportunity to influence the terms, whether he had been able to exercise any choice in agreeing to the terms or had any alternatives, whether the terms were expressed in intelligible language and readily available and whether the consumer understood them. In this respect, procedural good faith appears to be aimed at remedying any possible market failure in the form of lack of information and lack of choice.

Substantive good faith, on the other hand, involves an 'overall evaluation of the interests involved',[65] that is, it is related to the contractual terms themselves and focuses on whether and to what extent a term realises the interests of the consumer: so, for example, it has been suggested that good faith does more than exclude certain types of unacceptable conduct and includes terms causing such an *imbalance* that they should always be treated as being contrary to good faith and therefore unfair;[66] or that good faith encompasses all instances where one party has abused the social practice of making promises either by encouraging misplaced reliance or by securing *an unduly advantageous* transaction.[67]

If 'good faith' has to do with 'imbalance' or 'unduly advantageous' transactions, however, it is difficult to understand how it differs from the second part of the fairness test: a term which does not realise the interests of the consumer is a term that creates a 'significant imbalance', or anyway an 'imbalance', between the parties'

[64] Lord Bingham in *DGFT v FNB*, at 494. As noted by S Whittaker, this

> echoes the earlier observations of Bingham LJ (as he then was) in the Court of Appeal in *Interfoto Picture Library Ltd v Stiletto Visual Programmes Ltd* [1989] 1 QB 433, 429 made in the context of the treatment by English common law of unfair contract terms and before the enactment of the 1993 Directive.

See S Whittaker, 'Assessing the Fairness of Contract Terms: the Parties' "Essential Bargain", its Regulatory Context and the Significance of the Requirement of Good Faith' [2004] ZeuP 75, at p 86 fn 52.

[65] Recital 16 of Dir 93/13.

[66] H Beale, 'Legislative Control of Fairness: the Directive on Unfair Terms in Consumer Contracts' in J Beatson and D Friedmann (eds)*Good Faith and Fault in Contract Law* (Oxford, Clarendon Press, 1995) 245.

[67] Collins, above n 32, at 251. The distinction between substantive and procedural fairness found one of its first seminal discussions in by A Leff, 'Unconscionability and the Code—The Emperor's New Clause' (1967) 115 *University of Pennsylvania Law Review* 485.

rights and obligations and therefore overlaps, partially or totally, with this second requirement.[68]

Difficulties also arise when deciding the exact meaning and practical application of the 'significant imbalance' test. It is evident that 'significant imbalance' involves a lack of symmetry in parties' rights and obligations or that the seller's or supplier's rights or remedies are excessive and disproportionate; and that, on the contrary, 'balance' means that each risk placed on the consumer should be weighted against one placed on the business:

> for instance, a customer may buy goods which appear to carry a full warranty but find that the clause make the supplier sole judge of whether or not the goods are defective. The imbalance is that the seller can invoke a legal remedy against the buyer if the latter does not pay, but the buyer has no legal redress against the seller if the seller denies that the goods are faulty.[69]

It is difficult, however, to understand how this reasoning would apply, for example, to a clause excluding liability for consequential loss: 'since in the nature of things the seller cannot suffer consequential loss, the exclusion can only be balanced by adjustment in some other term in the buyer's favour'.[70]

Brownsword, echoed by Beale,[71] proposed that a clause should be judged unfair if, although it is compensated by a lower price, it exposes the customer to an unacceptable degree of risk; and an 'unacceptable' degree of risk is determined by reference to Rawl's 'veil of ignorance'. Applying this principle to 'significant imbalance' would mean that terms are fair when they could be accepted by rational agents who, without knowing on which side of the transaction they might stand, had to imagine themselves as parties to the transaction. Contracts which fail the test should not be upheld unless the losing party was consciously engaged in risk taking. Accordingly, it could be suggested that a term causes a 'significant imbalance' when it involves a risk that not only one customer would be reluctant to take, but so would most customers be.

Finally, it is not clear what the relationship between significant imbalance and good faith is. There are several possible combinations between the two notions.[72] The general view throughout Europe, supported by the wording of the Directive, is that the two requirements are cumulative,[73] that is, both must be satisfied for a term to be unfair. The same view, however, tends to confine the role of 'good faith' to that of being either a merely substantive requirement or of being 'ancillary' to

[68] See also R Browsword and G Howells 'The Implementation of the EC Directive on Unfair Term in Consumer Contracts—Some Unresolved Questions' (1995) JBL 255.

[69] H Beale, 'Unfair Contracts in Britain and Europe' (1989) *Current Legal Problems* 205.

[70] *Ibid* 205.

[71] *Ibid* 206.

[72] See the discussion in Law Commission Consultation Paper n 166, above n 19, at paras 3.57–3.62.

[73] See V Roppo,'Final Report from Workshop 3. The Definition of Unfairness' in *The Unfair Terms Directive: Five Years On*, Acts of the Brussels Conference, 1–3 July 1999 (Luxembourg, Office for Official Publications of the European Communities, 2000) 125.

[74] See for example M Tenreiro and E Ferioli, *Examen Comparatif des législations nationales transposant le Directive 93/13/CEE* in *The Unfair Terms Directive: Five Years On*, above n 10, at 17.

significant imbalance: this view has received some support from the European Commission[74] with the 'clearly political'[75] intention of avoiding the risk that good faith becomes a potentially harmful criterion for consumers.[76] A similar interpretation suggests that the function of good faith is to 'supplement' the test of significant imbalance so as to 'demonstrate irrefutably the inclusive nature of the assessment which the courts must undertake', this assessment requiring an 'overall evaluation of the different interests involved'.[77]

In line with this interpretation, Italian courts tend to assimilate the 'good faith' criterion to significant imbalance: a common formula used in decision making is that a term is unfair because it creates 'a significant imbalance of contractual duties and rights *which . . . is sufficient to render the term unfair*' (emphasis added):[78] good faith is, thus, completely ignored.

Similarly, the OFT does not appear to pay much attention to good faith when drawing up, in practice, the lists of various factors relevant to the fairness test. However, in their more theoretical explanations on the method of their work, they appear to favour a substantive approach to good faith: good faith does not

> equate with absence of bad faith in the narrow English sense of dishonest or deceptive conduct, in the way a term is likely to be used . . . We cannot challenge a term only if we have evidence that the supplier is likely to use it in bad faith. As previously noted, the mere absence of bad faith does not suffice to comply with the requirement of good faith. The legislation is directed at preventing contractual detriment generally, not just detriment that is caused by conscious malpractice . . .; the Directive, homing in as it does upon contractual 'imbalance' is concerned with drafting issues, not directly with the conduct of traders . . . For that reason, we take action where we consider that, on the balance of probabilities, a term involves a risk of consumer detriment, not merely where it could be proved that the detriment is likely to occur. . . . The task of the Director General is not to prove malpractice, nor to seek to impose penalties, but to identify and eliminate risks of consumer detriment in contract drafting.[79]

The Law Commission's current position is also to reject the idea that a term can be unfair unless there is both procedural and substantive unfairness, but rather that there are two routes to unfairness: substantive unfairness alone can make a term unfair,[80] but a term may also be unfair simply because of the circumstances in which it was incorporated into the agreement: for example, if the consumer had no reason to suspect that such a clause was in the contract.[81]

It seems, however that the fairness debate has so far concentrated on the ways that unfairness may arise (that is, for procedural or substantive reasons), but there is little discussion as to the *methods* of adjudication that courts use in their decision-making process on fairness. The task of the next few pages is therefore to

[75] Roppo, above n 73.

[76] Tenreiro and Ferioli, above n 74, at 17.

[77] Whittaker, above n 54, at 86.

[78] Tribunale di Roma 21 January 2000 in Foro Italiano 2046.

[79] Edwards, above n 16, at 17.

[80] Law Commission Consultation Paper no 166, above n 19, para 3.63.

[81] *Ibid* at paras 3.93 and 3.62.

review the practical application of the fairness test in Italy and England in an attempt to reformulate the terms of the fairness debate according to a different perspective.

DIFFERENT METHODS OF ADJUDICATION

Annex-based methods of adjudication

A common feature to the application of the fairness test in England and Italy is the importance of the grey list: correspondence with an item in the list, however, bears different consequences in the UK, where it raises a simple suspicion of unfairness, and in Italy, where it raises an actual presumption of unfairness. This is due to the different weight conferred to the list by the two legislators: according to article 33(2) of the Consumer Code, terms are 'presumed' to be unfair if their object or effect is among the ones included in the list; Regulation 5(5) UTCCR, on the other hand, defines Schedule 2 as an 'indicative and non-exhaustive list of the terms which *may* be regarded as unfair': accordingly, the OFT has undertaken the task of developing supplementary criteria that would help assess fairness.[82]

Apart from terms that exclude liability for the customer's death or personal injury caused by negligence, the validity of which appears to be a priori excluded, all the other terms listed in Schedule 2 of the Regulations are examined by the OFT in combination with a number of factors. Those include an assessment of whether a term has the potential to upset the original legal balance of the contract; to leave a significant number of consumers open to not getting what they were promised, paying more than what they bargained for, or obtaining no (or inadequate) redress for loss or damage caused by the trader's negligence. Whenever a term appears, on those grounds, suspicious, the OFT seeks to establish whether there are any other balancing provisions which, being detrimental to the supplier and linked to the term in question, tend to outweigh its effects: so, for example, a cancellation right for the trader might be considered fair if the consumer enjoys a right of equal extent and value (which does not necessarily mean a formal equivalence in rights to cancel). Alternatively, in the rest of the contract there may be qualifying provisions that remove the possibility of detriment in the term under suspicion. So, for example, terms that confer powers or safeguards to the supplier or subjecting the balance of the contract to changes to the detriment of the consumer are acceptable only (1) if narrow in effect; (2) if exercisable only for reasons stated in the contract which are clear and specific enough to ensure that the power of the trader cannot be used at will to suit the interests of the trader, or unexpectedly to the consumer; (3) if there is a duty on the supplier to give notice of any variation and the correspondent right of the consumer to cancel the contract.

[82] In February 2001, the OFT produced an *Unfair Contract Terms Guidance* (London, OFT, 2001) which is arranged according to the categories of unfair terms listed in Sch 2 to the Regulations (with two additional categories covering other types of unfairness); each category is then accompanied by a detailed explanation on why particular terms may or may not be held unfair.

The list of terms in Schedule 2 makes it clear that the Regulations introduce control on several types of terms, which were not previously covered by UCTA, even within its extended understanding of 'exemption clause'. Whereas UCTA can certainly challenge limitation of damages clauses and provisions which place obstacles in the way of legal claims and defences, such as elimination of the right of set-off, it does not reach, for example, the whole range of terms concerning agreed remedies: for example, UCTA cannot tackle retention of deposits from the consumer in breach of contract without an equivalent right to compensation for the consumer if the trader breaches the contract; terms which require the consumer to pay a disproportionately high sum in compensation for the breach; terms which confer discretionary power upon one contracting party to redefine contractual obligations and to determine whether breach of contract has occurred.

In this respect, Schedule 2 and the OFT guidelines certainly represent a useful aid to English lawyers in that they provide several examples of the variety and different forms of potentially unfair terms, beyond the ones which are already known under the UCTA case-law; but the Schedule does not represent the 'ultimate' authority on fairness.

In Italy, most of the case-law on unfair terms now concentrates on the application of the lists contained in articles 33(2) and 36 the Consumer Code. The lists provided by the legislator are wide enough to cover several types of potentially unfair terms and what is left to courts is the task of examining the practical effects of an allegedly unfair term and to verify whether or not it falls within one of the listed groups. So, for example, in the *Siremar* case the Tribunale di Palermo stated that a term that excludes the company's liability for all damages to persons and goods transported unless the consumer proves that the damage is due to the company's fault has the effect of introducing 'a reversal of the burden of proof (which) is *expressly forbidden* by article 1469-bis, para3 no 18' (now 33(2)(t)).[83] Particular success has been gained by article 33(2)(e) concerning terms that allow the professional to retain sums paid by the consumer where the latter does not conclude or cancels the contract without providing that the consumer receives from the trader twice that amount where the latter does not conclude or cancels the contract.[84]

Adjudication methods based on normative expectations

Another common feature to the Italian and English application of Directive 93/13 is that the fairness test has, in cases where a certain term affects consumers' statutory rights, revolved around the contract model provided by the legislator. So, for

[83] Tribunale di Palermo 3 February 1999 Foro Italiano 1999, I, 2085, at 2094. Similarly, the same court has held that a term that imposes on the consumer the payment of a deposit in case he withdraws from the contract without providing a similar obligation on the tour operator in case he cancels the contract was contrary to art 1469-bis No 5 (now art 33(2)(e) of the Consumer Code).

[84] Letter (d) of the annex mentions an amount which is equivalent, not double the amount paid by the consumer; the variation in the Italian implementation probably co-ordinates this provision with art 1385 cc on deposit which requires that the party who receives payment of a deposit pays twice that amount in the case where he cancels the contract.

example, the OFT has considered terms that deny buyers the right to full compensation where goods are mis-described or defective as potentially unfair under the Regulations (as well as void and unenforceable under other legislation). Similarly, the Corte d'Appello di Torino[85] has held that a term that replaces the remedies for non-conformity of the goods granted to the buyer by article 1490 cc with less effective remedies is unfair.

Beyond this prima facie similarity, the different characteristics of English and Italian law entail that this method of adjudication has different significance in the two systems. The detailed regulation in the Italian Civil Code or in separate legislation of the content and of the obligations attached to each type (*tipo*) of contract has allowed Italian courts to rely heavily on the balance envisaged by the legislator as the ideal point of reference of the fairness test (in particular the 'significant imbalance'); the OFT, on the other hand, has been unable to find in the English law of contract such an extensive description of the parties' obligations and has therefore been forced to resort to different criteria, that will be analysed in the following section.

In Italy, the ideal point of convergence between the parties' interests as envisaged by the legislator itself has been considered as the 'balance' with reference to which the 'significant imbalance' must be measured. In other words, the 'ideally balanced' contract is the one whose terms are established by the legislator itself by means of its *dispositive* provisions, that is, provisions which set out parties' rights and obligations with reference to each type of contract,[86] which can be derogated by the will of the parties and which therefore only apply where and when the contract does not envisage any different arrangements;[87] and the distance between the situation designed by the law and the one agreed upon by the parties, if not justified or elsewhere compensated, is the significant imbalance. So, for example, the Tribunale di Roma declared unfair a term establishing that where a certain loss was insured by different insurers, each of them was entitled to pay only a proportional share of the sum due. This, explained the court, reversed the rule of article

[85] Corte d' Appello di Torino 22 February 2000 in Giurisprudenza Italiana 2000, 2112, confirming Tribunale di Torino 16 April 1999 Foro Italiano 2000, I, 312.

[86] The distinction between *contratti tipici* and *atipici* is fundamental to Italian (and continental) contract law. In Title III of Book IV of the civil code (but also in separate laws) the legislator provides the legal framework for several types of contract (*contratti tipici*), ranging from sale to hire, from transport to agency, from banking to insurance contracts. Apart from some provisions which cannot be derogated by the parties, the rules provided for a certain type of contract are applicable to a transaction for all aspects which the parties do not choose to regulate themselves. However, parties are free to create *contratti atipici*, ie contracts of a type which is not envisaged by the law (as long as such contracts have a socio-economical purpose) but in this case the legal framework of the contract will have to be laid down by the parties themselves. For all aspects which are not regulated by the parties' agreement, the applicable rules will be the ones provided by the civil code (or other laws) for the type of contract which appears to be the closest to the one envisaged by the parties.

[87] Most of the rules of private law, as opposed to the rules of public law are '*dispositive*'. Usually the wording of a provision itself makes it clear whether it is *dispositiva* or *imperativa*: eg, art 1229 cc (any term that excludes liability for fraud of fault is void) is clearly *imperativa*. This basic distinction can be found in any textbook on obligations, such as Torrent Schlesinger, *Manuale di Diritto privato* (Milano, Giuffrè, 1995) 18–20.

1910 cc according to which each insurer is liable for the whole sum (but after paying he will be entitled to claim a partial refund from the other insurers).[88]

Even in cases where the contract under dispute does not prima facie fall within one of the 'tipi' regulated by the Consumer Code, courts would struggle to assimilate it to one of the models of the code in order to extract from there the set of obligations that tie parties to each other: so, for example, the *Pretura di Bologna*[89] found that a contract for the supply of private tuition by a private educational institute did not prima facie fall within the types regulated by the Consumer Code but at a closer look had many features in common with the type of contract envisaged by article 2230 cc (*contratto d'opera intellettuale*); to assess the fairness on certain terms contained in the contract between the institute and its students the court therefore referred to the model regulated by the above provisions.

This type of criterion is here called 'normative expectations'[90] as it relies on the expectations that may be generated by the existence of a set of legal rights embedded in the law (and that may have been altered by contractual agreement). This has, of course, very little to do with the expectations of the consumers, as consumers would very seldom know what exactly they are entitled to under the law.

Use of 'normative expectation'-based arguments is rather common in German law: as mentioned in Chapter 2, § 307 BGB expressly states that, in order to assess whether there is 'unreasonable disadvantage', one must take into account whether the provision at issue can be reconciled with essential basic principles of the statutory rule from which it deviates. Accordingly, in a case concerning the requirement that payment for a holiday package is made in advance, the BGH held that such a term would be fair, only if adequate guarantees of performance are provided to the holidaymaker (such as the handing over of the documents entitling him to the holiday).[91] To come to this solution, the court drew a parallel with the provisions of the BGB concerning the contract of supply, which prohibit any advance payment to the supplier.

This criterion has the advantage that it ensures a reasonable degree of predictability of the outcome of judicial decisions; however, it has a limited use, especially in countries where contract law is not codified or anyway not regulated in detail (as the OFT experience well demonstrates).

Adjudication methods based on reasonable expectations

In an individual action brought by a consumer against ENEL (Ente Nazionale Energia Elettrica), an Italian court had to examine, inter alia, the fairness of terms

[88] 28 October 2000 in Corriere Giuridico 2001, 385. See also Tribunale di Roma 21 January 2000, above n 78, at 2046 where the court declared unfair a term of a loan that allowed a security on the insolvent debtor's assets to a larger extent than the one established by art 190 cc.

[89] Pretura di Bologna 6 August 1998 Foro Italiano 1999, I, 384.

[90] Inspiration is here drawn from C Mitchell's 'Leading a Life of its own? The Roles of Reasonable Expectation in Contract Law' (2003) OJLS 639 but the definitions she gives of 'reasonable expectation' are slightly different from the ones given here.

[91] BGH 12 March 1987 in NJW c 1931.

that: (1) allowed ENEL to temporarily interrupt supply of energy in a set of listed circumstances and 'for any other needs'; (2) imposed on the customer the duty to pay any tax fee or any other fee related to the contract; (3) allowed termination of contract whenever the consumer failed to pay the bills within a very strict deadline and imposed on the consumer the duty to pay any expense incurred by ENEL in terminating or re-activating the contract. The answer to the question of the alleged unfairness of those terms is based on their common feature of giving rise to uncertainty for the consumer: due to those terms, the consumer is unable to foresee the financial consequences or anyway the effects of the contract. This amounts, according to the court, to

> a violation of objective good faith which imposes on each party, among other things, the duty to behave according to loyalty and clarity towards the other party in order to protect, as much as possible, his or her legal position.[92]

The application of good faith made by the court concerns neither the intelligibility and transparency of the language used nor the behaviour of the trader: it concerns the possibility for an individual to assess in advance his or her financial and legal position after signing a contract; its weight is that of an indicator of significant imbalance since the court later states that

> the imprecise and generic indication of the effects of a contract . . . gives rise to an unreasonable imbalance to the detriment of the consumer and accordingly the term must be considered unfair.

This is comparable to the approach that the OFT most commonly adopts in the application of the fairness test. As earlier mentioned, the OFT has identified a number of guidelines to unfairness in connection both with the terms included in Schedule 2 to the Regulations and with terms which are not in the list:[93] this includes considering whether a term allows the supplier to impose an unexpected financial burden on the consumer (eg an explicit right to demand payment of an unspecified amount at supplier's discretion); or makes the consumer carry risks which the supplier is better able to bear, remove or at least reduce by taking reasonable care (eg the risk of encountering foreseeable structural problems in installation work); or entitles the supplier to impose disproportionately severe penalties on the other or misleadingly threaten sanctions over and above those that can be really imposed.

A central feature of these 'indicators of unfairness' appears to be the concern that a significant number of consumers may be deprived of what they were promised, or would pay more than expected, or would obtain no (or inadequate) redress: in other words, all terms that render the consumer's position unforeseeable or that expose the consumer to unexpected disbursement appear to be regarded as potentially unfair. The leading rationale of the OFT's analysis appears therefore to be based on the idea that any term that deprives a consumer of what any reasonable consumer would expect from a certain contract is likely to be unfair.

[92] Tribunale di Palermo 7 April 1998 *I Contratti* 1998, 344.

[93] See terms listed in Group 18 of the OFT's *Unfair Contract Term Guidance* above n 82, at 41–51.

This seems to be the approach taken by the House of Lords in the case of *Director General of Fair Trading v First National Bank.*[94] In that case, the plaintiff Director General of Fair Trading (DGFT) sought an injunction pursuant to Regulation 8(2) of the Unfair Terms in Consumer Contracts Regulations 1994 restraining the defendant from:

1. including in any loan agreement a term making interest payable on the amount of any judgment obtained by the defendants for sums owed by the borrower under an agreement regulated by the Consumer Credit Act 1974;
2. enforcing or seeking to enforce any such term which had already been included in any existing agreement.

The reason for the existence of the term was that where a judgment is obtained under a contract for the loan of a principal sum owed by the borrower, the principal becomes due under the judgment and not under the contract: the contract merges in the judgment. If the contract contains a provision for the payment of an interest of the principal sum due, such term will merge in the judgment, which will accordingly govern also the entitlement of the creditor to claim interests. However, parties can expressly agree that a covenant to pay interests shall not merge in any judgment for the principal sum due, so that interests may still be charged under the contract.

According to the DGFT, such a term was unfair in that (1) it was unlikely to be noticed by the average borrower who, at the time of the judgment, would expect that if he discharged all the instalments under the judgment the debt would be cleared; (2) it deprived borrowers of the advantage afforded by the County Court (Interest on Judgment Debts) Order 1991, which excluded regulated agreements under the Consumer Credit Act 1974 from the imposition of interest on a judgment debt.

The application for the injunction was rejected in the High Court,[95] but later succeeded in the Court of Appeal;[96] upon further appeal, the House of Lords gave judgment against the DGFT and refused the injunction on grounds that the term was not unfair for a number of reasons, some of which will be analysed here.

The most interesting feature of the judgment is that it offers different views as to what expectations might be, including 'reasonable expectations'. Among the reasons given by the House Lord in favour of the fairness of the term one can read:

> if [the borrower's] attention were drawn to the impugned term . . . he might be well surprised at the need to spell this out, but he would surely not be at all surprised by the fact. It is what he would expect.[97]

The terms did not 'impose any further or unexpected liability upon [the borrower] not inherent in the basic transaction.' This was also the opinion of Evan LJ at first instance.

[94] [2001] 3 WLR 1297.
[95] [2000] 1 WLR 98.
[96] [2000] 2 WLR 1353.
[97] Lord Millett, above n 94, para 55.

All these criteria draw on the reasonable expectation of the ordinary consumer, that is, 'the objectively justified belief in the likelihood in some future event or entitlement'.[98] Terms that catch the consumer by surprise by imposing on him unexpected duties or deprive him of what he thought he was entitled to under the contract are considered to be in breach of the fairness requirement.

This criterion can ensure reasonably predictable decisions but has the drawback of having little innovative force: very often, consumers actually expect to find certain unfair terms in the contracts they sign, and it is therefore difficult to argue that their expectations are not fulfilled: in other words, if a certain unfair term is in common use, it will be held to match the reasonable expectation of the consumer and will not be considered as unfair; yet, one may think that the term is actually unfair and needs to be removed.

Adjudication methods based on contextual elements

In *DGFT v FNB* Lord Bingham also drew attention to the fact that the bank warns the consumer of the running interest by sending a letter to the defaulting borrower alerting him that interests continue to run;[99] for this reason, the consumer is no longer caught by surprise when he actually has to pay the interests due.

By shifting the focus of the fairness test from an assessment of the reasonable expectation of the ordinary custumer to the expectations of the specific customer, Lord Bingham's argument provides one example of what has earlier been called 'contextual justice':[100] although the case concerned a preventive action where no actual consumers were involved, the House of Lords placed emphasis on the conduct that the bank usually adopts towards its customers, thus taking into account specific circumstances occurring at the time when borrowers are in default with their payments.

Similarly, in *Westminster Building Company v Beckingham*[101] the High Court, in coming to the conclusion that an adjudication clause in a construction contract was not unfair, highlighted the fact that at the time of signing the contract the consumer had been assisted by a professional advisor; in a similar case,[102] where such an assistance had not been provided, the High Court gave judgment in favour of the consumer.

The contextual criterion has the advantage that it ensures that justice is made on a case-by-case basis but the level of predictability it generates is, as the UCTA experience shows, rather low. As discussed in Chapter 3, the contextual approach also presents the risk that it may easily lead to shifting the focus of the fairness test from the time of incorporation to the time when the contract is enforced: in *DGFT v FNB* Lord Bingham gave some weight to the argument that the bank used to send

98 Mitchell, above n 90, at 644.
99 [2001] 3 WLR 1297, 1310.
100 See Ch 4, pp 65–68.
101 [2004] EWHC 138.
102 *Picardi v Cuniberti* [2002] EWHC 2923.

the letter to its customers who were in default, thus implying that post-contractual conduct may be relevant to the fairness test: article 4(1) of Directive 93/13, on the other hand, requires that fairness of a term must be assessed 'having regard to the circumstances surrounding the conclusion of the contract'.

Another weakness of the contextual method is that, while it made perfect sense in the context of UCTA, which applied to all contracts (including business-to-business contracts and terms which had been negotiated), it is less easy to fit in the context of Directive 93/13, which specifically regulates contracts on standard forms, drafted in advance for an indeterminate number of contractual relationship with customers whose bargaining position is, by definition, one of inferiority. In other words, if the customer is a skilled lawyer who is able to understand the potentially detrimental effects of a term, he may be able, if he has sufficient bargaining power, to have the term changed: in this case, the Directive would no longer apply. If on the other hand, he does not manage to have the term changed, this means that he has not sufficient bargaining power and awareness that the term may operate in a way that may be unfavourable to him will not be of much comfort to him.[103]

Although the House of Lords, quite extraordinarily, applied criteria drawn from contextual method to preventive actions, it is pretty obvious that, in general, the contextual method of adjudication cannot be used in preventive actions: along these lines, the Tribunale di Torino has in one case refused to apply good faith to preventive actions brought by consumers' associations[104] on grounds that

> good faith must be understood in an objective sense as loyalty and correctness during the bargaining stage, that impose to the trader a duty to inform the consumer in detail about the terms in order to allow him an easy reading of the contract. This criterion does not appear to be usable in the case of preventive action given their abstract nature, in the same way as the 'circumstances at the moment of conclusion of the contract' . . . cannot be taken into account, since this must be attached to a practical case that does not exist in a preventive action.

Although the wording used is different, the Tribunale clearly referred to the contextual elements that may guide the fairness test.

That contextual elements are difficult to take into account in preventive actions is also confirmed by the OFT: for example, in assessing inequality of bargaining power between the parties (Schedule 2[3] to the Regulations) the OFT refers to abstract criteria and rather than looking at the position of the individual consumer (which would be impossible) they understands this criterion as relating to the trader's position in the market:

[103] Compare, on this point, the statement of the OFT that 'in no case has the argument that a term is intended to be applied in minor cases or as a shelter against unreasonable claims been accepted if the term at issue has the potential to upset the original legal balance of the contract' *Unfair Contract Terms Guidance*, above n 82, at 16.

[104] Tribunale di Torino 7 June 1999 in Foro Italiano 2000, I, 298; similar reasoning (by a different judge) can be found in Tribunale di Torino 16 April 1999 *ibid*, 312.

> we are not likely to accept unsupported professions of good faith from suppliers who are dominant in their markets and particularly those whom it is difficult for consumers to avoid continuing to deal with after an initial transaction.

Abstract fairness

Finally, there are some decisions that rely on criteria that can be defined as 'pure fairness', on standards of justice that are elaborated in a somehow more abstract fashion.

In *DGFT v FNB*,[105] the Court of Appeal emphasised that it was the fact that the term created an unfair surprise that made it contrary to good faith. In interpreting good faith, the court focused attention on the question whether a term which is not drawn to the customer's attention but which may operate in a way which the consumer might reasonably not expect to his disadvantage may offend the requirement of good faith. The court concluded that, in this respect, terms should not defeat the reasonable expectations of the consumer, who must be put in a position where he can make an informed choice. Does this mean that the Court of Appeal had a different perception of what consumers' expectations are as compared to the House of Lord? One cannot exclude that this may be so, but the most likely explanation is that the Court of Appeal was concerned not

> with what experience may lead the consumer to believe about interest payments, but with the normative issue of the substantive fairness of the term . . . The reference to reasonable expectation does not identify precisely why the clause is unfair and there are several possible grounds. Is it unfair because it may give rise to huge additional liability when the borrower thought he had extinguished the debt? because it was not brought to the borrower's attention? because the court rarely considers reducing the interest rate on post-judgment interests? or because it was contrary to the default position under general law?[106]

The answer to this seems to be that term simply appeared to the court to be unfair, and in this sense it was not 'reasonably expected'.

The abstract standard of fairness to which courts refer in these cases is often based on the idea of ensuring a symmetry of parties' duties and rights arising under the contract. In cases concerning terms allowing termination of the contract upon payment of a penalty, Italian courts have found unfairness where it appears that the other party is not entitled to the same right as the trader (who can, for example, terminate the contract at short notice and with no penalty due)[107] or to a similar one.[108] Behind the formal 'equality of weapons', courts have also questioned whether imposing the same right or duty on both parties has the same effect on them. The Tribunale di Roma, for example, has held that a term that gives to both parties to an insurance contract the right to cancel the contract after the

[105] Above n 94.
[106] Mitchell, above n 90, at 659.
[107] Tribunale di Palermo 2 June 1998 in Foro Italiano 1999, I, c 358.
[108] Tribunale di Torino 16 April 1999 in Foro Italiano 2000 I c 297.

occurrence of the loss covered by the policy creates a dramatic imbalance in favour of the insurer by increasing to the maximum possible extent the profit obtained from mass contracts and by reducing to the minimum the risk which he is willing to bear. Similarly, the same court held that a term in a loan agreement giving to both parties the right to cancel the contract with one day notice was unfair due the unreasonably short notice.[109]

This method of adjudication seems to be used rather frequently in German law: courts often refer to *Waffengleicheit* (parity of weapons), or to the *Aequivalenzprinzip* (principle of equivalence) as the guidelines driving their decisions. Just like the Tribunale di Roma, in assessing 'equivalence' they look at whether the similarity of weapons has the same effect for the consumer and for the trader:[110] for example, the BGH held to be unfair a term contained in a contract for the supply of water requiring that a customer whose water is also supplied by another supplier must pay a monthly charge, calculated on the basis of the highest consumption rate reached in previous months. The reason for the unfairness of the term was that were was no equivalence between performances, as the amount was calculated in a way that did not realistically reflect the costs that the supplier had to bear.

When such symmetry cannot be found, the research of the standard of fairness upon which the decision hinges becomes more difficult, and the reasoning may become muddled: as mentioned above, the reasons why the term in *DGFT v FNB* is unfair are not spelled out clearly by the Court of Appeal; the Tribunale di Torino, for example, held that a term providing a manufacturer's six-year guarantee against the rust of a car only if the owner took the car to periodical tests at the official Citroën dealer was not unfair, since the term was counter-balanced by the fact that the guarantee was given for a rather long lapse of time.[111] A more thoughtful answer, however, should have considered the extent to which the term allows the consumer to draw a clear picture of his/her position: the contract, for example, did not specify how often and at what charges the customer's car had to be taken for periodical tests—which is certainly an important element in determining whether the term gives rise to 'significant imbalance'.

This method may ensure fair results but it is difficult to apply where there is no symmetry of performances between parties' obligations to which one can refer and where there is not, as in Germany, a well-consolidated system of criteria that may guide its application: it would be difficult to apply, for example, in a case such as *DGFT v FNB*, as it would not be entirely clear where 'unfairness' is coming from, other than from the different perceptions judges have of as to what is fair and what is not, and as to who should bear the risk of non-performance: in *DGFT v FNB* the Court of Appeal must have made its own assumption as to who should bear the risk of the borrower not repaying in full and in due time: after all, the money-lending activity is, by its own nature, a risky one (and it is in view of such risks that banks charge interest rates).

109 Tribunale di Roma 21 January 2000 in Foro Italiano 2000, I, 2045.
110 BGH 30 May 1990 NJW 1990, II, c 2686.
111 Tribunale di Torino 7 June 1999, above n 104.

Methods of adjudication: concluding remarks

Although the case-law above examined shows that various methods of adjudication can, and usually do, co-exist within the same decisions, it is possible to identify the methods that tend to be more frequently used by national courts.

The most favoured method of the Italian courts is the annex-based one; this is immediately followed by 'normative expectations' approach, whereby courts seek their solution in the provisions of the civil code that regulate contractual arrangements and assess unfairness by reference to the *tipi* envisaged by the code as ideal models of contract balance: the further a term deviates from a default provision of the code, the higher the probability that it is found to be unfair. By so doing, courts have avoided to take into any account any considerations of socio-economical nature, such as whether consumers would 'reasonably expect' a certain term.

This shows that, as with the pre-Directive case-law, courts have not performed a highly creative role. Second, and more importantly, the courts' approach shows an understanding of the law as a closed system, with little relation to the social reality which it is meant to regulate. It has been explained that the reluctance of Italian courts to develop the poor cover of article1341 cc into a deeper form of control or to find other tools to interfere with unfair contractual arrangements has its roots in a particular conception of the law as a closed system, the 'purity' of which should not be contaminated by solutions that involve non-legal elements of reasoning: the solution to legal problems is to be found in the law itself, that is, in the provisions of the civil code. The use of Annex-based and normative expectations methods of adjudication reflects the same conception of the law.

Where the use of 'normative expectation'-based criteria has not been possible, courts have resorted to an 'abstract fairness' approach. Where possible, Italian courts try to ensure that there is formal and substantive symmetry between parties' rights and duties under the contract; where this is not possible, they appear to be unable to clearly identify and systematise the criteria governing its application, just as they had previously done with good faith (and unlike their German colleagues).

In England, some non-definitive guidance is provided by the Annex; for the rest, the absence of any detailed regulation of the content of different types of contract makes it more difficult to assess what is the ideal balance that the contract should achieve. Additionally, as Pollock's definition of contract as 'a promise or a set of promises recognized by the law' shows, contracts are perceived as an exchange of two sets of obligations which are somehow independent from each other; the interrelationship between the parties' obligations is therefore less important than it is in civil law, and this is also why doctrines of the type of *force majeure* developed at a relatively late stage. As a consequence, assessing one party's obligations in relation to the other's is not an operation which is commonly undertaken in common-law reasoning. To confirm this, it is sufficient to quote one comment made by a common lawyer to a decision of the OFT asking the amendment of a term that provided the possibility of getting compensation in case of cancellation of the contract only in favour of one party:

> what is noticeable about this approach is that the liability of the consumer in one scenario is looked at in conjunction with the liability of the seller or supplier in a different (but mirror image) scenario. This is a new development in English law. In the case of term (d) [of the annex] where the consumer forfeits sums to the seller or supplier where he (the consumer) does not conclude or perform the contract, English and Scots common law would focus on this side of the equation alone. Is the provision a deposit, and, if so, is it reasonable . . . In determining this sort of question the liabilities of the supplier in a reverse situation are not relevant.[112]

Accordingly, both the normative expectations and the abstract fairness criteria score pretty low in the judicial/OFT's records. On the other hand, the OFT and English courts seem to favour the principles of 'reasonable expectations' and the contextual method. The OFT's work of classification and systematisation of the 'indicators of unfairness' provides a clear and well-defined set of guidelines that allow, with a reasonable degree of certainty, advance assessment of the fairness of a term. The essence of the test lies in deciding whether a certain term deprives the consumer of what he would reasonably expect under a certain contract: such an assessment, however, is not made in relation to a specific context but it is made (due to the preventive nature of the actions brought by OFT) *in abstracto*. The decision of the House of Lords in *DGFT v FNB* includes elements drawn from both the reasonable expectations approach and the contextual approach. As with Italy, the methods of adjudication which are more popular among the common lawyers seem to reflect the ones that were used before the 1999 Regulations and which identified, as described in Chapter 4, the 'reasonable expectation' of the customer as the yardstick to determine whether a term is reasonable, whether it is incorporated into a contract, or how it has to be interpreted; occasionally, attention is paid to the specific features of the case which is being decided as per the common law tradition.

[112] C Willett 'Good Faith and Consumer Contract Terms' in Brownsword, Hird and Howells (eds) *Good Faith in Contract* above n 49, 85.

9

Conclusion: A European Tradition?

CONVERGENCE AND DIVERGENCE IN THE INTERPRETATION OF DIRECTIVE 93/13

AS STATED IN the Introduction, this book aimed to be a study in both comparative and EC law.

The comparative analysis has revealed that while Member States are well aware of the fact that European legislation has to be read 'as a single corpus of law binding across Europe',[1] the concepts and notions contained in Directive 93/13 (the Directive) are often interpreted, to various degrees, with reference to national legal traditions.

So, for example, the common law tradition of focusing on the reasonable expectations of the consumers and on the context of specific disputes deeply affects the way that English lawyers perceive the 'core terms' exclusion and the fairness test: as explained in Chapter 7, whether a term relates to the 'subject matter of the contract' or not is understood in the light of the reasonable expectation of the consumer, as well as the way that the bargain is presented to him and the way that the contract has been negotiated; and the fairness of a contract term is often evaluated in terms of consumers' reasonable expectations as far as preventive actions are concerned, in combination with contextual elements in the case of ex-post control. On the other hand, the traditionally abstract and impersonal nature of the Italian decision-making process has, for example, prompted doubts as to whether the persona 'consumer' could be a constitutionally acceptable means of determining the scope of protection against unfair terms; or has triggered an interpretation of the fairness test which is still largely based on the idea that the solution to legal problems should be found in the law itself.

In relation to some issues raised by the Directive, however, national courts' solutions seem to be converging. Sometimes this happens as a consequence of the intervention of the European Court of Justice (ECJ), that, through the Article 234 EC procedure provides a 'European dimension' to specific notions and concepts: this is the case, for example, with the notion of 'consumer', where the clarification provided by the ECJ has had the effect of dramatically altering the understanding of 'consumer' within the French and the English legal systems. In other cases convergence has occurred without the need for guidance by the ECJ: national courts

[1] Laws LJ in *R (Khatun and others) v Newham London Borough Council* [2005] QB 37 para 78

are sometimes aware of the special meaning that a certain concept has in EC law as opposed to the one it has in domestic law: one clear example is the way that common lawyers have handled the notion of 'good'. On some occasions, convergence has been the side effect of national courts' effort to enhance the effectiveness of the Directive by adopting the solution which is most favourable to the consumer: the desire to ensure the *effet utile* of the Directive and hence to adopt the most favourable interpretation for the consumer can probably explain convergence among national courts in relation, for instance, to the broad understanding of 'non-negotiated terms' (that ensures that Directive 93/13 is applied even where there has been some negotiation) and towards sanctioning lack of transparency with invalidity.

The high degree of divergence that persists in areas such as the definition of 'public service', 'contract', 'mandatory provision', 'core term', 'good faith' is explained by the fact that Directive 93/13 does not offer sufficient indications as to what exact meaning each of these concepts should have, or does so in an unclear way (as with the notion of 'good faith'): but this is a task which is usually entrusted to the ECJ through the preliminary rulings procedure.

Such a degree of divergence is, partly, an inevitable consequence of the nature of Directive 93/13 as a compromise among various legal traditions. The Directive borrowed from the French and the German systems the idea of 'significant imbalance' and that good faith involves an 'overall evaluation of the different interests involved'; but it closely resembles UCTA where it states (Recital 16) that good faith requires taking into account

> the strength of the bargaining positions of the parties, whether the consumer had an inducement to agree to the term and whether the goods or services were sold or supplied to the special order of the consumer.

These formulas may appear, to the naïve reader, as 'empty shells',[2] containers devoid of any clear meaning until a consolidated administrative and judicial practice or the Community court gives them some substance. In truth, such formulas are charged with meaning for those who interpret them: some parts of Recital 16 constitute an invitation, for a common lawyer, to refer to the reasonableness criteria used under UCTA; reference to contractual balance may well be understood by a German judge as an encouragement to apply the doctrine of *Waffengleicheit* or the *Aequivalenzprinzip*. Even Italian lawyers, who do not boast a proper 'tradition' in relation to unfair terms control, tend to adopt methods of adjudication that best reflect their legal thinking in deciding what 'contractual balance' is. In this sense, tradition is truly inescapable.

The aim of the 'European' part of this book has been to show that in some cases, as with the definition of 'public service' or 'mandatory', it is possible to distil from the existing Community *acquis* some enlightenment as to the interpretation that

[2] On the various different meanings of good faith see for example R Zimmermann and S Whittaker (eds) *Good Faith in European Contract Law* (Cambridge, CUP, 2000).

such concepts should be given in order to ensure the most effective and uniform application of European law; but in the cases where such a 'background' is missing, as with the definition of 'subject matter of the contract' the ECJ would have to start its hermeneutical analysis literally from scratch.

As the analysis in Chapter 8 demonstrates, methods of adjudication as to what is 'unfair' still very much reflect the ones used in the application of the previously existing domestic remedies. This is because there are no clear indications in the Directive (or in EC law in general) that one method of adjudication is more suitable than the other to ensure the attainment of the Directive's objectives. One may wonder whether it may be possible to identify such method by taking into account the aim and objectives of Directive 93/13.

It will be recalled from Chapter one that Directive 93/13 aims to achieve two objectives: increasing the level of consumer protection throughout Europe and reinforcing consumer confidence (as a way of contributing to the completion of the internal market).

As far as consumer protection is concerned, one needs to look for the solution which best ensures the achievement of the highest level of consumer protection. Although Community measures based on article 95 EC only have to ensure, according to para 3, a high (not the highest) level of consumer protection, the ECJ has so far interpreted Directive 93/13 so as to ensure the highest level of consumer protection.[3] It is difficult to identify a priori which of the methods of adjudication described at Chapter 8 can ensure the best outcome in terms of consumer protection: all criteria ensure, on average, the achievement of a similar standard, but not of similar results: a term may well be within the consumer's expectation but be considered unfair upon a more abstract assessment; a term which is reasonably expected by the consumer may be unfair because of the particular effects it has on a weak party; a term which is contrary to abstract fairness may be considered fair because the consumer is a particularly skilled one, or one who is well capable of bearing the loss. A Solomonic solution to the problem would entail that the method of adjudication to be applied in each case is the one which ensures, in the specific case, the most favourable outcome for the consumer. This solution may, however, be rather confusing for judges and little practicable as it would require a 'comparative review' of all criteria before a decision is made.

In terms of enhancement of consumer confidence, it has been explained in Chapter 2 that the rationale of the Directive is to ensure that consumers may be confident that, wherever they go, they can rely on a minimum threshold of protection, with no 'bad surprises': in other words, that their expectations as to what they will get under the contract will be fulfilled. This principle is reinforced by the ECJ in *Commission v Sweden*[4] where it held that

[3] See cases C–240/98 *Océano Grupo Editorial SA v Murciano Quintero* [2002] 1 CMLR 43; C–473/00 *Cofidis SA v Jean-Louis Fredout* [2002] ECR I–10875 and the Opinion of Tizzano AG in C–168/05 *Mostaza Claro v Centro Movil Milenium SL* nyr available at <http://www.curia.eu.int>

[4] C–478/99 [2002] ECR I–4147, para 18.

> it is essential that the legal situation resulting from national implementing measures be sufficiently precise and clear and that individuals be made fully aware of their rights so that, where appropriate, they may rely on them before the national courts. . . . The latter condition is of particular importance where the directive in question [Directive 93/13] is intended to confer rights on nationals of other Member States as is the case here.

This seems to suggest that the method of adjudication based on the 'reasonable expectations' is the most suitable to ensure consumer confidence. In addition, 'reasonable expectation' already enjoys the status of a well recognised parameter for adjudication in EC consumer law.[5] On the other hand, article 4 of Directive 93/13 requires that the unfairness of a term is assessed having regard to all the circumstances attending the conclusion of the contract, thus hinting at a contextual approach, while the reference in Recital 16 to an 'overall evaluation of the different interests involved', suggests a more abstract approach. Elements drawn from different criteria can also be found in *Océano*, where the ECJ has held that a term conferring jurisdiction on a court within whose territory the seller has his principal place of business was unfair as it was

> solely to the benefit of the seller and contained no benefit in return for the consumer. Whatever the nature of the contract, it thereby undermined the effectiveness of the legal protection of the rights which the Directive affords to the consumer. It was thus possible to hold that the term was unfair without having to consider all the circumstances in which the contract was concluded and without having to assess the advantages and disadvantages that that term would have under the national law applicable to the contract.[6]

As a result, the approach that courts should take towards the fairness assessment has not yet been spelled out clearly.

THE EUROPEAN COURT OF JUSTICE AS THE ENGINE OF EUROPEAN INTEGRATION?

One would expect that, in this respect, the ECJ will provide the necessary enlightenment through the Article 234 EC procedure. It must be borne in mind, however, that national courts are not always willing to generate the waves of the European tide which is, with increasing frequency, lapping the shores of domestic contract law. This is clear if one examines the House of Lords decision in *DGFT v FNB*.[7] In justifying the House of Lords' refusal to refer the case to the ECJ, Lord Bingham relied on the *acte clair* doctrine and observed that 'the language used in expressing

[5] See, eg, article 2(2) of Directive 1999/44/EC (OJ 1999 L171/12) providing that

> consumer goods are presumed to be in conformity with the contract if they . . . (d) show the quality and performance which are normal in goods of the same type and which the consumer can reasonably expect; article 4(2) of Directive 92/59/EEC (OJ 1992 L228/24) providing that the conformity of a product to the general safety requirement shall be assessed having regard . . . the safety which consumers may reasonably expect.

[6] Above n 3, para 23.

[7] [2001] 3 WLR 1297.

the [fairness] test, so far as applicable in this case, is . . . clear and not reasonably capable of differing interpretations'.[8] It is evident, on the other hand, that the questions at issue in the case were far from being *acte clair*. First, if the case had been 'clear' it would not have reached the House of Lords after the Court of Appeal had reversed the decision of the High Court which had in turn refused to award the injunction requested by the *DGFT*. Second, Lord Bingham himself suggested that 'Member States have no common concept of fairness or good faith', and it is exactly when concepts are vulnerable to the possibility of differing interpretations in differing Member States that questions need to be referred to the ECJ. Lord Bingham himself appeared to be well conscious of national courts' role under Article 234 Treaty when, sitting in the High Court in *Samex*[9] (a case concerning customs duties) a few years earlier, he expressed the following view:

> Sitting as a judge in a national court, asked to decide questions of Community law, I am very conscious of the advantages enjoyed by the Court of Justice. It has a panoramic view of the Community and its institutions, a detailed knowledge of the Treaties and of much subordinate legislation made under them, and an intimate familiarity with the functioning of the Community market which no national judge denied the collective experience of the Court of Justice could hope to achieve. Where questions of administrative intention and practice arise the Court of Justice can receive submissions from the Community institutions, as also where relations between the Community and non-Member States are in issue. Where the interests of Member States are affected they can intervene to make their views known . . . Where comparison falls to be made between Community texts in different languages, all texts being equally authentic, the multi-national Court of Justice is equipped to carry out the task in a way which no national judge, whatever his linguistic skills, could rival. The interpretation of Community instruments involves very often not the process familiar to common lawyers of laboriously extracting the meaning from words used but the more creative process of applying flesh to a spare and loosely constructed skeleton. The choice between alternative submissions may turn not on purely legal considerations, but on a broader view of what the orderly development of the Community requires. These are matters which the Court of Justice is very much better placed to assess and determine than a national court.[10]

Samex was, however, a case concerning customs duties, an area which is commonly accepted as being largely subject to European interference; *DGFT v FNB* raised issues that go straight to the core of a much more secluded and traditionally impermeable area of law. Yet, this would have been a perfect case to refer to the ECJ and the absence of an ECJ ruling on the fairness test is now lamented.[11]

The recent case-law of the ECJ shows that national courts may not be alone in their reluctance to involve the ECJ in the interpretation of the fairness test. In Freiburger *Kommunalbauten GmbH Baugesellschaft & Co KG v. Hofstetter*[12] the

[8] *Supra* note 8, 1307.

[9] *Commissioners of Customs and Excise v Samex ApS* [1983] 3 CMLR 194.

[10] *Ibid.* 210–11

[11] S Whittaker, 'Assessing the Fairness of Contract Terms: The Parties' "Essential Bargain", its Regulatory Context and the Significance of the Requirement of Good Faith' (2004) ZeuP 90.

[12] C–237/02 [2004] 2 CMLR 13 ECJ.

ECJ was asked to rule on the validity of a clause obliging the consumer to pay the price before performance of the obligations owed by the supplier (who was, in turn, under an obligation to provide a guarantee).

The court replied that the answer to the question whether a particular term in a contract is, or is not, unfair, lies with the national court: the jurisdiction of the court to interpret Community law does not extend to the interpretation of contractual terms at issue in a specific case before a national court.[13] The ECJ noted that article 4 of the Directive provides that the answer should be reached taking into account the nature of the goods or services for which the contract was concluded and by referring, at the time of conclusion of the contract, to all the circumstances attending the conclusion of the contract: in that respect, the consequences of the term under the law applicable to the contract must also be taken into account. This requires that consideration be given to the national law, rather than involving a question of Community law. The Court also distinguished the *Océano* case by pointing out that, in that specific case, the unfairness of the term was so obvious that it did not require any analysis of the underlying facts.

It is unusual for the ECJ not to accept the invitation to further refine Community legislation: they could certainly have done so without entering into the details of the case.

The problem may be with the way that Article 234 EC operates in relation to contract law. In this area, more than in others, certain notions and concepts of contract law already have a well-consolidated meaning in domestic law: this seems to be irrelevant, however, in a European context as the multi-lingual nature of Community law making and the peculiarity and specificity of European language and concepts exclude that domestic language can be nonchalantly used by national courts in interpreting European-derived legislation. Community law itself uses language peculiar to itself. The problem is that most words in the 'European dictionary' have not yet been defined: this is done, occasionally, by the ECJ who carries out such a task by depriving words of their 'national clothes' and giving them 'European' ones.

This is illustrated by the decision in *Leitner v TUI Deutschland GmbH & Co KG.*[14] The ECJ had to decide whether compensation under article 5 of the Package Holidays Directive[15] includes non-material damages caused by loss of enjoyment of the holiday. There was no express provision in the law of the referring country (Austria) to compensation for non-material damage of that kind, and it was submitted by the Austrian Government that the harmonisation sought by the directive consists only of defining a minimum level of protection for consumers of package holidays: it does

[13] Geelhoed AG at para 25.

[14] C–168/00, judgment of 12 March 2002 available at http://<www.curia.eu.int>

[15] Council Directive 90/314/EEC of 13 June 1990 on Package Travel, Package Holidays and Package Tours (Package Holidays Directive) OJ 1990 L158, 59.

> no more than set out a body of essential common rules concerning the content, conclusion and performance of package tour contracts without exhaustively regulating the entire subject, in particular matters relating to civil liability.[16]

The ECJ, on the other hand, took a broader approach to the scope of the directive and emphasised that different interpretations of 'compensation' within the Community would give rise to distortions of competition and undermine the effectiveness of consumer protection offered by the directive: the directive therefore implicitly recognised the existence of a right to compensation for damages other than personal injury. It is obvious that, in so doing,

> the ECJ may often unintentionally achieve outcomes that institutionally and politically the Community law-making bodies would have been unable to achieve (such as a common understanding of the extent of the right to compensation). This is due to the fact that the ECJ operates within an institutional and political framework which is free from the restraints and hindrances to which the European legislator is subject.[17]

One may therefore wonder whether there are any limits to the task that the ECJ is required to undertake.

Dougan notes[18] that consumer directives, being minimum harmonisation measures (at least they used to be, until a couple of years ago) are characterised by less need for uniformity as regards national remedies and procedures to enforce them. On the other hand, 'the problems of effectively enforcing consumer protection legislation are aggravated by sector-specific factors', such as the fact that many consumers are unaware of their rights or have little incentive to pursue them, as also noted by the ECJ in *Océano*. 'Such factors—Dougan argues—might well demand a high level of Community intervention in the domestic systems of judicial protection': this has been the case in *Océano*, and, if the ECJ is to follow the opinion of Tizzano AG, in the *Mostaza* case. Both cases concern enforcement of consumers' rights, rather than clarification of their substantive content.

Along the same lines, it is possible that, for example, the ECJ would demand that French courts disregard the doctrine of separation of power as laid down in the *arrêt Septfonds*[19] when it comes to deciding matters concerning the fairness of terms contained in contracts for the provision of public services. The concern for uniformity and effectiveness of the Directive 93/13 in procedural matters as opposed to the lack of interest as to the substantive definition of fairness may suggest that the ECJ does not see a need for uniformity in the substantive concepts of the Directive; this is equivalent to stating that, as suggested in the course of the analysis carried out in Chapter 2, the ECJ does not see Directive 93/13 as a measure of market integration, but simply as one of consumer protection: in order to ensure consumer protection, effectiveness and uniformity of remedies are far more important that the uniformity of substantive concepts.

[16] *Ibid* para 16.

[17] P Nebbia, case note on *DGFT v First National Bank* [2001] 3 WLR 1297 in (2004) CML Rev

[18] M Dougan, *National Remedies Before the Court of Justice* (Oxford, Hart, 2004) 211.

[19] Tribunal des Conflits 16 June 1923, Recueil Dalloz 1924, 3, 41.

Appendix I
Directive 93/13

Council Directive 93/13/EEC of 5 April 1993 on Unfair Terms in Consumer Contracts OJ L95/29

The Council of the European Communities,

Having regard to the Treaty establishing the European Economic Community, and in particular Article 100 A thereof,

Having regard to the proposal from the Commission [1],

In cooperation with the European Parliament[2],

Having regard to the opinion of the Economic and Social Committee[3],

Whereas it is necessary to adopt measures with the aim of progressively establishing the internal market before 31 December 1992; whereas the internal market comprises an area without internal frontiers in which goods, persons, services and capital move freely;

Whereas the laws of Member States relating to the terms of contract between the seller of goods or supplier of services, on the one hand, and the consumer of them, on the other hand, show many disparities, with the result that the national markets for the sale of goods and services to consumers differ from each other and that distortions of competition may arise amongst the sellers and suppliers, notably when they sell and supply in other Member States;

Whereas, in particular, the laws of Member States relating to unfair terms in consumer contracts show marked divergences;

Whereas it is the responsibility of the Member States to ensure that contracts concluded with consumers do not contain unfair terms;

Whereas, generally speaking, consumers do not know the rules of law which, in Member States other than their own, govern contracts for the sale of goods or services; whereas this lack of awareness may deter them from direct transactions for the purchase of goods or services in another Member State;

Whereas, in order to facilitate the establishment of the internal market and to safeguard the citizen in his role as consumer when acquiring goods and services under contracts which are governed by the laws of Member States other than his own, it is essential to remove unfair terms from those contracts;

Whereas sellers of goods and suppliers of services will thereby be helped in their task of selling goods and supplying services, both at home and throughout the

[1] OJ C 73, 24 March 1992, p 7.

[2] OJ C 326, 16 December 1991, p 108 and OJ No C 21, 25 January 1993.

[3] OJ C 159, 17 June 1991, p 34.

internal market; whereas competition will thus be stimulated, so contributing to increased choice for Community citizens as consumers;

Whereas the two Community programmes for a consumer protection and information policy[4] underlined the importance of safeguarding consumers in the matter of unfair terms of contract; whereas this protection ought to be provided by laws and regulations which are either harmonized at Community level or adopted directly at that level;

Whereas in accordance with the principle laid down under the heading 'Protection of the economic interests of the consumers', as stated in those programmes: 'acquirers of goods and services should be protected against the abuse of power by the seller or supplier, in particular against one-sided standard contracts and the unfair exclusion of essential rights in contracts';

Whereas more effective protection of the consumer can be achieved by adopting uniform rules of law in the matter of unfair terms; whereas those rules should apply to all contracts concluded between sellers or suppliers and consumers; whereas as a result inter alia contracts relating to employment, contracts relating to succession rights, contracts relating to rights under family law and contracts relating to the incorporation and organization of companies or partnership agreements must be excluded from this Directive;

Whereas the consumer must receive equal protection under contracts concluded by word of mouth and written contracts regardless, in the latter case, of whether the terms of the contract are contained in one or more documents;

Whereas, however, as they now stand, national laws allow only partial harmonization to be envisaged; whereas, in particular, only contractual terms which have not been individually negotiated are covered by this Directive; whereas Member States should have the option, with due regard for the Treaty, to afford consumers a higher level of protection through national provisions that are more stringent than those of this Directive;

Whereas the statutory or regulatory provisions of the Member States which directly or indirectly determine the terms of consumer contracts are presumed not to contain unfair terms; whereas, therefore, it does not appear to be necessary to subject the terms which reflect mandatory statutory or regulatory provisions and the principles or provisions of international conventions to which the Member States or the Community are party; whereas in that respect the wording 'mandatory statutory or regulatory provisions' in Article 1(2) also covers rules which, according to the law, shall apply between the contracting parties provided that no other arrangements have been established;

[4] OJ C 92, 25 April 1975, 1 and OJ C 133, 3 June 1981, 1

Whereas Member States must however ensure that unfair terms are not included, particularly because this Directive also applies to trades, business or professions of a public nature;

Whereas it is necessary to fix in a general way the criteria for assessing the unfair character of contract terms;

Whereas the assessment, according to the general criteria chosen, of the unfair character of terms, in particular in sale or supply activities of a public nature providing collective services which take account of solidarity among users, must be supplemented by a means of making an overall evaluation of the different interests involved; whereas this constitutes the requirement of good faith; whereas, in making an assessment of good faith, particular regard shall be had to the strength of the bargaining positions of the parties, whether the consumer had an inducement to agree to the term and whether the goods or services were sold or supplied to the special order of the consumer; whereas the requirement of good faith may be satisfied by the seller or supplier where he deals fairly and equitably with the other party whose legitimate interests he has to take into account;

Whereas, for the purposes of this Directive, the annexed list of terms can be of indicative value only and, because of the cause of the minimal character of the Directive, the scope of these terms may be the subject of amplification or more restrictive editing by the Member States in their national laws;

Whereas the nature of goods or services should have an influence on assessing the unfairness of contractual terms;

Whereas, for the purposes of this Directive, assessment of unfair character shall not be made of terms which describe the main subject matter of the contract nor the quality/price ratio of the goods or services supplied; whereas the main subject matter of the contract and the price/quality ratio may nevertheless be taken into account in assessing the fairness of other terms; whereas it follows, inter alia, that in insurance contracts, the terms which clearly define or circumscribe the insured risk and the insurer's liability shall not be subject to such assessment since these restrictions are taken into account in calculating the premium paid by the consumer,

Whereas contracts should be drafted in plain, intelligible language, the consumer should actually be given an opportunity to examine all the terms and, if in doubt, the interpretation most favourable to the consumer should prevail;

Whereas Member States should ensure that unfair terms are not used in contracts concluded with consumers by a seller or supplier and that if, nevertheless, such terms are so used, they will not bind the consumer, and the contract will continue to bind the parties upon those terms if it is capable of continuing in existence without the unfair provisions;

Whereas there is a risk that, in certain cases, the consumer may be deprived of protection under this Directive by designating the law of a non-Member country as the law applicable to the contract; whereas provisions should therefore be included in this Directive designed to avert this risk;

Whereas persons or organizations, if regarded under the law of a Member State as having a legitimate interest in the matter, must have facilities for initiating proceedings concerning terms of contract drawn up for general use in contracts concluded with consumers, and in particular unfair terms, either before a court or before an administrative authority competent to decide upon complaints or to initiate appropriate legal proceedings; whereas this possibility does not, however, entail prior verification of the general conditions obtaining in individual economic sectors;

Whereas the courts or administrative authorities of the Member States must have at their disposal adequate and effective means of preventing the continued application of unfair terms in consumer contracts,

had adopted this Directive:

Article 1

1. The purpose of this Directive is to approximate the laws, regulations and administrative provisions of the Member States relating to unfair terms in contracts concluded between a seller or supplier and a consumer.

2. The contractual terms which reflect mandatory statutory or regulatory provisions and the provisions or principles of international conventions to which the Member States or the Community are party, particularly in the transport area, shall not be subject to the provisions of this Directive.

Article 2

For the purposes of this Directive:

(a) 'unfair terms' means the contractual terms defined in Article 3;
(b) 'consumer' means any natural person who, in contracts covered by this Directive, is acting for purposes which are outside his trade, business or profession;
(c) 'seller or supplier' means any natural or legal person who, in contracts covered by this Directive, is acting for purposes relating to his trade, business or profession, whether publicly owned or privately owned.

Article 3

1. A contractual term which has not been individually negotiated shall be regarded as unfair if, contrary to the requirement of good faith, it causes a significant imbalance in the parties' rights and obligations arising under the contract, to the detriment of the consumer.

2. A term shall always be regarded as not individually negotiated where it has been drafted in advance and the consumer has therefore not been able to influence the substance of the term, particularly in the context of a pre-formulated standard contract.

The fact that certain aspects of a term or one specific term have been individually negotiated shall not exclude the application of this Article to the rest of a contract if an overall assessment of the contract indicates that it is nevertheless a pre-formulated standard contract.

Where any seller or supplier claims that a standard term has been individually negotiated, the burden of proof in this respect shall be incumbent on him.

3. The Annex shall contain an indicative and non-exhaustive list of the terms which may be regarded as unfair.

Article 4

1. Without prejudice to Article 7, the unfairness of a contractual term shall be assessed, taking into account the nature of the goods or services for which the contract was concluded and by referring, at the time of conclusion of the contract, to all the circumstances attending the conclusion of the contract and to all the other terms of the contract or of another contract on which it is dependent.

2. Assessment of the unfair nature of the terms shall relate neither to the definition of the main subject matter of the contract nor to the adequacy of the price and remuneration, on the one hand, as against the services or goods supplies in exchange, on the other, in so far as these terms are in plain intelligible language.

Article 5

In the case of contracts where all or certain terms offered to the consumer are in writing, these terms must always be drafted in plain, intelligible language. Where there is doubt about the meaning of a term, the interpretation most favourable to the consumer shall prevail. This rule on interpretation shall not apply in the context of the procedures laid down in Article 7(2).

Article 6

1. Member States shall lay down that unfair terms used in a contract concluded with a consumer by a seller or supplier shall, as provided for under their national law, not be binding on the consumer and that the contract shall continue to bind the parties upon those terms if it is capable of continuing in existence without the unfair terms.

2. Member States shall take the necessary measures to ensure that the consumer does not lose the protection granted by this Directive by virtue of the choice of the

law of a non-Member country as the law applicable to the contract if the latter has a close connection with the territory of the Member States.

Article 7

1. Member States shall ensure that, in the interests of consumers and of competitors, adequate and effective means exist to prevent the continued use of unfair terms in contracts concluded with consumers by sellers or suppliers.

2. The means referred to in paragraph 1 shall include provisions whereby persons or organizations, having a legitimate interest under national law in protecting consumers, may take action according to the national law concerned before the courts or before competent administrative bodies for a decision as to whether contractual terms drawn up for general use are unfair, so that they can apply appropriate and effective means to prevent the continued use of such terms.

3. With due regard for national laws, the legal remedies referred to in paragraph 2 may be directed separately or jointly against a number of sellers or suppliers from the same economic sector or their associations which use or recommend the use of the same general contractual terms or similar terms.

Article 8

Member States may adopt or retain the most stringent provisions compatible with the Treaty in the area covered by this Directive, to ensure a maximum degree of protection for the consumer.

Article 9

The Commission shall present a report to the European Parliament and to the Council concerning the application of this Directive five years at the latest after the date in Article 10(1).

Article 10

1. Member States shall bring into force the laws, regulations and administrative provisions necessary to comply with this Directive no later than 31 December 1994. They shall forthwith inform the Commission thereof.

These provisions shall be applicable to all contracts concluded after 31 December 1994.

2. When Member States adopt these measures, they shall contain a reference to this Directive or shall be accompanied by such reference on the occasion of their official publication. The methods of making such a reference shall be laid down by the Member States.

3. Member States shall communicate the main provisions of national law which they adopt in the field covered by this Directive to the Commission.

Article 11

Annex
Terms referred to in article (3) 1.
Terms which have the object or effect of:

(a) excluding or limiting the legal liability of a seller or supplier in the event of the death of a consumer or personal injury to the latter resulting from an act or omission of that seller or supplier;
(b) inappropriately excluding or limiting the legal rights of the consumer vis-à-vis the seller or supplier or another party in the event of total or partial non-performance or inadequate performance by the seller or supplier of any of the contractual obligations, including the option of offsetting a debt owed to the seller or supplier against any claim which the consumer may have against him;
(c) making an agreement binding on the consumer whereas provision of services by the seller or supplier is subject to a condition whose realization depends on his own will alone;
(d) permitting the seller or supplier to retain sums paid by the consumer where the latter decides not to conclude or perform the contract, without providing for the consumer to receive compensation of an equivalent amount from the seller or supplier where the latter is the party cancelling the contract;
(e) requiring any consumer who fails to fulfil his obligation to pay a disproportionately high sum in compensation;
(f) authorizing the seller or supplier to dissolve the contract on a discretionary basis where the same facility is not granted to the consumer, or permitting the seller or supplier to retain the sums paid for services not yet supplied by him where it is the seller or supplier himself who dissolves the contract;
(g) enabling the seller or supplier to terminate a contract of indeterminate duration without reasonable notice except where there are serious grounds for doing so;
(h) automatically extending a contract of fixed duration where the consumer does not indicate otherwise, when the deadline fixed for the consumer to express this desire not to extend the contract is unreasonably early;
(i) irrevocably binding the consumer to terms with which he had no real opportunity of becoming acquainted before the conclusion of the contract;
(j) enabling the seller or supplier to alter the terms of the contract unilaterally without a valid reason which is specified in the contract;
(k) enabling the seller or supplier to alter unilaterally without a valid reason any characteristics of the product or service to be provided;
(l) providing for the price of goods to be determined at the time of delivery or allowing a seller of goods or supplier of services to increase their price without in both cases giving the consumer the corresponding right to cancel the contract if the final price is too high in relation to the price agreed when the contract was concluded;

(m) giving the seller or supplier the right to determine whether the goods or services supplied are in conformity with the contract, or giving him the exclusive right to interpret any term of the contract;
(n) limiting the seller's or supplier's obligation to respect commitments undertaken by his agents or making his commitments subject to compliance with a particular formality;
(o) obliging the consumer to fulfil all his obligations where the seller or supplier does not perform his;
(p) giving the seller or supplier the possibility of transferring his rights and obligations under the contract, where this may serve to reduce the guarantees for the consumer, without the latter's agreement;
(q) excluding or hindering the consumer's right to take legal action or exercise any other legal remedy, particularly by requiring the consumer to take disputes exclusively to arbitration not covered by legal provisions, unduly restricting the evidence available to him or imposing on him a burden of proof which, according to the applicable law, should lie with another party to the contract.

2. Scope of subparagraphs (g), (j) and (l)

(a) Subparagraph (g) is without hindrance to terms by which a supplier of financial services reserves the right to terminate unilaterally a contract of indeterminate duration without notice where there is a valid reason, provided that the supplier is required to inform the other contracting party or parties thereof immediately.
(b) Subparagraph (j) is without hindrance to terms under which a supplier of financial services reserves the right to alter the rate of interest payable by the consumer or due to the latter, or the amount of other charges for financial services without notice where there is a valid reason, provided that the supplier is required to inform the other contracting party or parties thereof at the earliest opportunity and that the latter are free to dissolve the contract immediately. Subparagraph (j) is also without hindrance to terms under which a seller or supplier reserves the right to alter unilaterally the conditions of a contract of indeterminate duration, provided that he is required to inform the consumer with reasonable notice and that the consumer is free to dissolve the contract.
(c) Subparagraphs (g), (j) and (l) do not apply to:

—transactions in transferable securities, financial instruments and other products or services where the price is linked to fluctuations in a stock exchange quotation or index or a financial market rate that the seller or supplier does not control;
—contracts for the purchase or sale of foreign currency, traveller's cheques or international money orders denominated in foreign currency;

(d) Subparagraph (l) is without hindrance to price-indexation clauses, where lawful, provided that the method by which prices vary is explicitly described.

Appendix II
National Legislation

The Unfair Contract Terms Act 1977 (UCTA)

PART I AMENDMENT OF LAW FOR ENGLAND AND WALES AND NORTHERN IRELAND

1 Scope of Part I

(1) For the purposes of this Part of this Act, 'negligence' means the breach—

(a) of any obligation, arising from the express or implied terms of a contract, to take reasonable care or exercise reasonable skill in the performance of the contract;
(b) of any common law duty to take reasonable care or exercise reasonable skill (but not any stricter duty);
(c) of the common duty of care imposed by the Occupiers' Liability Act 1957 or the Occupiers' Liability Act (Northern Ireland) 1957.

(2) This Part of this Act is subject to Part III; and in relation to contracts, the operation of sections 2 to 4 and 7 is subject to the exceptions made by Schedule 1.

(3) In the case of both contract and tort, sections 2 to 7 apply (except where the contrary is stated in section 6(4)) only to business liability, that is liability for breach of obligations or duties arising—

(a) from things done or to be done by a person in the course of a business (whether his own business or another's); or
(b) from the occupation of premises used for business purposes of the occupier;

and references to liability are to be read accordingly but liability of an occupier of premises for breach of an obligation or duty towards a person obtaining access to the premises for recreational or educational purposes, being liability for loss or damage suffered by reason of the dangerous state of the premises, is not a business liability of the occupier unless granting that person such access for the purposes concerned falls within the business purposes of the occupier.

(4) In relation to any breach of duty or obligation, it is immaterial for any purpose of this Part of this Act whether the breach was inadvertent or intentional, or whether liability for it arises directly or vicariously.

2 Negligence liability

(1) A person cannot by reference to any contract term or to a notice given to persons generally or to particular persons exclude or restrict his liability for death or personal injury resulting from negligence.

(2) In the case of other loss or damage, a person cannot so exclude or restrict his liability for negligence except in so far as the term or notice satisfies the requirement of reasonableness.

(3) Where a contract term or notice purports to exclude or restrict liability for negligence a person's agreement to or awareness of it is not of itself to be taken as indicating his voluntary acceptance of any risk.

3 Liability arising in contract

(1) This section applies as between contracting parties where one of them deals as consumer or on the other's written standard terms of business.

(2) As against that party, the other cannot by reference to any contract term—

- (a) when himself in breach of contract, exclude or restrict any liability of his in respect of the breach; or
- (b) claim to be entitled—
  - (i) to render a contractual performance substantially different from that which was reasonably expected of him, or
  - (ii) in respect of the whole or any part of his contractual obligation, to render no performance at all,

except in so far as (in any of the cases mentioned above in this subsection) the contract term satisfies the requirement of reasonableness.

4 Unreasonable indemnity clauses

(1) A person dealing as consumer cannot by reference to any contract term be made to indemnify another person (whether a party to the contract or not) in respect of liability that may be incurred by the other for negligence or breach of contract, except in so far as the contract term satisfies the requirement of reasonableness.

(2) This section applies whether the liability in question—

- (a) is directly that of the person to be indemnified or is incurred by him vicariously;
- (b) is to the person dealing as consumer or to someone else.

5 'Guarantee' of consumer goods

(1) In the case of goods of a type ordinarily supplied for private use or consumption, where

loss or damage—

(a) arises from the goods proving defective while in consumer use; and
(b) results from the negligence of a person concerned in the manufacture or distribution of the goods,

liability for the loss or damage cannot be excluded or restricted by reference to any contract term or notice contained in or operating by reference to a guarantee of the goods.

(2) For these purposes—

(a) goods are to be regarded as 'in consumer use' when a person is using them, or has them in his possession for use, otherwise than exclusively for the purposes of a business; and
(b) anything in writing is a guarantee if it contains or purports to contain some promise or assurance (however worded or presented) that defects will be made good by complete or partial replacement, or by repair, monetary compensation or otherwise.

(3) This section does not apply as between the parties to a contract under or in pursuance of which possession or ownership of the goods passed.

6 Sale and hire-purchase

(1) Liability for breach of the obligations arising from—

(a) section 12 of the Sale of Goods Act 1979 (seller's implied undertakings as to title, etc);
(b) section 8 of the Supply of Goods (Implied Terms) Act 1973 (the corresponding thing in relation to hire-purchase),

cannot be excluded or restricted by reference to any contract term.

(2) As against a person dealing as consumer, liability for breach of the obligations arising from—

(a) section 13, 14 or 15 of the 1979 Act (seller's implied undertakings as to conformity of goods with description or sample, or as to their quality or fitness for a particular purpose);
(b) section 9, 10 or 11 of the 1973 Act (the corresponding things in relation to hire-purchase),

cannot be excluded or restricted by reference to any contract term.

(3) As against a person dealing otherwise than as consumer, the liability specified in subsection (2) above can be excluded or restricted by reference to a contract term, but only in so far as the term satisfies the requirement of reasonableness.

(4) The liabilities referred to in this section are not only the business liabilities defined by section 1(3), but include those arising under any contract of sale of goods or hire-purchase agreement.

7 Miscellaneous contracts under which goods pass

(1) Where the possession or ownership of goods passes under or in pursuance of a contract not governed by the law of sale of goods or hire-purchase, subsections (2) to (4) below apply as regards the effect (if any) to be given to contract terms excluding or restricting liability for breach of obligation arising by implication of law from the nature of the contract.

(2) As against a person dealing as consumer, liability in respect of the goods' correspondence with description or sample, or their quality or fitness for any particular purpose, cannot be excluded or restricted by reference to any such term.

(3) As against a person dealing otherwise than as consumer, that liability can be excluded or restricted by reference to such a term, but only in so far as the term satisfies the requirement of reasonableness.

(3A) Liability for breach of the obligations arising under section 2 of the Supply of Goods and Services Act 1982 (implied terms about title etc in certain contracts for the transfer of the property in goods) cannot be excluded or restricted by references to any such term.

(4) Liability in respect of—

(a) the right to transfer ownership of the goods, or give possession; or
(b) the assurance of quiet possession to a person taking goods in pursuance of the contract,

cannot (in a case to which subsection (3A) above does not apply) be excluded or restricted by reference to any such term except in so far as the term satisfies the requirement of reasonableness.

(5) This section does not apply in the case of goods passing on a redemption of trading stamps within the Trading Stamps Act 1964 or the Trading Stamps Act (Northern Ireland) 1965.

8 Misrepresentation

(This section substitutes the Misrepresentation Act 1967, s 3 and the Misrepresentation Act (Northern Ireland) 1967, s 3)

9 Effect of breach

(1) Where for reliance upon it a contract term has to satisfy the requirement of reasonableness, it may be found to do so and be given effect accordingly notwithstanding that the contract has been terminated either by breach or by a party electing to treat it as repudiated.

(2) Where on a breach the contract is nevertheless affirmed by a party entitled to treat it as repudiated, this does not of itself exclude the requirement of reasonableness in relation to any contract term.

10 Evasion by means of secondary contract

A person is not bound by any contract term prejudicing or taking away rights of his which arise under, or in connection with the performance of, another contract, so far as those rights extend to the enforcement of another's liability which this Part of this Act prevents that other from excluding or restricting.

11 The 'reasonableness' test

(1) In relation to a contract term, the requirement of reasonableness for the purposes of this Part of this Act, section 3 of the Misrepresentation Act 1967 and section 3 of the Misrepresentation Act (Northern Ireland) 1967 is that the term shall have been a fair and reasonable one to be included having regard to the circumstances which were, or ought reasonably to have been, known to or in the contemplation of the parties when the contract was made.

(2) In determining for the purposes of section 6 or 7 above whether a contract term satisfies the requirement of reasonableness, regard shall be had in particular to the matters specified in Schedule 2 to this Act; but this subsection does not prevent the court or arbitrator from holding, in accordance with any rule of law, that a term which purports to exclude or restrict any relevant liability is not a term of the contract.

(3) In relation to a notice (not being a notice having contractual effect), the requirement of reasonableness under this Act is that it should be fair and reasonable to allow reliance on it, having regard to all the circumstances obtaining when the liability arose or (but for the notice) would have arisen.

(4) Where by reference to a contract term or notice a person seeks to restrict liability to a specified sum of money, and the question arises (under this or any other Act) whether the term or notice satisfies the requirement of reasonableness, regard shall be had in particular (but without prejudice to subsection (2) above in the case of contract terms) to—

(a) the resources which he could expect to be available to him for the purpose of meeting the liability should it arise; and
(b) how far it was open to him to cover himself by insurance.

(5) It is for those claiming that a contract term or notice satisfies the requirement of reasonableness to show that it does.

12 'Dealing as consumer'

(1) A party to a contract 'deals as consumer' in relation to another party if—

(a) he neither makes the contract in the course of a business nor holds himself out as doing so; and
(b) the other party does make the contract in the course of a business; and
(c) in the case of a contract governed by the law of sale of goods or hire purchase, or by section 7 of this Act, the goods passing under or in pursuance of the contract are of a type ordinarily supplied for private use or consumption.

(2) But on a sale by auction or by competitive tender the buyer is not in any circumstances to be regarded as dealing as consumer.

(3) Subject to this, it is for those claiming that a party does not deal as consumer to show that he does not.

13 Varieties of exemption clause

(1) To the extent that this Part of this Act prevents the exclusion or restriction of any liability it also prevents—

(a) making the liability or its enforcement subject to restrictive or onerous conditions;
(b) excluding or restricting any right or remedy in respect of the liability, or subjecting a person to any prejudice in consequence of his pursuing any such right or remedy;
(c) excluding or restricting rules of evidence or procedure;

and (to that extent) sections 2 and 5 to 7 also prevent excluding or restricting liability by reference to terms and notices which exclude or restrict the relevant obligation or duty.

(2) But an agreement in writing to submit present or future differences to arbitration is not to be treated under this Part of this Act as excluding or restricting any liability.

14 Interpretation of Part I

In this Part of this Act—

'business' includes a profession and the activities of any government department or local or public authority;
'goods' has the same meaning as in the Sale of Goods Act 1979:
'hire-purchase agreement' has the same meaning as in the Consumer Credit Act 1974;
'negligence' has the meaning given by section 1(1);
'notice' includes an announcement, whether or not in writing, and any other communication or pretended communication; and
'personal injury' includes any disease and any impairment of physical or mental condition.

PART II

[*omissis*]

PART III

PROVISIONS APPLYING TO WHOLE OF UNITED KINGDOM

26 International supply contracts

(1) The limits imposed by this Act on the extent to which a person may exclude or restrict liability by reference to a contract term do not apply to liability arising under such a contract as is described in subsection (3) below.

(2) The terms of such a contract are not subject to any requirement of reasonableness under section 3 or 4: and nothing in Part II of this Act shall require the incorporation of the terms of such a contract to be fair and reasonable for them to have effect.

(3) Subject to subsection (4), that description of contract is one whose characteristics are the following—

(a) either it is a contract of sale of goods or it is one under or in pursuance of which the possession or ownership of goods passes; and
(b) it is made by parties whose places of business (or, if they have none, habitual residences) are in the territories of different States (the Channel Islands and the Isle of Man being treated for this purpose as different States from the United Kingdom).

(4) A contract falls within subsection (3) above only if either—

- (a) the goods in question are, at the time of the conclusion of the contract, in the course of carriage, or will be carried, from the territory of one State to the territory of another; or
- (b) the acts constituting the offer and acceptance have been done in the territories of different States; or
- (c) the contract provides for the goods to be delivered to the territory of a State other than that within whose territory those acts were done.

27 Choice of law clauses

(1) Where the law applicable to a contract is the law of any part of the United Kingdom only by choice of the parties (and apart from that choice would be the law of some country outside the United Kingdom) sections 2 to 7 and 16 to 21 of this Act do not operate as part of the law applicable to the contract.

(2) This Act has effect notwithstanding any contract term which applies or purports to apply the law of some country outside the United Kingdom, where (either or both)—

- (a) the term appears to the court, or arbitrator or arbiter to have been imposed wholly or mainly for the purpose of enabling the party imposing it to evade the operation of this Act; or
- (b) in the making of the contract one of the parties dealt as consumer, and he was then habitually resident in the United Kingdom, and the essential steps necessary for the making of the contract were taken there, whether by him or by others on his behalf.

(3) In the application of subsection (2) above to Scotland, for paragraph (b) there shall be substituted—

‘(b) the contract is a consumer contract as defined in Part II of this Act, and the consumer at the date when the contract was made was habitually resident in the United Kingdom, and the essential steps necessary for the making of the contract were taken there, whether by him or by others on

his behalf.’.

[*omissis*]

SCHEDULE 1

SCOPE OF SECTIONS 2 TO 4 AND 7

Section 1(2)

1 Sections 2 to 4 of this Act do not extend to—

(a) any contract of insurance (including a contract to pay an annuity on human life);
(b) any contract so far as it relates to the creation or transfer of an interest in land, or to the termination of such an interest, whether by extinction, merger, surrender, forfeiture or otherwise;
(c) any contract so far as it relates to the creation or transfer of a right or interest in any patent, trade mark, copyright [or design right], registered design, technical or commercial information or other intellectual property, or relates to the termination of any such right or interest;
(d) any contract so far as it relates—

    (i) to the formation or dissolution of a company (which means any body corporate or unincorporated association and includes a partnership), or
    (ii) to its constitution or the rights or obligations of its corporators or members;

(e) any contract so far as it relates to the creation or transfer of securities or of any right or interest in securities.

2 Section 2(1) extends to—

(a) any contract of marine salvage or towage;
(b) any charterparty of a ship or hovercraft; and
(c) any contract for the carriage of goods by ship or hovercraft;

but subject to this sections 2 to 4 and 7 do not extend to any such contract except in favour of a person dealing as consumer.

3 Where goods are carried by ship or hovercraft in pursuance of a contract which either—

(a) specifies that as the means of carriage over part of the journey to be covered, or
(b) makes no provision as to the means of carriage and does not exclude that means,

then sections 2(2), 3 and 4 do not, except in favour of a person dealing as consumer, extend to the contract as it operates for and in relation to the carriage of the goods by that means.

4 Section 2(1) and (2) do not extend to a contract of employment, except in favour of the employee.

5 Section 2(1) does not affect the validity of any discharge and indemnity given by a person, on or in connection with an award to him of compensation for pneumoconiosis attributable to employment in the coal industry, in respect of any further claim arising from his contracting that disease.

SCHEDULE 2

'GUIDELINES' FOR APPLICATION OF REASONABLENESS TEST

Sections 11(2), 24(2)

The matters to which regard is to be had in particular for the purposes of sections 6(3), 7(3) and (4), 20 and 21 are any of the following which appear to be relevant—

(a) the strength of the bargaining positions of the parties relative to each other, taking into account (among other things) alternative means by which the customer's requirements could have been met;
(b) whether the customer received an inducement to agree to the term, or in accepting it had an opportunity of entering into a similar contract with other persons, but without having to accept a similar term;
(c) whether the customer knew or ought reasonably to have known of the existence and extent of the term (having regard, among other things, to any custom of the trade and any previous course of dealing between the parties);
(d) where the term excludes or restricts any relevant liability if some condition is not complied with, whether it was reasonable at the time of the contract to expect that compliance with that condition would be practicable;
(e) whether the goods were manufactured, processed or adapted to the special order of the customer.

[*omissis*]

The Unfair Terms in Consumer Contracts Regulations 1999 (UTCCR)

SI 1999 No 2083

Whereas the Secretary of State is a Minister designated for the purposes of section 2(2) of the European Communities Act 1972 in relation to measures relating to consumer protection:

Now, the Secretary of State, in exercise of the powers conferred upon him by section 2(2) of that Act, hereby makes the following Regulations:—

Citation and commencement

1. These Regulations may be cited as the Unfair Terms in Consumer Contracts Regulations 1999 and shall come into force on 1st October 1999.

Revocation

2. The Unfair Terms in Consumer Contracts Regulations 1994 are hereby revoked.

Interpretation

3.—(1) In these Regulations—
'the Community' means the European Community;

'consumer' means any natural person who, in contracts covered by these Regulations, is acting for purposes which are outside his trade, business or profession;
'court' in relation to England and Wales and Northern Ireland means a county court or the High Court, and in relation to Scotland, the Sheriff or the Court of Session;
'Director' means the Director General of Fair Trading;
'EEA Agreement' means the Agreement on the European Economic Area signed at Oporto on 2nd May 1992 as adjusted by the protocol signed at Brussels on 17th March 1993;
'Member State' means a State which is a contracting party to the EEA Agreement;
'notified' means notified in writing;
'qualifying body' means a person specified in Schedule 1;

'seller or supplier' means any natural or legal person who, in contracts covered by these Regulations, is acting for purposes relating to his trade, business or profession, whether publicly owned or privately owned;
'unfair terms' means the contractual terms referred to in regulation 5.

(2) In the application of these Regulations to Scotland for references to an 'injunction' or an 'interim injunction' there shall be substituted references to an 'interdict' or 'interim interdict' respectively.

Terms to which these Regulations apply

4.—(1) These Regulations apply in relation to unfair terms in contracts concluded between a seller or a supplier and a consumer.

(2) These Regulations do not apply to contractual terms which reflect—

(a) mandatory statutory or regulatory provisions (including such provisions under the law of any Member State or in Community legislation having effect in the United Kingdom without further enactment);
(b) the provisions or principles of international conventions to which the Member States or the Community are party.

Unfair Terms

5.—(1) A contractual term which has not been individually negotiated shall be regarded as unfair if, contrary to the requirement of good faith, it causes a significant imbalance in the parties' rights and obligations arising under the contract, to the detriment of the consumer.

(2) A term shall always be regarded as not having been individually negotiated where it has been drafted in advance and the consumer has therefore not been able to influence the substance of the term.

(3) Notwithstanding that a specific term or certain aspects of it in a contract has been individually negotiated, these Regulations shall apply to the rest of a contract if an overall assessment of it indicates that it is a pre-formulated standard contract.

(4) It shall be for any seller or supplier who claims that a term was individually negotiated to show that it was.

(5) Schedule 2 to these Regulations contains an indicative and non-exhaustive list of the terms which may be regarded as unfair.

Assessment of unfair terms

6.—(1) Without prejudice to regulation 12, the unfairness of a contractual term shall be assessed, taking into account the nature of the goods or services for which the contract was concluded and by referring, at the time of conclusion of the contract, to all the circumstances attending the conclusion of the contract and to all the other terms of the contract or of another contract on which it is dependent.

(2) In so far as it is in plain intelligible language, the assessment of fairness of a term shall not relate—

(a) to the definition of the main subject matter of the contract, or
(b) to the adequacy of the price or remuneration, as against the goods or services supplied in exchange.

Written contracts

7.—(1) A seller or supplier shall ensure that any written term of a contract is expressed in plain, intelligible language.

(2) If there is doubt about the meaning of a written term, the interpretation which is most favourable to the consumer shall prevail but this rule shall not apply in proceedings brought under regulation 12.

Effect of an unfair term

8.—(1) An unfair term in a contract concluded with a consumer by a seller or supplier shall not be binding on the consumer.

(2) The contract shall continue to bind the parties if it is capable of continuing in existence without the unfair term.

Choice of law clauses

9. These Regulations shall apply notwithstanding any contract term which applies or purports to apply the law of a non-Member State, if the contract has a close connection with the territory of the Member States.

Complaints—consideration by Director

10.—(1) It shall be the duty of the Director to consider any complaint made to him that any contract term drawn up for general use is unfair, unless—

(a) the complaint appears to the Director to be frivolous or vexatious; or
(b) a qualifying body has notified the Director that it agrees to consider the complaint.

(2) The Director shall give reasons for his decision to apply or not to apply, as the case may be, for an injunction under regulation 12 in relation to any complaint which these Regulations require him to consider.

(3) In deciding whether or not to apply for an injunction in respect of a term which the Director considers to be unfair, he may, if he considers it appropriate to do so, have regard to any undertakings given to him by or on behalf of any person as to the continued use of such a term in contracts concluded with consumers.

Complaints—consideration by qualifying bodies

11.—(1) If a qualifying body specified in Part One of Schedule 1 notifies the Director that it agrees to consider a complaint that any contract term drawn up for general use is unfair, it shall be under a duty to consider that complaint.

(2) Regulation 10(2) and (3) shall apply to a qualifying body which is under a duty to consider a complaint as they apply to the Director.

Injunctions to prevent continued use of unfair terms

12.—(1) The Director or, subject to paragraph (2), any qualifying body may apply for an injunction (including an interim injunction) against any person appearing to the Director or that body to be using, or recommending use of, an unfair term drawn up for general use in contracts concluded with consumers.

(2) A qualifying body may apply for an injunction only where—

(a) it has notified the Director of its intention to apply at least fourteen days before the date on which the application is made, beginning with the date on which the notification was given; or
(b) the Director consents to the application being made within a shorter period.

(3) The court on an application under this regulation may grant an injunction on such terms as it thinks fit.

(4) An injunction may relate not only to use of a particular contract term drawn up for general use but to any similar term, or a term having like effect, used or recommended for use by any person.

Powers of the Director and qualifying bodies to obtain documents and information

13.—(1) The Director may exercise the power conferred by this regulation for the purpose of—

(a) facilitating his consideration of a complaint that a contract term drawn up for general use is unfair; or
(b) ascertaining whether a person has complied with an undertaking or court order as to the continued use, or recommendation for use, of a term in contracts concluded with consumers.

(2) A qualifying body specified in Part One of Schedule 1 may exercise the power conferred by this regulation for the purpose of—

(a) facilitating its consideration of a complaint that a contract term drawn up for general use is unfair; or
(b) ascertaining whether a person has complied with—

(i) an undertaking given to it or to the court following an application by that body, or
(ii) a court order made on an application by that body,

as to the continued use, or recommendation for use, of a term in contracts concluded with consumers.

(3) The Director may require any person to supply to him, and a qualifying body specified in Part One of Schedule 1 may require any person to supply to it—

(a) a copy of any document which that person has used or recommended for use, at the time the notice referred to in paragraph (4) below is given, as a pre-formulated standard contract in dealings with consumers;
(b) information about the use, or recommendation for use, by that person of that document or any other such document in dealings with consumers.

(4) The power conferred by this regulation is to be exercised by a notice in writing which may—

(a) specify the way in which and the time within which it is to be complied with; and
(b) be varied or revoked by a subsequent notice.

(5) Nothing in this regulation compels a person to supply any document or information which he would be entitled to refuse to produce or give in civil proceedings before the court.

(6) If a person makes default in complying with a notice under this regulation, the court may, on the application of the Director or of the qualifying body, make such order as the court thinks fit for requiring the default to be made good, and any such order may provide that all the costs or expenses of and incidental to the

application shall be borne by the person in default or by any officers of a company or other association who are responsible for its default.

Notification of undertakings and orders to Director

14. A qualifying body shall notify the Director—

(a) of any undertaking given to it by or on behalf of any person as to the continued use of a term which that body considers to be unfair in contracts concluded with consumers;
(b) of the outcome of any application made by it under regulation 12, and of the terms of any undertaking given to, or order made by, the court;
(c) of the outcome of any application made by it to enforce a previous order of the court.

Publication, information and advice

15.—(1) The Director shall arrange for the publication in such form and manner as he considers appropriate, of—

(a) details of any undertaking or order notified to him under regulation 14;
(b) details of any undertaking given to him by or on behalf of any person as to the continued use of a term which the Director considers to be unfair in contracts concluded with consumers;
(c) details of any application made by him under regulation 12, and of the terms of any undertaking given to, or order made by, the court;
(d) details of any application made by the Director to enforce a previous order of the court.

(2) The Director shall inform any person on request whether a particular term to which these Regulations apply has been—

(a) the subject of an undertaking given to the Director or notified to him by a qualifying body; or
(b) the subject of an order of the court made upon application by him or notified to him by a qualifying body;

and shall give that person details of the undertaking or a copy of the order, as the case may be, together with a copy of any amendments which the person giving the undertaking has agreed to make to the term in question.

(3) The Director may arrange for the dissemination in such form and manner as he considers appropriate of such information and advice concerning the operation of these Regulations as may appear to him to be expedient to give to the public and to all persons likely to be affected by these Regulations.

Howells

SCHEDULE 1

QUALIFYING BODIES

[*omissis*]

SCHEDULE 2

REGULATION 5(5)

Indicative and non-exhaustive list of terms which may be regarded as unfair

1. Terms which have the object or effect of—

(a) excluding or limiting the legal liability of a seller or supplier in the event of the death of a consumer or personal injury to the latter resulting from an act or omission of that seller or supplier;
(b) inappropriately excluding or limiting the legal rights of the consumer vis-à-vis the seller or supplier or another party in the event of total or partial non-performance or inadequate performance by the seller or supplier of any of the contractual obligations, including the option of offsetting a debt owed to the seller or supplier against any claim which the consumer may have against him;
(c) making an agreement binding on the consumer whereas provision of services by the seller or supplier is subject to a condition whose realisation depends on his own will alone;
(d) permitting the seller or supplier to retain sums paid by the consumer where the latter decides not to conclude or perform the contract, without providing for the consumer to receive compensation of an equivalent amount from the seller or supplier where the latter is the party cancelling the contract;
(e) requiring any consumer who fails to fulfil his obligation to pay a disproportionately high sum in compensation;
(f) authorising the seller or supplier to dissolve the contract on a discretionary basis where the same facility is not granted to the consumer, or permitting the seller or supplier to retain the sums paid for services not yet supplied by him where it is the seller or supplier himself who dissolves the contract;
(g) enabling the seller or supplier to terminate a contract of indeterminate duration without reasonable notice except where there are serious grounds for doing so;
(h) automatically extending a contract of fixed duration where the consumer does not indicate otherwise, when the deadline fixed for the consumer to express his desire not to extend the contract is unreasonably early;

(i) irrevocably binding the consumer to terms with which he had no real opportunity of becoming acquainted before the conclusion of the contract;
(j) enabling the seller or supplier to alter the terms of the contract unilaterally without a valid reason which is specified in the contract;
(k) enabling the seller or supplier to alter unilaterally without a valid reason any characteristics of the product or service to be provided;
(l) providing for the price of goods to be determined at the time of delivery or allowing a seller of goods or supplier of services to increase their price without in both cases giving the consumer the corresponding right to cancel the contract if the final price is too high in relation to the price agreed when the contract was concluded;
(m) giving the seller or supplier the right to determine whether the goods or services supplied are in conformity with the contract, or giving him the exclusive right to interpret any term of the contract;
(n) limiting the seller's or supplier's obligation to respect commitments undertaken by his agents or making his commitments subject to compliance with a particular formality;
(o) obliging the consumer to fulfil all his obligations where the seller or supplier does not perform his;
(p) giving the seller or supplier the possibility of transferring his rights and obligations under the contract, where this may serve to reduce the guarantees for the consumer, without the latter's agreement;
(q) excluding or hindering the consumer's right to take legal action or exercise any other legal remedy, particularly by requiring the consumer to take disputes exclusively to arbitration not covered by legal provisions, unduly restricting the evidence available to him or imposing on him a burden of proof which, according to the applicable law, should lie with another party to the contract.

2. Scope of paragraphs 1(g), (j) and (l)

(a) Paragraph 1(g) is without hindrance to terms by which a supplier of financial services reserves the right to terminate unilaterally a contract of indeterminate duration without notice where there is a valid reason, provided that the supplier is required to inform the other contracting party or parties thereof immediately.
(b) Paragraph 1(j) is without hindrance to terms under which a supplier of financial services reserves the right to alter the rate of interest payable by the consumer or due to the latter, or the amount of other charges for financial services without notice where there is a valid reason, provided that the supplier is required to inform the other contracting party or parties thereof at the earliest opportunity and that the latter are free to dissolve the contract immediately.

Paragraph 1(j) is also without hindrance to terms under which a seller or supplier reserves the right to alter unilaterally the conditions of a contract of indeterminate duration, provided that he is required to inform the consumer with reasonable notice and that the consumer is free to dissolve the contract.

(c) Paragraphs 1(g), (j) and (l) do not apply to:

—transactions in transferable securities, financial instruments and other products or services where the price is linked to fluctuations in a stock exchange quotation or index or a financial market rate that the seller or supplier does not control;—contracts for the purchase or sale of foreign currency, traveller's cheques or international money orders denominated in foreign currency;

(d) Paragraph 1(l) is without hindrance to price indexation clauses, where lawful, provided that the method by which prices vary is explicitly described.

French Consumer Code: Article L 132-1

In contracts concluded between *professionnels* and *non-professionnels* or consumers, terms are unfair when their object or effect is to create a significant imbalance between parties' rights and obligations to the detriment of the consumer.

It is possible to determine, by means of *décrets* of the *Conseil d'Etat*, enacted after the opinion of the Commission envisaged by article L 132-2, the types of terms which must be regarded as unfair in accordance with para 1.

An Annex to the present code includes an indicative and non-exhaustive list of terms that may be regarded as unfair if they satisfy the conditions under para 1. This is without prejudice the requirement that, in case of a dispute on a contract containing one of these terms, the claimant must prove the unfair nature of the term.

These provisions are applicable whatever the form and means of support of the contract are. The same applies to order forms, invoices, guarantees, delivery notes, notes or tickets containing terms, whether freely negotiated or not, or references to pre-established standard conditions.

Without prejudice to the rules of interpretation of articles 1156 to 1161, 1163 and 1164 of the civil code, the unfair nature of a term must be appreciated by reference, at the time of conclusion of the contract, to all circumstances attending its conclusion, as well as all to the other terms of the contract. Equally, it must be appreciated with reference to the terms contained in another contract whenever the conclusion or performance of the two contracts legally depend one on the other.

Unfair terms are deemed as not written.

The appreciation of the unfair nature as per para 1 does not concern the definition of the subject matter of the contract or the adequacy of the price or remuneration to the good sold or the service offered as long as the terms are drafted in a plain, intelligible way.

Terms other than the ones declared unfair shall continue to bind the parties if the contract is capable of continuing in existence without the unfair terms.

The provisions of this article are provisions of *ordre public*.

Annex: terms referred to at para 3 of article L 132-1

1. Terms having as their object or effect:
   (a) excluding or limiting the legal liability of the *professionnel* in the event of the death of a consumer or personal injury to the latter resulting from an act or omission of that *professionnel*;

(b) inappropriately excluding or limiting the legal rights of the consumer vis-à-vis the *professionnel* or another party in the event of total or partial non-performance or inadequate performance by the *professionnel* of any of the contractual obligations, including the option of offsetting a debt owed to the *professionnel* against any claim which the consumer may have against him;

(c) making an agreement binding on the consumer whereas performance by the *professionnel* is subject to a condition whose realization depends on his own will alone;

(d) permitting the *professionnel* to retain sums paid by the consumer where the latter decides not to conclude or perform the contract, without providing for the consumer the right to receive compensation of an equivalent amount from the *professionnel* where the latter is the party cancelling the contract;

(e) requiring any consumer who fails to fulfil his obligation to pay a disproportionately high sum in compensation;

(f) authorizing the *professionnel* to dissolve the contract on a discretionary basis where the same facility is not granted to the consumer, or permitting the *professionnel* to retain the sums paid for services not yet supplied by him where it is the *professionnel* himself who dissolves the contract;

(g) enabling the *professionnel* to terminate a contract of indeterminate duration without reasonable notice except where there are serious grounds for doing so;

(h) automatically extending a contract of fixed duration where the consumer does not indicate otherwise, when the deadline fixed for the consumer to express his desire not to extend the contract is unreasonably early;

(i) irrevocably binding the consumer to terms with which he had no real opportunity of becoming acquainted before the conclusion of the contract;

(j) enabling the *professionnel* to alter the terms of the contract unilaterally without a valid reason which is specified in the contract;

(k) enabling the *professionnel* to alter unilaterally without a valid reason any characteristics of the product or service to be provided;

(l) providing for the price of goods to be determined at the time of delivery or allowing a *professionnel* to increase their price without in both cases giving the consumer the corresponding right to cancel the contract if the final price is too high in relation to the price agreed when the contract was concluded;

(m) giving the *professionnel* the right to determine whether the goods or services supplied are in conformity with the contract, or giving him the exclusive right to interpret any term of the contract;

(n) limiting the *professionnel*'s obligation to respect commitments undertaken by his agents or making his commitments subject to compliance with a particular formality;

(o) obliging the consumer to fulfil all his obligations where the *professionnel* does not perform his;

(p) giving the *professionnel* the possibility of transferring his rights and obligations under the contract, where this may serve to reduce the guarantees for the consumer, without the latter's agreement;

(q) excluding or hindering the consumer's right to take legal action or exercise any other legal remedy, particularly by requiring the consumer to take disputes exclusively to arbitration not covered by legal provisions, unduly restricting the evidence available to him or imposing on him a burden of proof which, according to the applicable law, should lie with another party to the contract.

2. Scope of subparagraphs (g), (j) and (l)

(a) Subparagraph (g) is without hindrance to terms by which a supplier of financial services reserves the right to terminate unilaterally a contract of indeterminate duration without notice where there is a valid reason, provided that the supplier is required to inform the other contracting party or parties thereof immediately.

(b) Subparagraph (j) is without hindrance to terms under which a supplier of financial services reserves the right to alter the rate of interest payable by the consumer or due to the latter, or the amount of other charges for financial services without notice where there is a valid reason, provided that the supplier is required to inform the other contracting party or parties thereof at the earliest opportunity and that the latter are free to dissolve the contract immediately.

Subparagraph (j) is also without hindrance to terms under which a *professionel* reserves the right to alter unilaterally the conditions of a contract of indeterminate duration, provided that he is required to inform the consumer with reasonable notice and that the consumer is free to dissolve the contract.

(c) Subparagraphs (g), (j) and (l) do not apply to:

—transactions in transferable securities, financial instruments and other products or services where the price is linked to fluctuations in a stock exchange quotation or index or a financial market rate that the *professionnel* does not control;

—contracts for the purchase or sale of foreign currency, traveller's cheques or international money orders denominated in foreign currency;

(d) Subparagraph (l) is without hindrance to price-indexation clauses, where lawful, provided that the method by which prices vary is explicitly described.

Bürgerliches Gesetzbuch (BGB)

BOOK 2 LAW OF THE OBLIGATIONS

SECTION 2: FORMATION OF CONTRACTUAL OBLIGATIONS BY MEANS OF STANDARD BUSINESS TERMS

§ 305 Incorporation of standard business terms into the contract

(1) Standard business terms are all contractual terms pre-established for a multitude of contracts which one party to the contract (the user) presents to the other party upon the conclusion of the contract. It is irrelevant whether the provisions appear as a separate part of a contract or are included in the contractual document itself, how extensive they are, what script is used for them, or what form the contract takes. Contractual terms do not constitute standard business terms where they have been individually negotiated between the parties.

(2) Standard business terms are incorporated into the contract only if, during the conclusion of the contract, the user

1. expressly draws the other party's attention to them, or if, because of the way in which the contract is concluded, an express reference to them is unreasonably difficult, he draws his attention to them by means of a clearly visible sign at the place where the contract is concluded and
2. gives the other party, in a reasonable manner that also appropriately takes account of any physical handicap of the other party discernible by the user, the possibility of gaining knowledge of their content,

and if the other party agrees that they are to apply.

(3) Subject to observance of the requirements set out in subsection (2) above, the parties may agree in advance that particular standard business terms will apply to a particular type of legal transaction.

§ 305a Incorporation in special cases

Even if the requirements set out in § 305 (2) Nos 1 and 2 are not observed, if the other party agrees to their application:

1. railway tariffs and regulations adopted with the approval of the competent transport authority or on the basis of international conventions and terms of transport, authorised in accordance with the Passenger Transport Act, of trams, trolley buses and motor vehicles in scheduled services are incorporated into the transport contract;

2. standard business terms published in the official journal of the regulatory authority for Post and Telecommunications and kept available in the user's business premises are incorporated

(a) into contracts of carriage concluded away from business premises by the posting of items in post boxes,
(b) into contracts for telecommunications, information and other services that are provided directly and in one go by means of remote communication and during the provision of a telecommunications service, if it is unreasonably difficult to make the standard business terms available to the other party before conclusion of the contract.

§ 305b Precedence of individually negotiated terms

Individually negotiated terms take precedence over standard business terms.

§ 305c Surprising and ambiguous clauses

(1) Provisions in standard business terms which in the circumstances, in particular in view of the outward appearance of the contract, are so unusual that the contractual partner of the user could not possibly have expected them, do not form part of the contract.

(2) In case of doubt, standard business terms are interpreted against the user.

§ 306 Legal consequences of non-incorporation and invalidity

(1) If all or some standard business terms have not become part of the contract or are invalid, the remainder of the contract continues to be valid.

(2) Where provisions have not become part of the contract or are invalid, the content of the contract is determined by the statutory rules.

(3) The contract is invalid if one party would suffer unreasonable hardship if he were bound by the contract even after the amendment provided for in subsection (2) above.

§ 306a No circumvention

The rules in this section apply even if they are circumvented by other arrangements.

§ 307 Review of subject-matter

(1) Provisions in standard business terms are invalid if, contrary to the requirement of good faith, they place the contractual partner of the user at an unreasonable disadvantage. An unreasonable disadvantage may also result from the fact that the provision is not clear and comprehensible.

(2) In case of doubt, an unreasonable disadvantage is assumed if a provision

1. cannot be reconciled with essential basic principles of the statutory rule from which it deviates, or
2. restricts essential rights or duties resulting from the nature of the contract in such a manner that there is a risk that the purpose of the contract will not be achieved.

(3) Subsections (1) and (2) above, and §§ 308 and 309 apply only to provisions in standard business terms by means of which provisions derogating from legal rules or provisions supplementing those rules are agreed. Other provisions may be invalid under subsection (1), sentence 2, above, in conjunction with subsection (1), sentence 1, above.

§ 308 Clauses whose validity is subject to appraisal

In standard business terms the following terms, in particular, are invalid:

1. (period for acceptance or performance)
   a provision by which the user reserves the right to an unreasonably long or inadequately specified period for acceptance or rejection of an offer or for performance; this does not include reservation of the right to perform only after expiry of the period for revocation or return under §§ 355 (1) and (2) and 356;
2. (additional period for performance)
   a provision by which the user, in derogation from legislative provisions, reserves the right to an unreasonably long or inadequately specified additional period within which to perform;
3. (right of termination)
   the stipulation of a right for the user to free himself, without an objectively justified reason specified in the contract, of his duty to perform; this does not apply to a contract for the performance of a recurring obligation;
4. (right of amendment)
   the stipulation of the user's right to alter or depart from the promised performance, unless, taking into account the user's interests, the stipulation to alter or depart from performance is reasonable for the other party;

5. (fictitious declarations)
   a provision whereby a declaration of the user's contractual partner is deemed or not deemed to have been made by him if he does or fails to do a particular act, unless

   a) he is allowed a reasonable period within which to make an express declaration and
   b) the user undertakes to draw to his attention at the beginning of the period the particular significance of his conduct; this does not apply to contracts in which the whole of Part B of the contracting rules for award of public works contracts is incorporated;

6. (fictional receipt)
   a provision which provides that a declaration by the user of particular importance is deemed to have been received by the other party;

7. (winding-up of contracts)
   a provision by which, in the event that one of the parties to the contract terminates the contract or gives notice to terminate it, the user can demand

   a) unreasonably high remuneration for the utilisation or use of a thing or a right or for performance made, or
   b) unreasonably high reimbursement of expenditure;

8. (unavailability of the object of performance)
   a stipulation permitted under 3. above of the user's right to free himself of his obligation to perform the contract if the object of the performance is not available, unless the user agrees

   a) to inform the other party immediately of the unavailability, and
   b) immediately to refund counter-performance by that party.

§ 309 Clauses whose invalidity is not subject to appraisal

Even where derogation from the statutory provisions is permissible, the following are invalid in standard business terms:

1. (price increases at short notice)
   a provision which provides for an increase in the remuneration for goods or services that are to be supplied within four months of the conclusion of the contract; this does not apply to goods or services supplied in the course of a recurring obligation;

2. (right to refuse to perform)
   a provision by which

   a) the right under § 320 of the contractual partner of the user to refuse to perform is excluded or restricted, or

b) a right of retention of the contractual partner of the user, in so far as it arises from the same contractual relationship, is excluded or restricted, in particular by making it subject to recognition by the user of the existence of defects;

3. (prohibition of set-off)
a provision by which the contractual partner of the user is deprived of the right to set off a claim which is undisputed or has been declared final and absolute;

4. (notice, period for performance)
a provision by which the user is relieved of the statutory requirement to give notice to the other party to perform or to fix a period for performance or supplementary performance by him;

5. (lump-sum claims for damages)
stipulation of a lump-sum claim by the user for damages or for compensation for reduction in value, if

a) the lump sum in the cases in question exceeds the damage expected in the normal course of events or the reduction in value which normally occurs, or
b) the other party is not given the express right to prove that damage or reduction in value has not occurred or is materially lower than the lump sum agreed;

6. (penalty)
a provision by which the user is entitled to receive payment of a penalty in the event of non-acceptance or late acceptance of performance, delay in payment or in the event that the other party withdraws from the contract;

7. (exclusion of liability for death, injury to body and health and for gross fault)

a) (death and injury to body and health)
exclusion or limitation of liability for losses arising out of death, injury to body or health caused by negligent breach of duty by the user or a deliberate or negligent breach of duty by his statutory agent or a person employed by him to perform the contract;

b) (gross fault)
exclusion or limitation of liability for other losses caused by a grossly negligent breach of duty by the user or a deliberate or grossly negligent breach of duty by a statutory agent of the user or by a person employed by him to perform the contract;

a) and b) above do not apply to restrictions of liability in the terms of transport, authorised in accordance with the Passenger Transport Act, of trams, trolley buses and motor vehicles in scheduled services, in so far as they do not derogate, to the detriment of passengers, from the Regulation concerning the terms of transport by tram and trolley bus and by motor vehicles in scheduled services of 27 February 1970; b) above does not apply to restrictions of liability for State-approved lottery or raffle contracts.

8. (other exclusions of liability in the event of breach of duty)

a) (exclusion of the right to withdraw from the contract)
a provision which, upon a breach of duty for which the user is responsible and which does not consist in a defect of the thing sold or the work, excludes or restricts the other party's right to withdraw from the contract; this does not apply to the terms of contract and tariff rules referred to in no. 7 on the conditions set out therein;

b) (defects)
a provision by which, in contracts for the supply of new, manufactured things or of work,

aa) (exclusion and reference of claims to third parties)
claims against the user on account of a defect as a whole or with regard to individual elements of it are excluded entirely, restricted to the assignment of claims against third parties, or which make the pursuit of legal proceedings against third parties a condition precedent;

bb) (restriction to supplementary performance)
claims against the user are restricted, entirely or with regard to individual elements, to a right to supplementary performance, unless the other party is given an express right to claim a price reduction if supplementary performance is unsuccessful or, except where the defects liability is in respect of building work, to choose to terminate the contract ;

cc) (expenditure incurred in the course of supplementary performance)
the user's obligation to bear the expenditure necessary for supplementary performance, in particular the costs of carriage, transport, labour and materials, is excluded or restricted;

dd) (withholding of supplementary performance)
the user makes supplementary performance conditional on the prior payment of the entire price or, having regard to the defect, an unreasonably high proportion thereof;

ee) (time-limit for notice of defects)
the user fixes a period within which the other party must give notice of non-obvious defects which is shorter than the period permitted under ff) below;

ff) (facilitation of limitation)
facilitates the limitation of claims on account of defects in the cases set out in § 438 (1), no. 2 and § 634a (1), no. 2, or, in other cases, results in a limitation period of less than one year from the date on which the statutory period of limitation begins; this does not apply to contracts in which the whole of Part B of the contracting rules for award of public works contracts is incorporated;

9. (period of recurring obligations)
in a contractual relationship concerning the periodic delivery of goods or the periodic supply of services or work by the user,

   a) a contract duration which binds the other party for more than two years,
   b) a tacit extension of the contractual relationship which binds the other party for a period of more than one year in each particular case, or
   c) to the detriment of the other party, a period of notice to terminate the contract which is more than three months prior to the expiration of the initial or tacitly extended period of the contract;

   this does not apply to contracts for the supply of things sold as a unit, to insurance contracts or contracts between the owners of copyrights and of claims and copyright collecting societies within the meaning of the Protection of Copyrights and Related Rights Act;

10. (change of contract partner)
a provision whereby in sales contracts, contracts for the supply of services or contracts for work a third party assumes or may assume the rights and obligations of the user under the contract, unless the provision

   a) specifies the third party by name, or
   b) gives the other party the right to withdraw from the contract;

11. (liability of an agent on conclusion of the contract)
a provision by which the user imposes on an agent who concludes the contract for the other party,

   a) the agent's own liability or duty to perform the contractual obligation without having made an express and separate declaration in that regard, or
   b) where the agent lacks authority, liability which exceeds that under § 179;

12. (burden of proof)
a provision by which the user alters the burden of proof to the detriment of the other party in particular by

   a) imposing the burden in respect of circumstances which fall within the scope of the user's responsibility, or
   b) requiring the other party to acknowledge particular facts;

   Subsection b) above does not apply to acknowledgments of receipt which are separately signed or bear a separate, qualified electronic signature;

13. (form of notices and declarations)
a provision by which notices or declarations to be given to the user or third parties are subject to a stricter requirement than the need for writing or to special requirements with regard to receipt.

§ 310 Scope of application

(1) § 305 (2) and (3) and §§ 308 and 309 do not apply to standard business terms which are proffered to a businessperson, a legal person governed by public law or a special fund governed by public law. In those cases § 307 (1) and (2) nevertheless applies to the extent that this results in the invalidity of the contractual provisions referred to in §§ 308 and 309; due regard must be had to the customs and practices applying in business transactions.

(2) §§ 308 and 309 do not apply to contracts of electricity, gas, district heating or water supply undertakings for the supply to special customers of electricity, gas, district heating or water from the supply grid unless the conditions of supply derogate, to the detriment of the customer, from Regulations on general conditions for the supply of tariff customers with electricity, gas, district heating or water. The first sentence applies mutatis mutandis to contracts for the disposal of sewage.

(3) In the case of contracts between a businessperson and a consumer (consumer contracts) the rules in this section apply subject to the following provisions:

1. Standard business terms are deemed to have been proffered by the businessperson, unless the consumer introduced them into the contract;
2. §§ 305c (2) and §§ 306, 307 to 309 of the present Act and Article 29a of the Introductory Act to the Civil Code apply to pre-established conditions of contract even if they are intended for use only once and in so far as, because they are pre-established, the consumer could not influence their content.
3. When deciding whether there has been unreasonable detriment under § 307 (1) and (2) the circumstances surrounding the conclusion of the contract must also be taken into account.

(4) This section does not apply to contracts in the field of the law of succession, family law and company law or to collective agreements and private- or public-sector works agreements. When it is applied to labour contracts, appropriate regard must be had to the special features of labour law; § 305 (2) and (3) is not to be applied. Collective agreements and public and private sector works agreements are equivalent to legal rules within the meaning of § 307 (3).

Relevant Provisions of the Italian Civil Code (*codice civile*)

Article 1229 Exemption clauses

Any agreement that excludes or restricts the liability for cases of fraud or gross negligence is void.

Any agreement exempting or limiting liability in cases where the act of the debtor or his auxiliaries constitutes a breach of duties arising from rules of public order is void.

Article 1341 Standard form contracts

Standard terms of contract prepared by one of the parties are effective as to the other, only if at the time of formation of the contract the latter knew of them, or should have known of them by using ordinary diligence.

In any case, some specific types of clauses are not effective unless specifically approved in writing. Such clauses are those which establish, in favour of him who has prepared them in advance, limitations on liability, the power of withdrawing from the contract or suspending its performance, or which impose time limits involving forfeitures on the other party, limitations on the power to raise defences, restrictions on contractual freedom in relations with third parties, tacit extension or renewal of the contract, arbitration clauses, or derogations from the competence of courts.

Article 1342 Contract made by forms or formularies

In contracts made by subscribing to forms or formularies prepared for the purpose of regulating certain contractual relationships in a uniform manner, terms added to such forms or formularies prevail over the original terms of said forms or formularies when they are incompatible with them, even though the latter have not been struck out.

This does not affect the application of Art 1341(2).

Article 1370 Interpretatio contra proferentem

Terms contained in standard terms contracts (1341) or in forms or formularies (1342) which have been prepared by one of the contracting parties must be interpreted, in case of doubt, in favour of the other party.

Relevant provisions of the Italian Consumer Code (*Codice del consumo*) dlgs 6 settembre 2005, no 206

PART I GENERAL PROVISIONS

TITLE I

General provisions and aims

[*omissis*]

Art 3

Definitions

1 For the purposes of the present Code the following meanings are to be given:

a) consumer or user: the natural person who acts for purposes which are outside the business or professional activity he may carry out;
b) consumers' or users' associations: the entities which have as their exclusive statutory aim the protection of the interests and of the rights of consumers or users;
c) professional: the natural or legal person who acts within the framework of his business or professional activity, or his intermediary ;

[*omissis*]

PART III RELATIONSHIPS WITH THE CONSUMER

TITLE I

Of consumer contracts in general

Art 33

Unfair terms in a contract between a professional and a consumer

1. Terms in a contract between a consumer and a professional are regarded as unfair when, in spite of the good faith, they cause a significant imbalance in the rights and obligation arising out of the contract to the detriment of the consumer.

2. Unless otherwise proven, terms will be presumed to be unfair when their object or effect is to:

a) Exclude or limit the liability of the professional in the event of death or injury to the consumer resulting from an act or omission of the professional;
b) Exclude or limit the actions or legal rights of the consumer vis-à-vis the professional or another party in the event of total or partial non-performance or inadequate performance by the professional;
c) Exclude or limit the possibility for the consumer to offset a debt owed to the professional against any credit which the consumer may have against him;
d) Make an agreement binding on the consumer whereas performance by the professional is subject to a condition whose realisation depends on his own will alone;
e) Allow the professional to retain sums paid by the consumer where the latter does not conclude the contract or cancels it, without providing for the consumer to receive compensation of twice that amount from the professional where the latter does not conclude the contract or cancels it;
f) Require any consumer who fails to perform his obligation or does it with delay to pay a disproportionately high sum as agreed damage, penalty or as any other type of compensation;
g) Authorise the professional to cancel the contract where the same facility is not granted to the consumer, or permit the professional to retain, even in part, the sums paid for performance not yet carried out by him where it is the professional himself who dissolves the contract;
h) Enable the professional to terminate a contract of indeterminate duration without reasonable notice except where there are serious grounds for doing so;
i) Impose a deadline on the consumer to express his desire not to extend the contract which is unreasonably early in respect of the expiry of the contract;
l) Bind the consumer to terms with which he had no opportunity of becoming acquainted before the conclusion of the contract;
m) Enable the professional to unilaterally alter the terms of the contract or any characteristics of the product or service to be provided without a valid reason specified in the contract
n) Provide for the price of goods or services to be determined at the time of delivery or supply;
o) Allow the professional to increase the price of the goods or services without giving the consumer the corresponding right to cancel the contract if the final price is too high in relation to the price agreed when the contract was concluded;
p) Give the professional the right to determine whether the goods or services supplied are in conformity with the contract, or give him the exclusive right to interpret any term of the contract;
q) Limit the professional's obligation to respect commitments undertaken by his agents or making his commitments subject to compliance with a particular formality;

r) Limit or exclude the possibility for the consumer to refuse to fulfil all his obligations where the professional does not perform his;
s) Give the professional the possibility of transferring his rights and obligations under the contract, even with the previous consent of the consumer, where this may reduce the guarantees for the consumer;
t) Restrict the consumer's right to take legal action by imposing time limitations, unconditioned duties to perform, derogation to the competence of courts prescribed by the law, restrictions on the evidence available to him, impositions on him of a burden of proof which, according to the applicable law, should lie with another party to the ontract, or restrictions to his freedom to contract with thirds;
u) Establishing as competent forum a court that sits in a place which is different from the consumer's place of residence or domicile;
v) Subject the transfer of a right or the acceptance of an obligation to a conditions whose realisation depends on the professional's own will alone while the consumer is immediately bound, save for the provision of Art 1355C.c.

3. If the contracts concerns the supply of financial services of indeterminate duration, the professional can, without prejudice to nos h) and m) of paragraph 2:

a) terminate unilaterally the contract without notice where there is a valid reason, provided that the supplier is required to inform the consumer immediately;
b) alter the conditions of the contract where there is a valid reason, provided that the supplier is required to inform the consumer with reasonable notice and that the consumer is free to cancel the contract.

4. If the contracts concerns supply of financial services, the professional can alter, without notice, as long as there is a valid reason, in derogation to nos n) and o) the interest rate or any other charge for the supply of the financial service agreed at the moment of conclusion of the contract, provided that the supplier is required to inform the consumer immediately and that the consumer is free to cancel the contract.

5. Nos h), m), n) and o) of paragraph 2 do not apply to contract concerning securities, financial instruments and other products or services where the price is linked to fluctuations in a stock exchange quotation or index or a financial market rate that the seller or supplier does not control and do not apply to contracts for the purchase or sale of foreign currency, traveller's cheques or international money orders denominated in foreign currency.

6. Nos n) and o) do not apply to price-indexation clauses, where lawful, provided that the method by which prices vary is explicitly described.

Art 34

Assessment of the unfair nature of terms

1. The unfairness of a term is assessed by taking into account the nature of the goods or services for which the contract was concluded and by referring to the circumstances attending the conclusion of the contract and to the other terms of the contract or of another contract to which it is related or dependent.

2. Assessment of the unfair nature of the terms shall relate neither to the definition of the main subject matter of the contract nor to the adequacy of the price of the goods or services as long as these elements are identified in plain, intelligible language.

3. Terms which reproduce statutory provisions or provisions which reproduce provisions or implement principles contained in international conventions to which all EU Members States or the EU are part shall not be regarded as unfair.

4. Terms or parts of terms which have been individually negotiated shall not be regarded as unfair.

5. In contracts made by signing forms or contracts drafted in advance to regulate in a uniform way certain contractual relationships, the burden of proving that terms, or parts of terms, even though unilaterally drafted, have been individually negotiated with the consumer, lies on the professional.

Art 35

Form and interpretation

1. In the case of contracts where all or certain terms offered to the consumer are in writing, these terms must always be drafted in plain, intelligible language.

2. Where there is doubt about the meaning of a term, the interpretation most favourable to the consumer shall prevail.

3. The rule of para 2 shall not apply in the cases regulated by article 37.

Art 36

Voidability of unfair terms

1. Terms regarded as unfair under article 33 and 34 shall not be binding but the contract will continue to bind the parties for the rest.

2. Terms which, even though negotiated, have as their object or effect to:

   a) Exclude or limit the liability of the professional in the event of the death or personal injury to the consumer resulting from an act or omission of the professional;

b) Exclude or limit the actions or legal rights of the consumer vis-a -vis the professional or another party in the event of total or partial non-performance or inadequate performance by the professional;
c) Bind the consumer to terms with which he had no opportunity of becoming acquainted before the conclusion of the contract;

shall be regarded as voidable.

3. Terms will be voidable only to the advantage of the consumer and voidability can be raised by the judge by his own motion.

4. A retailer has the right to claim compensation from the supplier for the damages he may have suffered where terms in the retailer's contract have been declared unfair.

5. Terms according to which the law of a non-Member country is the law applicable to the contract are avoidable if they have the effect of depriving the consumer of the protection ensured by the present chapter where the contract has a closer connection with the territory of a Member State of the European Union.

Art 37

Preventive actions

1. The associations which are representative of consumers' interests mentioned by article 137, professional associations, Chambers of Commerce, Industry, Craftsmanship and Agriculture can bring legal actions against professionals or professional's associations who use or who recommend the use of standard contract terms and can apply to the competent court for interim relief measures in order to prevent them from using terms which have been declared unfair according to this chapter.

2. The interim measure can be awarded, in case of fair and urgent reasons, in accordance with Art 669-bis ff. of the code of civil procedure.

3. The court can order that the decision is published in one or more newspapers, of which at least one must have national circulation.

4. Preventive actions taken by consumers' associations shall, for whatever is not covered by the present article, be regulated by article 140.

Art 38

Other applicable provisions

1. Contracts between consumer and professionals shall be regulated by the civil code in all respects that are not regulated by the present code.

Index

Ingram Content Group UK Ltd.
Milton Keynes UK
UKHW020147140323
418511UK00002B/16/J

9 781841 135946